Design In
Built Environment

Today architecture and other fields in the built environment face the steep task of answering complex questions pertaining to sustainability, performance, and adaptability.

How are these disciplines to accomplish these difficult tasks at such an immense pace?

How might architectural practice renovate itself accordingly?

Worldwide it is becoming increasingly clear that different modes of research are emerging which are triggered directly by the need to renovate practice. One significant prevailing mode is what has come to be known as 'research by design'.

This book delivers an overview of this pluralistic domain. Bringing together a range of leading architects, architectural theorists, and designers, it outlines the developments in current practice from leading individuals based in the USA, UK, Australia, Japan, and Europe. Edited by a recognized expert, this book exposes the undercurrent of research that is taking place and how this will contribute to the renovation of architectural practice.

Michael U. Hensel is an architect, researcher, and writer. He is Professor for Architecture at the Oslo School of Architecture where he directs the Research Centre for Architecture and Tectonics. He is a board member of the OCEAN Design Research Association, of the SEA, the Sustainable Environment Association, and of BIONIS, the Biomimetics Network for Industrial Sustainability.

Design Innovation for the Built Environment

Research by design and the renovation of practice

Edited by
Michael U. Hensel

Routledge
Taylor & Francis Group

LONDON AND NEW YORK

First published 2012
by Routledge
2 Park Square, Milton Park, Abingdon, Oxon OX14 4RN

Simultaneously published in the USA and Canada
by Routledge
711 Third Avenue, New York, NY 10017

Routledge is an imprint of the Taylor & Francis Group, an informa business

British Library Cataloguing in Publication Data
A catalogue record for this book is available from the British Library

Library of Congress Cataloging in Publication Data
Hensel, Michael U.
Design innovation for the built environment : research by design and the
renovation of practice / Michael U. Hensel.
p. cm.
Includes bibliographical references and index.
 1. Architecture—Research. 2. Architectural practice. I. Title. II. Title:
Research by design and the renovation of practice.
NA2000.H46 2012
720.72—dc23
2011032846

ISBN: 978-0-415-59664-0 (hbk)
ISBN: 978-0-415-59665-7 (pbk)
ISBN: 978-0-203-12974-6 (ebk)

Typeset in Univers
by FiSH Books, Enfield

Printed and bound in Great Britain by
TJ International Ltd, Padstow, Cornwall

To my late father Ulli. Alas, you had to return home. You will always be missed.

Contents

Contents

List of contributors

Mark Burry is Professor of Innovation and Spatial Information (SIAL) at RMIT University in Melbourne Australia, as well as founding director of RMIT's Design Institute, and holds numerous visiting professorships. He is also executive architect and researcher to the Temple Sagrada Familia in Barcelona, Spain, and member of the Australian Research Council College of Experts. He has internationally published on two main themes: the life and work of the architect Antoni Gaudí in Barcelona, and putting theory into practice with regard to 'challenging' architecture.

As consultant architect to the Temple Sagrada Família since 1979, Mark Burry has been a key member within the local design team based on site in Barcelona, untangling the mysteries of Gaudí's compositional strategies for his greatest work, especially those coming from his later years, the implications of which are only now becoming fully apparent as they are resolved for building purposes. On February 18, 2004, in recognition of his contribution to this project, Professor Burry was given the prestigious award 'Diploma i la insignia a l'acadèmic corresponent' and the title *Senyor Il.lustre* by the Reial Acadèmia Catalana de Belles Arts de Sant Jordi. In May 2006 Mark was awarded an Australian Research Council Federation Fellowship and he was recently the recipient of the USA Association for Computer Aided Design in Architecture (ACADIA) Award for Innovative Research. For further information see: http://www.sial.rmit.edu.au/People/mburry+Biography.php.

Eva Castro is Director of the Landscape Urbanism programme and has been teaching at the Architectural Association School of Architecture, London (AA) since 2003. She studied architecture and urbanism at the Universidad Central de Venezuela and subsequently completed the AA Graduate Design programme with Jeff Kipnis. She is co-founder of Plasma Studio and GroundLab. She is winner of the Next Generation Architects Award, the Young Architect of the Year Award, the Contract World Award and the HotDip Galvanising Award. Her work is published and exhibited worldwide. Plasma and GroundLab are currently lead designers for the International Horticultural Fair in Xi'an, China, a 37ha landscape with a wide range of buildings which was opened in 2011.

Halina Dunin-Woyseth is an architect and professor at the Oslo School of Architecture and Design (AHO). Since 1990 she has been the founding head of AHO's Doctoral Programme. Her professional, teaching and research experience originated in urban design and spatial planning-related issues. During the recent decade she has been mainly involved in issues of knowledge in the design professions. She has lectured extensively at the doctoral level and supervised PhD students in Norway and abroad, and she has been commissioned as an evaluator by several research councils in Scandinavia and has also experience from assessing EU-funded research.

Mehran Gharleghi is an architect and director of Studio Integrate together with Amin Sadeghy. He received his BA Degree from Tehran University of Science and Technology and his Master of Architecture from the Emergent Technologies and Design programme at the Architectural Association. His dissertation won international awards such as 'AA Fab Research Cluster Symposium 2009' and 'International prize for sustainable Architecture-2010'. He collaborated with the most prominent architect in Iran, Hadi Mirmiran, and worked for Plasma Studio and Foster and Partners in London. He has won several competitions and design awards. He lectured at The House of Architecture in Graz in 2011, Smart Geometry09, AA Fab Research Cluster Symposium and ACADIA 2009. Mehran Gharleghi has been interviewed in the book entitled *Conversation With the Young Architect* by Dr Nasrine Faghih in which he discusses the current role of the young architect. Mehran Gharleghi and Amin Sadeghy exhibited their 'Responsive Pneumatic Systems' research at London's Design Festival 2009.

Michael U. Hensel [Dipl. Ing. Grad Dipl Des AA] is an architect, researcher, writer and educator. He is a founding member of OCEAN (1994) and served as founding chairman of the OCEAN Design Research Association (2008). He is currently board member of OCEAN and of BIONIS – The Biomimetics Network for Industrial Sustainability – and served as editorial board member for JBE (*Journal of Bionic Engineering*), Elsevier Scientific Press. Currently he is professor and director of the Research Centre for Architecture and Tectonics at AHO – The Oslo School of Architecture and Design in Oslo in Norway. Previously he taught for 16 years at the Architectural Association School of Architecture in London, has held visiting professorships and taught and lectured in Europe, the Americas, Asia and Australia. His research interests and efforts include formulating the theoretical and methodological framework for performance-oriented architecture and developing a biological paradigm for design and sustainability of the built environment. He has written extensively on this and other topics in architecture and urban design. Forthcoming publications include: *AD Primer Performance-oriented Design – Towards an Inclusive Approach to Architectural Design and the Built Environment* (2011, AD Wiley); and with D. Sunguroğlu Hensel *et al.* (2013) *The Handbook for Sustainable Traditional Buildings Analysis* (2013, John Wiley & Sons).

Christopher Hight is an associate professor and Director of Undergraduate Studies at the Rice University School of Architecture in Houston, Texas, where he is pursuing design and research on architecture's potential at the nexus of social, natural and subjective ecologies within the built environment.

Reinhard Kropf is an Austrian architect and researcher educated at the University of Science in Graz and the Oslo School of Architecture and Design (AHO), where he studied under Christian Norberg-Schulz. In 1996, together with Siv Helene Stangeland he founded the architectural office Helen & Hard in Stavanger on the west coast of Norway. Helen & Hard have received several awards for their work, including the Norwegian National Award for Building and Environmental Design for the Pulpit Rock Mountain Lodge. They have exhibited internationally, including at the Venice Biennale, the Lisbon Biennale and Manifesta 7. In 2008, the firm was selected with eight others to represent European architectural offices in the travelling exhibition 'New Trends of Architecture'. They have won several competitions including the Norway Pavilion at Expo Shanghai 2010 and have an extensive body of built work. Helen & Hard have written, published and lectured extensively in Europe, North America and Asia about their research on sustainable practices and methods.

David Leatherbarrow is Professor of Architecture, Chairman of the Architecture PhD Program, and Associate Dean at the University of Pennsylvania, where he has taught architectural design, history, and theory since 1984. Before Penn he taught at Cambridge University and the University of Westminster. He has also visited and taught at many universities in the USA and abroad. David Leatherbarrow earned his Bachelor of Architecture Degree at the University of Kentucky and his PhD in Art at the University of Essex. His books include *Architecture Oriented Otherwise* (2009, Princeton Architectural Press), *Topographical Stories: Studies in landscape and architecture* (2004, University of Pennsylvania Press), and *Surface Architecture* (2005, MIT Press), written in collaboration with Mohsen Mostafavi. Earlier books include *Uncommon Ground: Architecture, technology and topography*; *The Roots of Architectural Invention: Site, enclosure and materials* (2002, MIT Press); and *On Weathering: The life of buildings in time* (1993, MIT Press), again with Mostafavi. In addition to these books he has published over 80 scholarly articles. In the past, his research has focused on various topics in the history and theory of architecture, gardens, and urbanism; more recently his work has concentrated on the impact of contemporary technology on architecture and the city.

Henry Mainsah is a visiting researcher at the Oslo School of Architecture and Design. He has a PhD from the Department of Media and Communication, University of Oslo where he currently lectures on subjects such as media, cultural identity, and globalization. His doctoral thesis focused on the role played by digital online media in the construction of identity among ethnic minority youth. His research interests include cultural studies, migration studies, media studies, visual culture, and design ethnography.

Einar Sneve Martinussen is a designer and researcher working with interactive products, technology and urban and cultural studies. He holds a Master's Degree in Design from the Oslo School of Architecture and Design and has a background from architecture and urbanism. Martinussen's work includes research on mobile technologies, interaction design and product development; he lectures about physical computing and technologies as materials for design. Details of projects can be found at www.einarsnevemartinussen.com.

Andrew Morrison is Professor of Interdisciplinary Design and coordinates design research at the Institute of Design, Oslo School of Architecture and Design (AHO). He has published in new media, applied discourse studies and various fields of interaction and communication design. His recent books include *Inside Multimodal Composition* and *Exploring Digital Design* (2011, Hampton Press). Andrew leads the

YOUrban research project and NarraHand. He is course leader of the PhD school at AHO, active in the Nordes Design Research conferences, and formerly head of Communication Design research at InterMedia, University of Oslo.

Fredrik Nilsson is architect SAR/MSA, professor of Architectural Theory at Chalmers University of Technology, and Partner and Head of Research and Development at White Arkitekter AB, Sweden. He has taught and lectured widely, and has written especially on contemporary architecture, architectural theory and philosophy with a special interest in the epistemology of architecture and the inter-action between conceptual, theoretical thinking and practical design work. Nilsson is author and editor of several books and frequently publishes articles, architectural criticism and reviews of books.

Hidetoshi Ohno (born 1949, Japan) received his Doctor's Degree in 1997 at the University of Tokyo. After working for Fuhimiko Maki for many years, he became a professor at the Department of Socio-Cultural Environmental Studies, Graduate School of Frontier Sciences and Department of Architecture, Faculty of Engineering at the University of Tokyo. He is a practising architect, with many works rewarded in Japan. His main field of interests are architectural and urban design, and planning. Major publications in English include 'Hong Kong: Alternative Metropolis', Special Issue of SD, March 1992, Kajima Publishing Institute, and 'Fibercity Tokyo 2050', JA Special Issue No. 63, 2006, also partially published in Germany, France and Taiwan.

Bruno Peeters (born 1968, Belgium) received his Masters Degree in Architecture in 1993 at the Department of St.-Lucas, Brussels. After working for Kisho Kurokawa in Tokyo and Europe for several years he established his own office, and became a professor at the St.-Lucas Department of Architecture. Since 2007 he has been the architectural design chairman and coordinator of the Diploma-Projects, and in charge of the new EU Ausmip R&DaR exchange programme. His main fields of interest are architectural and urban design, and he is currently a Japan Foundation Fellow at the Department of Socio-Cultural Environmental Studies, University of Tokyo.

Alfredo Ramirez is an architect and co-founder of GroundLab. He studied Architecture in Mexico City, and the AA graduate programme Landscape Urbanism in 2005. He has practised in several architectural offices and institutions in Mexico City, Madrid and London where he has concentrated on architectural and urban design projects such as the Olympic master plan for London 2012. At GroundLab he has won and developed several competitions, workshops, exhibitions and projects, including the winning entry 'Deep ground' for Longgang City international competi-tion master plan and the ongoing development of the international horticultural exhibition project in Xian. Alfredo is also a Studio Master of the Landscape Urbanism Design Master at the AA and collaborates with Fundacion Metropoli.

Amin Sadeghy is an architect and director of studio integrate together with Mehran Gharleghi. He received his BA Degree from Tehran University of Science and Technology and his Master of Architecture from the Emergent Technologies and Design programme at the Architectural Association. He has been collaborating with prominent architects in Iran since 2000 and currently works for Fosters and Partners in London. He has won several design awards, such as International honourable mention for sustainable design. His Dissertation in Emtech in collaboration with Mehran Gharleghi won two international awards, 'AA Fab Research Cluster Symposium 2009' and 'International Prize for Sustainable Architecture'. He lectured at The House of Architecture in Graz in 2011, AA Fab Research Cluster Symposium 2009 and his work was presented in Acadia 2009 and Smart Geometry conference 2009. Mehran Gharleghi and Amin Sadeghy exhibited their 'Responsive Pneumatic Systems' research at London's Design Festival 2009.

Birger Sevaldson [dipl NCAD MNIL PhD] is professor at the Institute of Design at AHO – Oslo School of Architecture and Design and a principal researcher in OCEAN Design Research Association. He is a designer working in a broad field of design and architecture. He has been in private practice since 1986. His practice spans from architecture, interior to furniture and product design. It also includes experimental architecture and several art installations in collaboration with the composer Natasha Barrett.

He has been developing concepts in design computing and his doctoral thesis from 2005 is a summary of this research. He has been collaborating in OCEAN since 1997 and the OCEAN Design Research Association since its inception in 2008. The experimental design projects resulting from this collaboration have been published worldwide. He has defined systems-oriented design as a designerly way of systems thinking and systems practice and has published numerous articles on the topics of design computing, design research methodology and systems-oriented design. He is a member of the Council of the Design Research Society.

He has lectured and taught in Norway, Europe, Asia and USA and has participated in educational evaluation committees internationally amongst them for the Ministry of Culture in Denmark and the Higher Education and Training Award Council in Ireland.

Siv Helene Stangeland is a Norwegian architect and researcher based in Stavanger, Norway. Together with Reinhard Kropf, she founded the architectural office Helen & Hard in 1996. Siv Helene Stangeland studied at the University of Barcelona and at the Oslo School of Architecture and Design AHO, under Christian Norberg-Schulz. She has taught at AHO, NTNU (Trondheim), Chalmers University (Gothenburg) and KTH (Stockholm). Helen & Hard have received several awards for their work, including the Norwegian National Award for Building and Environmental Design for the Pulpit Rock Mountain Lodge. They have exhibited internationally, including at the Venice Biennale, the Lisbon Biennale and Manifesta 7. In 2008, the firm was selected with eight others to represent European architectural offices in the travelling exhibition 'New Trends of Architecture'. They have won several competitions including the Norway Pavilion at Expo Shanghai 2010 and have an extensive body of built work. Helen & Hard have written, published and lectured extensively in Europe, North America and Asia about their research on sustainable practices and methods.

Defne Sunguroğlu Hensel [MSc EmTech AA Dipl RIBA II] is an architect, interior architect, and researcher. Currently she serves as a board member in the OCEAN

Design Research Association. She studied architecture Part I at Kent University and completed her degree at the Architectural Association, where she also gained her MSc in the Emergent Technologies and Design Programme. Currently, she is working on her PhD entitled *Multiple Performance Integration Models Based on Wood and Clay Based Systems* as a stipend-funded PhD research fellow at AHO Oslo School of Architecture and Design. She received the Buro Happold studentship (2006) to pursue her research into Complex Brick Assemblies; the Holloway Trust Award (2006) for a significant contribution to the construction industry; a stipend by BDA – the Brick Development Association (2007); the Anthony Pott Memorial Award (2007) for detailed analysis and research of Eladio Dieste's work; as well as the CERAM Industrial Category Award (2007). She held innovation fellowships, and lectured, taught and exhibited internationally and her work has been published widely. Most recently she co-edited: Ertas H., Hensel M. and Sunguroğlu Hensel D. (Eds) (2010). *Turkey – At the Threshold*. London: AD Wiley.

Inger-Lise Syversen is an architect who through comprehensive international and teaching experience has gained considerable pedagogical skills within sustainable architectural conservation. Her experiences as a lecturer and networker in East Africa (1991–) have entailed a focus on capacity building, institutional cooperation and architectural heritage conservation. Syversen delivered her PhD thesis with focus on architectural heritage in East Africa (2007). She also has thorough experience from working at the highest political level in the Nordic Council of Ministers with main responsibility for the development of Nordic international cooperation within higher education and research. Syversen is a professor at Chalmers University of Technology – Chalmers Architecture at the Department of Sustainable Development and Design – with responsibility for Architectural Conservation and Transformation in the Master studios. Since 1995 she has had the responsibility for designing Master courses in the Nordic, as well as the East African context.

Jeffrey P. Turko [AA Dipl. RIBA II] is the founder of the design practice NEKTON. He is currently Vice Chairman of the OCEAN Design Research Association and has collaborated on projects such as Landsc[r]aper – Urban Ring Bridge, the World Centre for Human Concerns and most recently the MM tent (aka Membrella). He studied and taught at the Architectural Association School of Architecture in London. He currently teaches architecture at the postgraduate diploma level at the University of East London School of Architecture and Visual Arts where he has been a senior lecturer since 2001. He has published his work and writings in numerous international architecture journals. He has been practising since 1999 and has been a registered architect in The Netherlands since 2001.

Julian Vincent is a biologist who spent the last eight years of his university career as a professor of mechanical engineering. His 300+ publications cover biomechanics of animals and plants (mostly materials), texture of food, smart materials, techniques of TRIZ, and more. In his retirement he is collecting consultancies and professorships and continues lecturing and writing and doing a few experiments. His ambition is to make biomimetics the new engineering and to play his banjo in Carnegie Hall.

Preface

Dear reader,

This book gathers together a series of efforts in the rapidly developing field of research by design and the renovation of practices involved in design innovation and the making of the built environment. The picture that emerges shows this field to be fundamentally pluralistic, as well as inter- and often transdisciplinary. The diverse efforts that constitute this field seem to gradually create new collaborative alliances between practice and education through research.

While some of the efforts portrayed in this book are evidently different in aim, scope, scale, methodological approach, and so on, and are often couched within different theoretical frameworks, some obviously also share numerous traits and may even seem complementary in character. When selecting the content for this book and arranging it into a particular sequence of chapters it was therefore necessary to withstand the temptation to streamline where differences prevail, or to keep apart what seems related.

Unfortunately quite a number of distinguished experts whose significant efforts should have been portrayed here were not able to contribute due to their demanding schedules. In addition, the size constraints of the publication had to be met. Yet, it has also never been the intention to produce an encyclopaedic volume or even one that generally seeks to be inclusive of a broadly representative range of existing approaches. Instead it is the intention to contribute to initiating both an increasingly broader and more nuanced discussion of the theme at hand. Hopefully this book will be one in a series of such efforts. Furthermore, it is my hope that this endeavour will contribute to the understanding that research by design is far from being an undefined field, but instead is a pluralistic field of highly specific localized efforts. Surely this book can only be one part of the puzzle towards a clear and productive discourse on research by design and design innovation for the built environment. At any rate it is my hope that the book is informative and inspiring towards this end.

Michael U. Hensel

Holmsbu, June 2011

Acknowledgements

My sincere gratitude to all those who have had vital formative impacts on my colleagues and me in the pursuit of our collaborative interests and efforts: the late Robin Evans, the late Hassan Fathy, Jeffrey Kipnis, Frei Otto, Julian Vincent, but also David Attenborough and Werner Herzog in their ceaseless curiosity and brilliance. Without them the interest and efforts that led to the writing of this book would not have seen the light of day.

I would like to offer my warm gratitude to the contributors to this book, some of whom have been long-time companions and collaborators, as well as to Caroline Mallinder whose advice has been of key importance to the development of the project. Many thanks also to Laura Williamson and Alanna Donaldson at Routledge, Sarah Fish, Ann King, Caroline Hamilton and FiSH books for their continual and diligent collaboration.

Last, but certainly never least, I would like to thank my wonderful wife Defne, my mother, and Jojo and Donny for their loving understanding and support when once again one must do what one must do, whatever time and effort it might take.

Introduction to design innovation for the built environment – research by design and the renovation of practice

Michael U. Hensel

> When there is a solution, it is no longer a real problem.
> When there is an answer, it is no longer a real question.
> For at that point, the problem is part of the solution and the answer is
>   part of the question.
> And then nothing remains but solutions without problems and answers
>   without questions.
> O, happy days when we had only questions without answers and
>   problems without solutions!
>
> (Baudrillard 1990: 223)

This book introduces a series of efforts in research by design and the renovation of practices involved in design innovation and the making of the built environment. Selecting the contributions from an exceedingly wide and pluralistic field was both a challenging and enlightening task. In order to establish a position to start from it was of use to examine the view of eminent people in the field on the topic at hand. The distinguished German architect and researcher Frei Otto, for instance, portrayed the state of research in architecture and engineering as follows:

> The big new ecological and biological tasks require a global and integrated way of thinking and designing, especially when dealing with works of great dimensions and significant technological components. In the majority of cases even the best architects or artistically gifted engineers are not yet capable to cope with these challenges.
>
> Today neither architects nor engineers carry out notable research. They don't get involved with either the humanities or the natural sciences. They don't even try to approach problems dealing with medicine, biology, or ethology, and they don't arrive at developments worthy of mention even in the common area of construction. Up until

1

now, the construction industry only supports research projects that can produce short-term benefits.

To elevate the quality of construction, basic interdisciplinary research must begin at once, with long-term objectives that are passed on through many generations.

(Songel 2008: 13)

Determining whether architects or engineers currently do or do not carry out notable research obviously depends entirely on the criteria for assessment and also on what is seen as a valid mode of research and the associated production of knowledge. Many an architect or engineer might beg to disagree with Frei Otto today at a time when the claim to conduct research by design is becoming increasingly ubiquitous. A growing number of practitioners today go as far as claiming that to practise is to research. Conversely, an equally increasing number of experts are rejecting this notion and the claim that commonplace design practice or general inquiries geared towards the realization of a design – such as to call a contractor to acquire information about materials, for instance – constitutes actual research. As seems obvious from the quote above, Frei Otto is not inclined to view such activities as 'notable research'. Instead he calls for an integrated and interdisciplinary approach with research goals and benchmarks for inquires set by the complexity of contemporary ecological and biological problems, with far-reaching consequences for the built environment, with approaches rooted in the humanities and/or the natural sciences, and relating to long-term research objectives. The call for disciplinary relations to humanities and the natural sciences requires inherently a detailed understanding of their specific modes of inquiry and knowledge production. Are these modes directly to be applied to design innovation for the built environment or are intermediary or modified modes required? This is where some of the current notions of research by design begin to be instrumental, as they present the possibility of interlinking the different research modes of the humanities, the empirical (social and natural), interdisciplinary, applied and formal sciences. This realization led over time to new inter- and transdisciplinary modes of inquiry and knowledge production, as several authors point out in various chapters of this book.

In order to examine a number of these developments more specifically this book combines chapters that elaborate specific research by design efforts as they have evolved in various contexts over recent decades with chapters that introduce particular current approaches and others that emphasize promising disciplinary affiliations that can help advance design innovation for the built environment. Obviously this book can only introduce a few selected developments. Consequently the aim is not to provide an encyclopaedic volume or even one that seeks to be generally inclusive of the broad range of existing approaches. Obviously such a goal cannot be accomplished, not only because of a great wealth of activities that have emerged in recent times, but also because of both the acceleration of the diversification and convergences of efforts across the field of research by design and the numerous impacts these efforts have, which may either make them increasingly ubiquitous or bring them into greater focus across the research by design community and the practices involved in the making of the built environment. All this implies that the field of design innovation through research by design is and will continue to be inherently heterogeneous and evolving. While some feel thus inclined to state that research by design is a diffuse and poorly defined mode of inquiry, the following chapters will hopefully demonstrate that there is indeed a great amount of clarity and long-term perspective and objectives in many of the approaches that can be listed under the label of research by design. And in so doing the multitude of approaches also help clarify collectively what research by design might imply in general.

The subjects of interest and inquiry represented by the approaches selected for this book span across scales of magnitude – from the micro-scale of materials to urban design – and diverse disciplinary affiliations. Ultimately, what emerges in the majority of cases is a trans-scalar and transdisciplinary characteristic that is shared between the approaches and that aims for a complex understanding of a research by design problem and an equally complex resolution of the inquiry. Here one can clearly detect the eventual impact of recent theories in complexity theory and systems thinking across the disciplines and across the efforts portrayed here within. This entails more often than not the willingness and ability to suspend entrenched beliefs and clichés in what may or may not constitute valid design problems and related relevant research modes and methods. It would seem therefore that improving on the quality and complexity of questions asked in framing areas of inquiry might be one of the first and foremost contributions of research by design towards design innovation for the built environment. To help shed light on some of these aspects and to offer them to a productive discussion is the endeavour of this book.

Bibliography

Baudrillard, J. (1990) *Cool Memories*. London: Verso.

Songel, J. M. (2008) *A Conversation with Frei Otto*. New York: Princeton Architectural Press.

Chapter 1

The project of design research

David Leatherbarrow

> *The general system of the sciences and the arts is a kind of labyrinth, a twisting road, which the mind enters without really knowing the route it ought to take.*
>
> Jean le Rond d'Alembert, Encyclopédie (Paris, 1751)

> *The external conditions which are set for [the scientist] by the fact of experience do not permit him to let himself be too much restricted in the construction of his conceptual world by the adherence to an epistemological system. He, therefore, must appear to the systematic epistemologist as a type of unscrupulous opportunist.*
>
> Albert Einstein (Schilpp 1951: 683)

> *Science knows no bare facts at all ... the facts that enter our knowledge are already viewed in a certain way and are, therefore, essentially ideational.*
>
> Paul Feyerabend (Feyerabend 2010: 3)

If *design research* in architecture is to amount to more than a slogan used by professionals advertising their services or professors seeking promotion, if it is to inaugurate a renewal of architecture's cultural role and a redefinition of its disciplinary task, then the nature of the project it proposes needs to be clarified. When any new theme activates a flurry of discussion, one always wonders if interest will fade just as quickly as it surfaced, either because its ideas are not really new or its promises are unrealistic. But even if this were the case, it would still be necessary to understand the origin of the fashion and the prestige of the promise.

Among architects and educators today, the proposal for design research is generally understood as follows: the design of buildings is not only a professional practice but also a form of inquiry, a sister or brother in the growing family of research disciplines at work in the world today. The older siblings are well known, the highly regarded research fields in the natural sciences: physics, chemistry, and biology, for example. In the next generation are the social sciences: economics, political science, and sociology. Also related are the fields in which the basic sciences are applied: medicine, engineering, and law. This last group is more akin to architecture, for these academic disciplines are also professions. The problem with architecture is that it also has family ties to disciplines beyond the sciences, in painting, urban design, and landscape architecture, even literature and poetry. Furthermore, artistic practices are not only non-scientific, they are purposeless; beauty is its own reward – at least according to modern aestheticians. But these categories – natural science, social science, the arts – together with the terms that designate them are no less subject to debate and misuse than the words 'design' and 'research' with which we began.

Design research: a contradiction in terms?

One reason that the notion of design research appears to be new in architecture is that these two terms seem to pose a contradiction, at least when long-standing conceptions are allowed. Each activity would seem to have different objects, methods, and times.

Considering its objects, design is the means by which something new is brought into being. Like work, it involves effort, but unlike tasks that are performed repetitively, design's labour is essentially progressive, advancing beyond current conditions rather than stabilizing or reaffirming what is already given. Moreover, design work couples manual with intellectual effort, in ways that repetitive kinds of work often do not; production follows preconception. The opposite seems to be true of research. The objects into which research inquires are presumed to exist at the beginning of the investigation, even if their existence is only hypothesized. While the facts of the case may be hidden, research presumes they can be discovered because they are already *there*, waiting to be found, then documented, for others, at present and in future. For discoveries to be made, researchers must follow leads, probing overlooked conditions, seeing beyond distractions. They must also free themselves from prejudgments. Research methods are meant to open inquiry to the phenomena themselves. But unlike the outcomes of design productivity, these phenomena do not derive from the research process. Observation is not generation.

The procedures by which design and research reach their goals also suggest their incompatibility. Design invention authors originals; its outcomes are stamped with the sign of the new. Admittedly, study, thought, and experiment sometimes set the stage for innovative work, but lessons from the past neither foreshadow nor predetermine groundbreaking proposals. Imagination of unforeseen possibilities advances design's operations. It proceeds by acts of will, as if by fiat, strengthened by firm conviction and enlivened by inspiration. Research, by contrast, is nothing if not methodical, requiring prolonged and careful study. If one takes the natural sciences as a model, the procedures of serious research are worked out in advance; its inquiries follow a plan. Moreover, a basic sense of objectivity governs its steps, so that other researchers can follow the same procedures and reach the same conclusions. The validity of outcomes rests upon a thesis of non-subjectivity and transparent communication. Research today involves teamwork. Just as observation in research is not meant to be generative, its methods are never internalized. Passion may drive research, but it is never as personal as creative expression.

The third reason that design and research seem to resist one another is that each operates in a different timeframe: design's advances move into the future, while research resides in the present. A bridge between the *not yet* and the *now* can be built if design's productivity is construed as planning, if the future is drawn back into the present, or seen as a set of arrangements that have been made in advance of its beginning. But we have stressed the contrary: design is not planning, or not always and only that; it ventures into the subjunctive, toward a horizon of possibilities, and does so imaginatively. Research, on the other hand, holds its ground. It makes no claims on times to come because it is sharply attuned to what is given here and now, particularly what is given beneath or behind appearances, the real facts of the case. Because now and then are distinct moments, research and design seem to be irreconcilable practices.

Modification and discovery

Were these opening comments a summary of actual practices occurring today, one would conclude that the prospect for design research is not particularly encouraging. Yet neither account is accurate. Although commonplace, they caricature both practices. Design never proceeds by fiat and research is never disinterested. The possibilities envisaged in creative practice are only persuasive when they can be understood as real possibilities. The observational work of disciplined research represents genuine insight when it discovers phenomena that were previously unknown. Finally, while invention in architecture always intends conditions that do not exist at present, the spaces and settings that result always retain elements and qualities that predate the project. Even the most progressive patterns of inhabitation always transform past practices.

Two terms that are relatively familiar in architecture – modification and discovery – should help us get closer to the actual practices of design and research and to see the real possibilities of their cooperation.

'No new architecture can arise without modifying what already exists' (Gregotti 1996: 67). Any of the essential topics of architectural design – the site, programme or construction materials – can be understood as the 'what already exists' that is subject to modification. Insofar as the work is to be built, for example, it must be built somewhere, in some place that precedes the project, with some materials that were available to construction before it commenced. Work on an existing site and with existing materials always involves the alteration of subject matter that bears the stamp of the anterior, even if it is so recent a past that it seems contemporary. Furthermore, some aspects of the subject matter drawn into the project's beginning persist through its realization. The alterations to which sites and materials are subjected never change them beyond recognition. Even if the slope of the soil is levelled, subsurface conditions persist. Similarly, timber that is sawn, sanded, and stained still shows its grain. The sorts of change that result from construction can be significant but never absolute. The same is true for program modification. New works can certainly offer new types of accommodation, but these provisions will only be sensible if they are sufficiently familiar to invite appropriation. The inevitability of modification is especially evident in urban architecture, for primary topics of design, such as frontality and orientation, are *conferred upon* the project as much as they *result from* it. The thesis of modification is neither a constraint on invention nor a restriction on divergence; in fact it requires the latter as the measure of the project's particularity.

What modification is to design, discovery is to research. Research brings into visibility what it observes. Only an unwarranted act of faith would assume that the subject matter of such discoveries predates the investigation. Evidence of this point is amply supplied by modern science. Experimental procedures in modern science do not confirm theories as much as they perform them. Research today is not understood as the dispassionate observation of empirical phenomena. Scientific study is a controlled form of participation in a process of discovery and disclosure. One well-known version of *performative science* is the thesis of 'constructive realism' (Wallner 1994; Spaulding 1918). The practising scientist does not describe phenomena but contributes to their construction. Truth is not observed and then documented but approximated, according to conditions that vary. Fritz Wallner has written: 'we understand what we have constructed. We cannot understand anything else' (Wallner 1994: 23). Because this thesis has close affinities with the eighteenth-century arguments of Giambattista Vico, we should not be surprised to discover that, despite long-standing assumptions about 'objectivity', it has been a basic premise of three centuries of modern science.

Research yesterday and today

Today's wide enthusiasm for research in all fields is rooted in a long tradition. For two centuries, centres of learning have turned from *doctrina* to research. The recent and periodic calls for the restoration of canonical studies attest to the overwhelming movement in the opposite direction. The battle-cry for university reform announced by Wilhelm von Humboldt in the late eighteenth century signalled an offensive that has been victorious on all fronts. He defined the replacement of inherited wisdom by research as 'the transition to [a] science which has not yet been completely discovered' (Gadamer 1992: 48). Professors still teach, but a university's greatness is measured by the volume and quality of its *research output*. While the transmission of knowledge is necessary in higher education, it is insufficient for society's greatest need: the advancement of learning.

But the renunciation of academic learning has occurred outside universities, too. The most strident claims for new beginnings made by early modernist architects included an attack on academicism. Le Corbusier's condemnation of the academy is perhaps the most well known. Chapter One of *Precisions* announced a decisive preliminary for all who seek a new architecture: 'To Free Oneself Entirely From Academic Thinking' (Le Corbusier 1991: 24ff.). Promising a 'new spirit' for the 'new world' (the Americas), he described his programme of study as the result of twenty-five years of 'step by step research' (Le Corbusier 1991: 25). That he was promoting a 'doctrine' had to be admitted, but he maintained that his findings were open to examination, built up in accordance with the laws of logic, and arrived at with no regard to received wisdom. His first step – ours, too – involved quitting 'the pillow of ancient habits' so that he could 'go into the unknown to forge a new attitude for thought.' This meant shaking himself free from the 'ruling and omnipotent mechanism of [the] academies.' How had they obtained such a tight grip? By offering security of knowing in a time of transition. So that we would be clear on what to avoid, he outlined the basic characteristics of the academician: (1) the person who does not judge by himself, (2) the one who accepts results without verifying causes, (3) who believes in absolute truths, and (4) the one who does not involve his own self in the question being asked. The fourth characteristic is most debilitating, for acting in accordance with slogans and submission to the constraint of the academies suffocates the creative spirit. The engineer is the preferred alternative, the patient researcher who observes phenomena, analyses them, and then calculates. Although he never suggested this type of practice would be sufficient for architecture, he did describe his studio as *l'atelier de la recherché patiente*. In truth, however, his image of himself at work oscillated between scientist, artist, and monk.

The *modern* approach to design research did not begin in the twentieth century, nor did the movement away from received wisdom. Both can be seen in the late seventeenth century. Already at that time the academies promoted the kind of inquiry we associate with science: observation, description, logical inference, and disinterested investigation. Rejecting pathetic appeals to ancient learning, Claude Perrault criticized the 'docility of men of letters' for their 'spirit of submission ingrained in their way of studying and learning' (Perrault 1993: 58). Apparently, their submissiveness had been common for centuries. While the scholars of the monasteries deserved some praise for preserving knowledge against the ravages of time and invading armies, their belief (in God) constrained their spirit of inquiry and limited 'the freedom needed for scrupulous investigation,' transferring the respect that is due sacred things to things that are not, things such as architecture, which invite examination, criticism, and censure (Perrault 1993: 57–58).

The rejection of doctrine we see in seventeenth-century architecture was an outgrowth of a much more comprehensive attack on received wisdom carried out in the preceding decades. This polemic set the stage for the valorizations of research that has reached such heights in our time. Of the many sources that documented the history of this movement, perhaps the most incisive was Bernard Palissy, who was not only a great scientist, but also a designer of fountains, gardens, grottos, ceramics, and sculpture. Palissy's *Discours admirable* is basically one long invective against the professors of the Sorbonne. 'I assure you, dear reader, that you will learn more about natural history from the facts contained in this book [which documents the results of research in his 'workshop'] than you would learn in fifty years devoted to the study of the theories of the ancient philosophers' (Palissy 1957: 26–27). Another important aspect of his research and workshop is that their orderly arrangements would allow any visitor to be his own instructor, tracing the steps Palissy had followed, in order to reach the same conclusions. Just as traditional wisdom was to be doubted method was to be trusted.

While it may seem odd to suggest that research could be undertaken in a studio or workshop, scientific advances in our time often occur outside university settings. In recent decades we have witnessed the steady increase of research centres, institutes, and foundations. Some have close ties with universities, others operate independently. Many graduates face a choice between work in these centres or the university, which often amounts to a choice between work in the basic sciences and applied fields. But even work in the basic sciences is no longer centred in academic institutions – still less in teaching programmes – because the institutional support for research is often non-academic. The massive and thorough-going transformation of society through industrialization has had its effect on universities as much as on any of the institutions of modern life. Anyone involved in research today knows that the question concerning funding determines the scope, setting, and personnel of study programmes. Advanced research is costly, prohibitively so if external support is not obtained. In many fields, close alliances between the academy and industry have formed, ostensibly for mutual benefit; support of inquiry allows privileged access for applications. What were once distinct spheres of activity now completely interpenetrate one another. Study programmes in medicine, for example, are commonly seen as extensions of the *research industry*. Corporations not only supply funding, they propose topics. But the alliance between the academy and business is not without its critics, for the fundamental purpose of science, the advancement of understanding, together with its characteristic style of thought, free inquiry – independent of applications – and critique, including self-critique, is often compromised by the push toward practical results. Can application-oriented testing undertaken in contemporary research centres be accurately described as scientific inquiry? A modern scientist is, I think, best prepared to answer this question.

From fact to probability

Four decades ago, one of the twentieth century's most distinguished physicists offered cautionary comments about the research industry. Describing the transition from free inquiry to applied research, Werner Heisenberg wrote: 'In earlier days art and science were the cultural adornment of life, an adornment which could be afforded in good times but which had to be dispensed with in bad, since other cares and obligations claimed priority' (Heisenberg 1974a: 91). Today, by contrast, research is 'the seed corn from which economic prosperity, the right organization of state affairs, the national health and much else are due to grow.' Writing only a decade or so after the end of World War II, Heisenberg was not altogether confident about the use to which modern science had been put in the twentieth century. He worried that the great influence which science and technology had had on the shaping of the world had more often than not 'brought destruction rather than order' (Heisenberg 1974b: 65). Indeed, the atomic bombs had fallen on Japan only fifteen years before. While science can promise to alleviate want, to cure diseases, or bring military victory, it can also lead to chaos if its purposes are not 'understood as parts of a larger pattern, a higher order of things.' Historically, the inquiry into the higher order of things was the chief purpose of science.

More than anyone else in modern physics, Heisenberg understood the fundamental changes that science had undergone in the modern period, changes we tend to ignore in our uncritical allegiance to concepts of impartiality and objectivity. The shift he describes from closed to open systems, or certainty to probability is fascinating because it points to common ground between scientific disciplines and those we tend to think are non-scientific, such as architecture.

Heisenberg explained that Isaac Newton had greater aspirations than the establishment of mathematical laws for natural phenomena; more basically, he wanted to explain the laws of mechanics as a universal science. The working-out of this project was so successful that in subsequent decades other scientists adopted the premise that the nature and behaviours of an exceedingly wide range of phenomena could be explained by these laws. So great was the prestige of the method, Heisenberg reports, that in the nineteenth century, mechanics was coextensive with science. Astronomy, for example, was seen as celestial mechanics. But as a result of investigations into phenomena such as electromagnetism, by the last decades of that century cracks started to appear in the system. Matters got worse with more subtle phenomena: the velocity of light, the behaviour of nuclear particles, the forces of chemical valency, and so on. The details of this history, the emergence of relativity theory and quantum mechanics, are less important than the summary observations Heisenberg offered. He insisted that it was incorrect to assert that Newtonian mechanics is false because it cannot explain field phenomena. One must say instead that 'Classical mechanics is a consistent self-enclosed scientific theory,' correct where its concepts can be applied, but only in those applications. Devastating as such a conclusion may have been for traditional thinking, the consequences were clear: a closed theory such as Newton's 'contains no certain statements about the world of experience' (Heisenberg 1974a: 42–45). What can be established mathematically is only to a small extent an 'objective fact'; it is more largely a survey of possibilities. From this point onward, the concepts of probability, possibility, and potential reality were seen to occupy the centre of theoretical interpretation in science.

Research as project making

Design practice can be understood as a form of scientific research when both are seen as *projective* activities. First, science. One of the key dimensions of the 'uncertainty principle' in modern physics is the *conditional* character of its explanations. Heisenberg observed that the position and momentum of a particle could not be defined simultaneously, for the measurement of one particle caused others to appear in what he called 'in-actual' positions. Assertions of fact, he said, had to be replaced by interpretations of possibility because the phenomena under study offered themselves to observation *variably*.

Project making in architecture is, of course, similarly interpretative and conditional, at least when design is seen as projection, not production. New techniques and instruments of representation promise to close the gap between phases of project making typically called design development and production. (I am referring to the rosy claims made in the advertising of new software packages, for building information modelling especially.) Whether or not those promises are kept, the distinction has great force in contemporary practice. Production assumes that much if not most of the work of design development has been finished. Production, like the project and progress, is oriented toward the future. But the accomplishment it represents – the completion or near completion of development – insulates the procedure against future interferences. With the deadline in view, production frees itself from alternate possibilities, distilling the process to technique alone, in order to lay hold of the work's final stage. This conversion of design into planning draws the yet-to-come back into the now, placing the future in the grasp of the present.

Production, then, is the means by which the product discards its preliminaries, severing the link between formation and form. While this temporal bracketing can be seen as a reduction of potentials and content, it is also a moment of coordination and concentration of all the energies that brought the work to its present state.

Like probability in science, projection in architecture remains within the limits of the likely. It is always and only an incomplete prefiguration of a final product, foreshadowing an outcome that has formed itself in the space between discovery and recollection. This means both the future and the past have roles to play. Before it can anticipate anything final the project must redefine its relationship to what exists, partly tearing itself away from the present, partly remaining there, creating a tension between the two. A break is refused and adhesions are allowed, according to the principle of modification whereby the project adheres to the conditions of its genesis.

Project making in architecture is no more certain of its outcome than research in modern sciences. One cannot say projects develop by chance, but their outcomes are far from pre-given. Retrospectively, the results make sense, but during the work's unfolding, the process is not entirely clear where it is going. It could be described as a kind of blind logic that creates itself along the way. Its path is often indirect, detouring after advancing, then turning back, renewing beginnings, and moving forward once again. Perhaps it could be described as a mixture of chance and reason: chances must be taken because repetitions get us nowhere, yet reason must intervene because the problems with which we began have not been solved. Such a process is less a matter of foresight and calculation than of cunning, requiring alertness to possibilities as they emerge. Theories in architecture tend to be more emancipated, problem-solving more enmeshed. Project making preserves and surpasses given conditions. It is not the kind of 'experimentation' whose techniques close the work in on itself, nor a method untainted by extra-disciplinary involvements. Project making requires movement away from its own techniques toward conditions that are not of its own making, an eccentric procedure dedicated to the unseen potential of the world it seeks to remake. This account of the architectural project suggests an approach to design research that is both more confident and more modest than is often assumed. To summarize my argument and guide this approach I will outline four basic premises for the project of design research:

1. when the actual methods of scientific research are kept in mind, and their similarity to project making understood, architecture's membership in the research community ceases to be a question;
2. knowledge is advanced in design research through creative practices not technical procedures, no matter how up-to-date the techniques may be, for the real distinction is between projective and product-oriented thinking;
3. innovation is misconstrued if it assumes adhesions to inherited culture can be completely severed or allowed without review, the principle of modification posits the rootedness of every tearing away;
4. the real subject matter of design research seen projectively is the world in which architecture finds its place, a world that is at once historical, cultural, and natural.

Bibliography

Feyerabend, P. (2010) *Against Method*, London: Verso.

Gadamer, H.-G. (1992) 'The Idea of the University', *On Education, Poetry, and History: Applied Hermeneutics*, Albany: State University of New York.

Gregotti, V. (1996) 'Modification', *Inside Architecture*, Cambridge, Mass.: MIT Press.

Heisenberg, W. (1974a) 'Closed Theory in Modern Science' [1948], *Across the Frontiers*, New York: Harper & Row.

Heisenberg, W. (1974b) 'Science and Technology in Contemporary Politics' [1960], *Across the Frontiers*, New York: Harper & Row.

Heisenberg, W. (1974c) 'Problems in Promoting Scientific Research' [1963], *Across the Frontiers*, New York: Harper & Row.

Le Corbusier (1991) *Precisions* [1930], Cambridge, Mass.: MIT Press.

Palissy, B. (1957) *The Admirable Discourse of Bernard Palissy* [1580], Urbana Champaign: University of Illinois Press.

Perrault C. (1993) *Ordonnance* [1683], Santa Monica: Getty.

Schilpp, P. A. (ed.) (1951) *Albert Einstein: Philosopher Scientist*, Chicago: Open Court.

Spaulding, E. G. (1918) *The New Rationalism*, New York: Henry Holt.

Wallner, F. (1994) *Constructive Realism*, West Lafayette, IN: Purdue University Press.

Chapter 2

One step towards an ecology of design: fields of relations and bodies of knowledge

Christopher Hight

As 'design research' has become increasingly ubiquitous within the contemporary academy its meaning has become increasingly diffused. It could be that like 'design' itself, the term has as many different definitions as there are practices that align themselves with it. Nevertheless, one adherent strain emerged in a newly public manner in the mid-1990s as a 'new' paradigm for architectural education and practice aligned to then emerging digital design processes, a Deleuze-derived new materialism, as well as Post-Fordist paradigms of a global information economy and production. Since then, such design research has become synonymous with innovations linked to complex geometry, parametric design and material experimentation. To the extent that my education, teaching and research has participated and sought to develop such practices, this chapter is a reflection on a shared project that has developed over almost two decades and which has reached a maturity that suggests it is time for both an assessment and transformation. Around the time of its emergence I argued that, 'the first movement in design research is to re-search architecture for its refracted resemblance, to route out its alignments with rationality and realism which appear only when we are anamorphically displaced from our habitual vantage point' (Hight 2005: 201). That is to say, design research should not be understood as continuing the ill-fated attempts to turn design into a science or to compensate for it not being so, but rather as offering methods and approaches that seek to enrich the specificity of architectural knowledge while opening it to extra-disciplinary potentials. In the mid-1990s science and technology offered such a potential for renovation.

Heretofore, design research has been commonly understood as applicable to post-graduate (post-professional) and other upper degree work. This is understandable for many reasons, including accreditation limitations, the expertise inculcated by such programs, and because expanding or transgressing disciplinary boundaries is, paradoxically, facilitated by having a group of students trained within a normative practice. If one understands design research as a claim regarding the nature of architectural knowledge, practice and its education, then it could be usefully generalized as a model rather than adhering to a narrower band of inquiry.

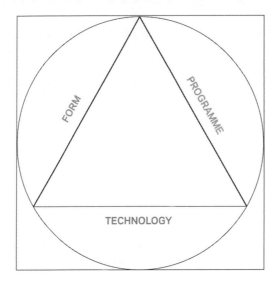

2.1
A diagram of the 'body of knowledge of architecture' as a Vitruvian triumvirate.

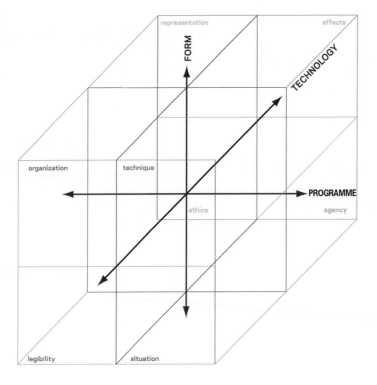

2.2
The discipline as a contingent 'field of relations' organized as a gradient of three-vector fields.

Lines of dissent

Here 'design research' does not mean normative research about how one should design nor anthropological studies of how design practice occurs but is itself a theoretical conjecture, namely that design practice constitutes a distinctive form of knowledge production and intellectual inquiry (Cross 1999; Findeli 1999). In his seminal text on design research, Stanford Anderson also situated it as a way of linking theory to practice, treating the contingencies of discrete projects as points along one or many research programmes. For him, such research should be rigorous in the way that Lakatos argued scientific practice is rigorous, but not in the science of naive rationalism (Anderson 1984: 147–148). Rather than an opposition of instrumentalism or autonomous formalism, Anderson's framing and examples suggest that the specificity and advancement of architectural knowledge can both enfold what have been heretofore understood as extrinsic criteria as well as the source of agency for the discipline. Accordingly, design research is inherently related to attempts to renovate practice and theory through each other, such as Stan Allen's understanding of architecture as a 'material practice' rather than a semiotic (Allen 2000) and to Sarah Whiting's and Bob Somol's conception of 'projective practices' (Somol and Whiting 2002), to which I will return. In such formulations issues of method and technique are necessarily epistemological because if it is understood as research, design produces new objects of inquiry and makes claims as to their significance. Empirical analysis and materials are often a central part of such design research, which in turn often seems to affiliate itself to sciences. But design research should not be understood as an updated version of 'design science' discourses of the 1960s. Indeed, design research is symptomatic of a broader epistemological transformation in which the privileged status of architecture as the metaphor for systematic reason has been displaced because architectonics of knowledge seem themselves less empirically accurate as ways of understanding the production of knowledge even in the natural sciences (Hight 2005: 200).

Design research marked a shift from 'critical practices' to 'innovation' and the adjunct promises of positioning architecture as a 'projective' or 'material' practice, through three operations. First, it was to incubate differentially advanced architectures that spoke to the newly shimmering global information economy and cyberspace. It seemed simply impossible to continue to argue for architecture of resistance from an avant-garde position. Indeed, as Kenneth Frampton argued, the possibility of maintaining a cogent critical programme was to position architecture in the rear-guard (Frampton 1983: 20). An emerging generation believed that architecture needed to reinvent itself to remain relevant after what was – and often still is – understood as a philosophical, technological and social 'revolution' of a global economy and information technology. Programmes such as the Architectural Association's Graduate Design Program initiated by Jeffery Kipnis were platforms to research alternative capacities for architectural thought and its agency (Hensel 2011). Kipnis was among the first to attempt to recognize that the critical programmes of the 1970s and 1980s had reached both maturity and an impasse and that the material conditions of architectural thought were to be problematized as a site for research in two directions he described as 'informed' programmatically and by 'deformation'

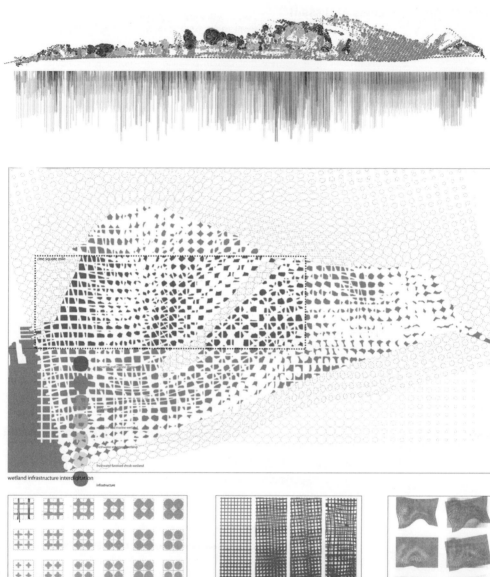

field notation

wetland | development blending

field moire diagrams

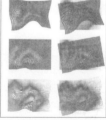

abstract machine

2.3a
This project by Jason Pierce researched Moiré effect, or interference pattern, as a way of staging the relationship between landscape and architecture, atmosphere and performance. From a graduate core studio at the Rice School of Architecture taught by Christopher Hight and Michael Robinson, 2009.

2.3b

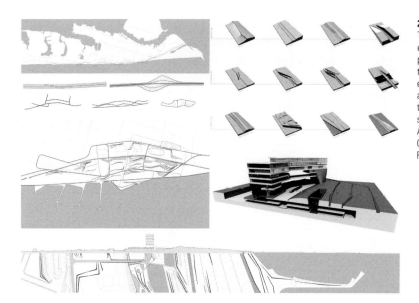

2.4
This project by Peter Muessig examined the 'line' in both plan and section, delaminating the edge produced by an existing seawall between city and sea into a negotiated terrain. From a graduate core studio at the Rice School of Architecture taught by Christopher Hight and Michael Robinson, 2009.

of surfaces (Kipnis 1991, 1993). By 1995 the graduate programme had been transformed into the Architectural Association's Design Research Laboratory under the leadership of Brett Steele, Patrick Schumacher and Tom Verebes, and immediately thereafter the AA's graduate school would host two other design research-based programmes: Landscape Urbanism, headed by Ciro Najlie and Moshen Mostafavi and Emerging Technologies, led by Michael Hensel and Michael Weinstock. Patrik Schumacher's texts at the time positioned the design research programme of the DRL as an extension of Kipnis's deforming and informing architecture, but take on a significant inflection. For him, the 'negativities' of critical theory proved unable to track the complex and multiple conditions of late-capitalist society, and new social orders demanded formal innovation (Schumacher 2000). In a different way, Brett Steele positioned design research as a mechanism through which architecture could pragmatically engage issues such as branding and globalization.

Second, design research became a method for training architects for hybrid, or transdisciplinary, practices that would lead the transformation. Significantly, the very idea of the 'discipline' as a clearly bounded body of knowledge was seen as problematic, and 'design' was aimed at interdisciplinary diffusion (with particular links to product design, landscape, digital design, internet protocols, etc.). Landscape urbanism emerged as a design research agenda, which, as Charles Waldheim argued, signalled a disciplinary realignment between landscape, urbanism and architecture. The crucible of the modern industrial metropolis had been succeeded by the post-metropolitan sprawl, for which landscape and systems was the common substrate, the autonomous objects then thought through architecture. Frampton himself claimed that by the mid-1990s even the rear-guard position within architecture was co-opted and that only reconfiguration or even dissolution of the disciplinary boundaries into a general idea of 'environmental design' offered a possible line of resistance to capital (Frampton 1994: 83–93; Shannon 2006: 160).

One can locate a similar realignment in the Emerging Technologies programme at the AA between architecture, industrial design and engineering. While both programmes of design research could respect architecture as an autonomous discipline, they also knew that post-Fordism substantially reconfigured the urban and technical contexts for which the modernist discursive formation of architecture was calibrated. That is to say, there was a historical moment when normative, perhaps even hegemonic, boundaries of the discipline could still be assumed at least as a straw man. The history of modern architecture is character-ized by an anxiety regarding the nature of its discipline, perennially unsure about itself and looking to other fields. Rather than attempting to call for 'disciplinarity,' design research sought to exploit this condition. This can be understood as a process of introjection, in which a problem cannot be articulated within the discipline either because it is so central to the conditions of its possibility or because it locates the discipline's exteriority. The other fields are therefore enfolded into the space of the architectural thought, which through this process is transformed (Hight 2008).

Third, and following from the first two, design was approached not as the solving of problems, but as a particular form of synthetic intellectual inquiry and as a process for the production of concepts. Such concepts were not extrinsic ideas that would be represented or signified by architecture in a semiotic manner, but rather propositions that were intrinsic to the material practices of design (Allen 1999). The entire discourses surrounding emergence and biomimesis in architecture can also be understood as positioning architecture's agency and intellectual cogency as a material practice (cf. Hensel and Menges 2006). To do so was to position the architect as a vital agent of change within the world rather than providing critical commentary upon it. Not insignificantly, design research programmes such as those at the AA replaced the independent thesis with an extended project pursued under the research umbrellas defined by the professors, a model adopted by many other programs (Hight 2005: 29–33). Similarly, at the AA there was an institutional shift of the centre of gravity from the Diploma school, which featured units, run by 'Masters' as highly autonomous ateliers, to the graduate programmes run under a laboratory model more akin to that found in scientific research settings (Higgott 2007:153–188; cf. http://www.aaschool.ac.uk/AALIFE/LIBRARY/aahistory.php).

Today, the generative conditions of design research have been supplanted by the maturation and proliferation of programmes and practices. We have shifted from a few outliers to a generation of expert practices that are now running their own laboratories. This proliferation of a model of education, however, raises issues that are rather different from the conditions of fifteen or so years ago. For one, the boundaries of disciplinarily are at once much more diffused even as there seems an ever-increasing locus of expertise vying for ubiquity. For example 'parametricism' is being promulgated and resisted as a universal style. While seek-ing to displace critical theory, design research leveraged oppositional strategies and 'radical' neo-avant-gardism. For example, if modern architecture was governed by the 'poem of the right angle' and straight line of rationalism (Ingraham 1998), design research charted the orderings of curvilinearity and the 'function of the oblique'. Such an ideological opposition is no longer capable of propelling a discourse in part because it has been so successful in displacing the once dominant construct. In

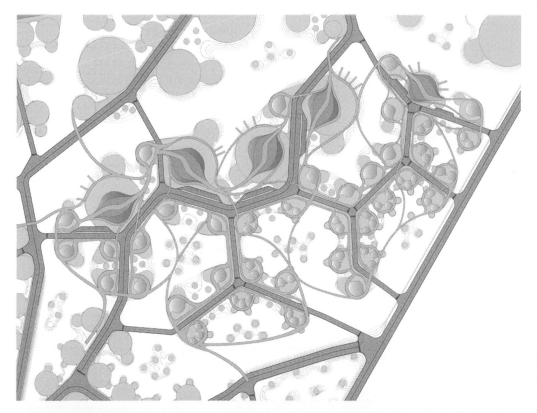

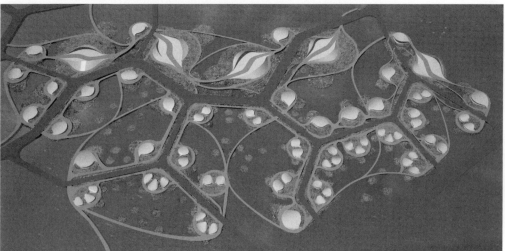

2.5a
Amy Westermeyer combined research on the industrial ecologies of dredging with geometric research on Voronoi patchwork organizations to design a site that would evolve in time from a remediation field into a resort community embedded in the wetlands created through these processes. From a graduate core studio taught by Christopher Hight and Michael Robinson, 2009.

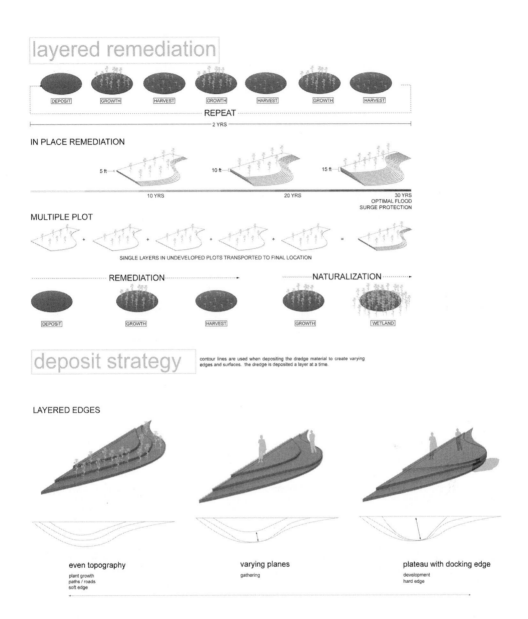

layered remediation

DEPOSIT GROWTH HARVEST GROWTH HARVEST GROWTH HARVEST

---- REPEAT ----

2 YRS

IN PLACE REMEDIATION

5 ft   10 ft   15 ft

10 YRS   20 YRS   30 YRS
OPTIMAL FLOOD
SURGE PROTECTION

MULTIPLE PLOT

+ + + + =

SINGLE LAYERS IN UNDEVELOPED PLOTS TRANSPORTED TO FINAL LOCATION

---- REMEDIATION ----   ---- NATURALIZATION ----

DEPOSIT   GROWTH   HARVEST   GROWTH   WETLAND

deposit strategy

contour lines are used when depositing the dredge material to create varying edges and surfaces. the dredge is deposited a layer at a time.

LAYERED EDGES

even topography
plant growth
paths / roads
soft edge

varying planes
gathering

plateau with docking edge
development
hard edge

2.5b

such a condition, design research becomes a pedagogy of refinement and horizontal variation rather than a laboratory of evolutionary differentiation. The methods of instruction can also become similarly 'conventional' and normative. When coupled to the demand for the 'new' this can render the products of design research as

2.6
Third-year undergraduate students Ryan Botts and Philip Poon designed an urban park that captures surface water run-off and remediates it before it enters a bayou, employing the same geometries to stage a programme that links the street level to the water level. Studio at the Rice School of Architecture taught by Christopher Hight and Michael Robinson, 2008.

simply part of the churn. Sarah Whiting has described this as a condition of simple 'accumulation' and 'exhaustive proliferation' that is emblematic rather than transformative (Whiting 2009). Paradoxically, therefore, once design as research transforms from a disruption to convention and becomes a new paradigm, this very success threatens to undermine the innovation upon which the entire idea of design research depends. We seem to have passed the 'revolutionary' paradigm shift and entered a new period of normalcy. This does not suggest that design research should be abandoned but expanded and decoupled from the particular practices to which it has been adhered.

Coordinating disciplinarity

How does one educate an architect to constitute a projective form of practice within such a condition? How does one remain committed to a progressive agenda, neither capitulating into the proliferation of variation with little criteria of differentiation nor calling for a return to an essentialist definition of 'disciplinarily'? First, one might try to survey the current terrain and plot its coordinate geography.

Recently, Bob Somol has offered a triangulation of what can be understood as three primary rhetorics of architectural thought: Politics, Fiction and Science (Somol 2010). In turn these operate in three different pairings: Political Fiction, Political Science and Science Fiction. The latter is deployed to develop a critical position on the now prevalent discourses on design research wedded to parametric, scripted and otherwise programmed digital design processes and often coupled to ideas and formalisms of emergence and performativity. For Somol the frequent references to natural models and to engineering logics in such design research programmes suggests a creeping 'scientism' that displaces the political dimension of design. Moreover, Somol notes how this coupling not only employs references to science and nature but also does so in that it requires 'elegant' and 'intricate' integration to the extent that such work requires extreme control and even re-imagining not only of the design process, but also of fabrication and construction. While examples of such architecture are being constructed, often through state-of-the-art technologies, the work continually pushes towards a retreating horizon of imminent technological innovation. This scientistic futurism, Somol suggests, places this idiom in the domain of 'Science + Fiction = Science Fiction'. Common discourses of 'sustainability' and infrastructural derived design, on the other hand, belong to the genre of 'Political Science' in that it employs scientific and technical factors often as ways of making moralist claims and even imperatives that determine design. In contrast, Somol champions architecture as a literature of political fiction (Somol 2010), a genre of what amounts to Baudrillardian simulacra.

It is worth noting that Somol's feat of ideological jujitsu is only possible because of the proliferation and maturation of the two other rhetorics to such an extent that they produce a disciplinary anxiety about the relevancy of architectural practice and the cogency of autonomy. Yet, as I have just argued, at the historical moment of its formulation, 'design research' was inherently ideological and coupled to discourses of post-humanism as much as to science. That is to say, in the mid-1990s it is reasonable to suggest that references to scientific and technical factors were themselves a political and ideological lever designed to displace the mature

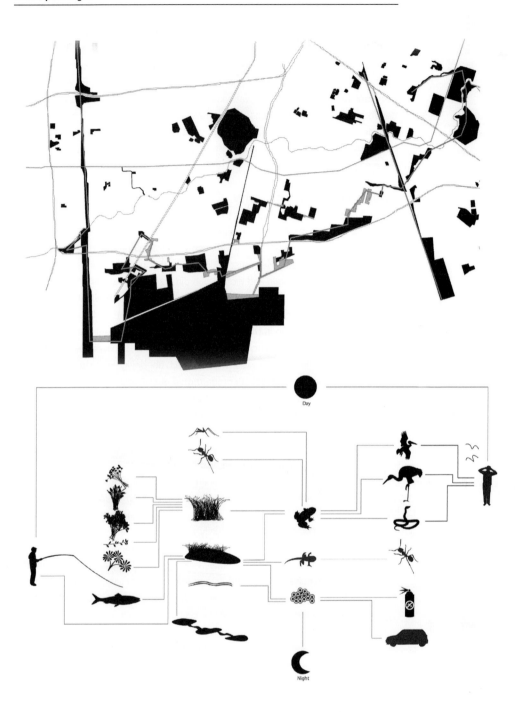

2.7a
Weijia Song, a third-year undergraduate student, researched the potential of linking isolated patchworks of green into an ecological network by employing infrastructural rights-of-way that cut across the urban fabric in Houston. In the design, a keystone species of frog is reintroduced into an operative landscape produced through a fanning and stepped geometry that allows both pockets of human and non-human habitats and linear corridors of connection. Studio at the Rice School of Architecture taught by Christopher Hight and organized with Neeraj Bhatia.

Slow Moving Water
Remediation Pools   Houston Toad Habitats
Retention Ponds

-20'
-15'
-10'
-5'
0-5'

2.7b

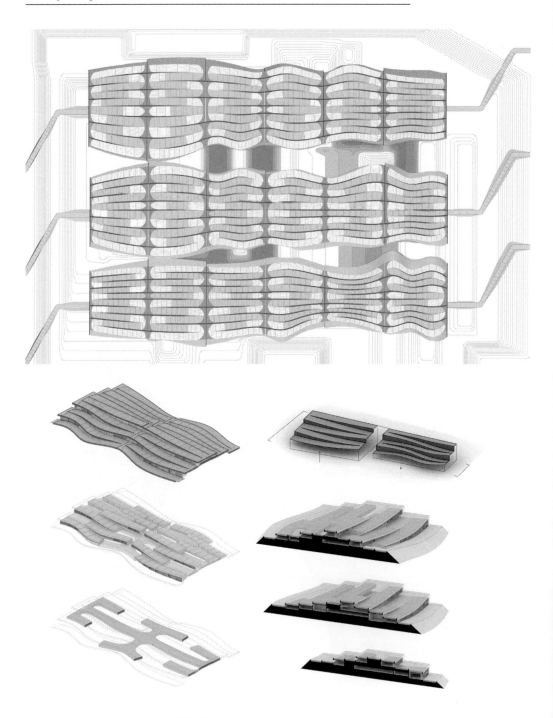

2.8a
Using Grasshopper-Rhino, third-year undergraduate Peter Stone developed a design that combines housing and urban agriculture that opportunizes the existing topography of the site to maximize irrigation and minimize regional flooding, creating an architecture and ecological sponge. Studio at the Rice School of Architecture taught by Christopher Hight and organized with Neeraj Bhatia.

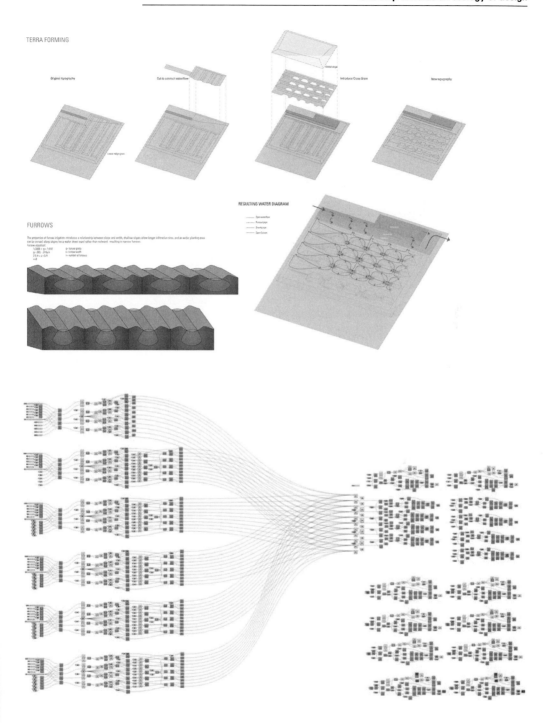

TERRA FORMING

Original topography

Cut to connect waterflow

Introduce Cross Grain

New topography

FURROWS

RESULTING WATER DIAGRAM

2.8b

2.9
Undergraduate students
examining how to translate
material prototype
experiments into digital
geometries. Rice School of
Architecture, 2006.

paradigm of political fiction that then dominated the elite academy (one tied to Marxism, critical theory, semiotics, deconstruction and literature). The problem arises when this ideologically 'critical' operation of displacement becomes *de rigueur*.

More importantly, Somol's triad of science, politics and fiction could be understood as a twenty-first-century version of the Vitruvian triumvirate firmitatis, utilitatis, venustatis. Perhaps because of a deep disciplinary investment in stability, architects seem to love tripods when delineating itself as a field of knowledge. What distinguishes Somol's formulation from that of classical architecture is that he repeatedly kicks one of the legs out from under the table of architectural thought to construct instead a series of purposefully unstable pairs. Furthermore, these couplings are not truly dialectical, as synthesis is not presented as necessary or even perhaps desirable. Or to put it in the Derridian rhetoric of the late 1980s, one of the three terms is in a state of erasure (e.g., Political Fiction Science). The tripod of architectural knowledge, which in classical Vitruvian terms provides a foundational structure of knowledge, is presented as an inherently unstable relationship of signifiers. Somol's argument suggests a dynamic of continually rotating and provisional alignments defined by what these shifting signifiers exclude.

Interestingly, Somol's triad more closely maps onto Kant's tripartite architectonic of knowledge. As we know, Kant divided metaphysics into three faculties, each of which was the subject of one of his epochal books: *Critiques of Pure Reason, of Practice Reason* and *of Judgment*. Both the Vitruvian and the Somolian terms map more or less directly onto knowledge of objective ordering and structure, of use and agency, and finally of subjective qualities. Of all these, the subjective has always been the most problematic and generative in that it operated as that which adheres the other two, completing Kant's architectonics of knowledge, but in a way

2.10
A material performance
workshop led by Michael
Hensel within a studio at the
Rice School of Architecture by
Christopher Hight and Michael
Robinson, 2007.

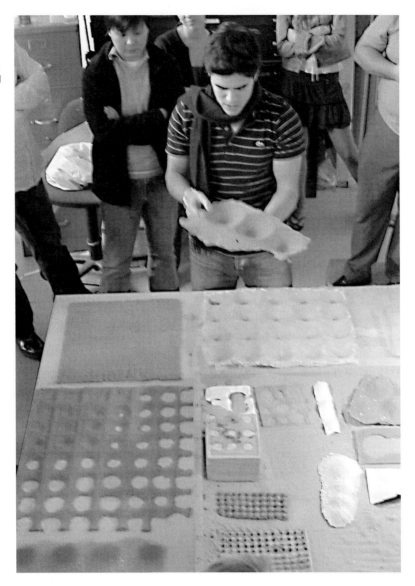

that is itself highly unstable. Kant's *Critique of Judgment* is itself divided into two
sections on aesthetics and teleological judgment addressing questions of the beau-
tiful and artistic practice in the former and biological process and forms in the latter.
Design itself can be understood as a bridge between these two sections. Once the
Kantian revolution sundered the transparency between phenomena and noumena, a
discipline such as architecture characteristically swerves from cultural and natural
referents as a way of girding its discourses and claiming a truth or agency for certain
forms of practice.

Now we can see that Somol's triplet operates as a refrain in the very
conditions of possibility of architectural thought or aesthetic practice modernity. The

point here is not to embrace or return to a Kantian schema, let alone make a claim to some sort of classically timeless and invariant foundation of knowledge. Instead, such a stable figure suggests putting onto the table the conditions of architecture as a discipline constituted in and through modernity or architectural propositions possible within a modern episteme. Rather than understand the persistent return and restatement of such a formulation as evidence of extrinsic categories, we might understand them as providing a map or coordinate system of the space of architectural knowledge in modernity. This mapping is not the territory, but neither is it simply empirical insofar that it triangulates and articulates the problems that can become explicitly positioned and redraws the terrain.

Towards an ecology of the architectural mind

The problem therefore is not simply to shift from one couple back to the other, but to understand what might be at stake in approaching architecture as such a field of triangulated relationships. Perhaps it is useful to shift away from the metaphor of the 'body of knowledge' for understanding disciplinarity of 'architecture'. Such a latent Vitruvian model of the body suggests clear delineations of interiors, boundaries and contexts with apparent teleological ends. This organism moves through historical time and may evolve but nevertheless retains a continuous and singular identity and autonomy. However, today, this formal model, itself at least as architectural as it is corporal, is less useful or descriptive than a spatial model in which disciplinarity is approached as a 'field of relations'. Rather than a bounded set of hierarchical parts integrated into a whole that adapts to context, a 'field' suggests a topological surface constructed through the material practices at any given moment and which can be continually enfolded to produce different configurations and constellations. Any identify or coherence through time is therefore provisionally determined in terms of representation and subject matter, an epiphenomenon produced by the manner in which one operates in the field. This, in other words, shifts from an anatomical-architectonic metaphor to an ecological-informational model. If the use of ecology seems foreign to the discipline of architecture, one should recall the classical isomorphism between the 'body' and the architectonic as model. If one wants to displace such humanist and classical epistemologies, one needs to be able to construct a concept of disciplinary coherence that does not repeat ad nauseum humanist concepts of identity, boundary and coherence.

Another triplet is useful to introduce here: Felix Guattari's 'three ecologies' of Subjective, Social, Natural life worlds (Guattari 2000: 23–69). Guattari adapted these terms from Gregory Bateson's theories of an 'ecology of mind' and did so to avoid the idea that these three constitute some sort of fundamental trinity or discrete worlds that one might synthesize into a unity. Bateson's definition of ecology depends on a recursive relationship between living systems and information as the relationship between a discrete system (an organism, a body, a discipline) to the 'context' of other systems (environment, other disciplines, etc.) that it negotiates and constructs as a concept and representation to itself via its organization of sensory inputs. For Bateson, ecology is 'study of the interaction and survival of ideas and programs (i.e., differences, complexes of differences, etc.) in circuits' (Bateson 1972: 491). The 'mind' is not singular, but the multiple 'minds' or subsystems organized in relationship to other such 'minds'. Every mind is immanent to other minds and participates in their construction, not an object set apart from its context (Bateson 1972: 466). This understanding of ecology is useful as an alternative model to the 'body of knowledge' insofar as it offers a way of defining specific relationships and transmission of information across multiple identities or systems within dynamic context as well as the related transformation of these things in time. In that regard, Guattari's Subject, Social and Natural ecologies are best understood not as categories nor closed domains so much as abstract planes similar to those that Guattari proposed with Deleuze in their last book, *What is Philosophy*. They argue, 'Philosophy, art and science are not the mental objects of an objectified brain but the three aspects under which the brain becomes subject … They are the three planes, the rafts on which the brain plunges into chaos' (Deleuze and Guattari 1994: 210). An analogy might be to Bateson's ecological minds, three fields with three attractors, setting up a complex gradient; these attractors are not things or abstract idealities but rather the systemic aggregation of concrete and specific material conditions, constraints and practices (phenomena rather than fundamental categories). Though Guattari's short essay is characteristically sweeping if evocative, if understood in relationship to Deleuze's sustained and more rigorous attempts to invert Kant's transcendental idealism into a sort of transcendental empiricism (just as Foucault attempted to replace the transcendental a priori with the historical a priori), we have the ability to specify and differentiate modes of operation and the production of knowledge without the need for reification of categories or ideologies.

What would happen if we understood design research as the production of an architectural 'brain becoming subject'? Could we understand 'Science, Politics and Fiction', or 'firmitatis, utilitatis, venustatis' as three coordinate planes roughly corresponding to Natural, Social and Subjective matters of fact, through which design constructs figures of relationships, across which the historicity of concepts accrues and novelty arises through enfolding? For example, around the Social attractor we can group those architectural problems such as programme, space and agency; around the Natural, material, structure and environment; around the Subjective, effects, form and representation. These of course are further specified by any design problem of thesis. The point is that within this field, specific things are assembled into various combinations as a mode of practice, and as a line of inquiry. The media of architecture – drawings, diagrams, modelling, materials writing, etc. – can all be understood as the means through which such constellations are constructed, examined, developed, translated, recombined. That is, they do not exist

2.11
An array of diagrammatic design models. Studio at the Rice School of Architecture taught by Christopher Hight and organized with Neeraj Bhatia.

outside the practices of architecture as a mode of inquiry or research into the construction of design worlds, and which allow the discipline to address a wide spectrum of issues through the specificity of the discipline, now understood not as cohering to a singular identity or dialectic but to an irreducible multiplicity. This field of relations supports the project of proliferation while allowing that within the multiplication of streams of research, which require increasing specificity. Design here becomes the production of concepts in a field space coordinated by three planes rather than as a dialectic or tripartite architectonic of reason. These three terms are not essential components of an objectified understanding of what constitutes architecture, but epiphenomenal platforms for plunging into a field of material conditions of architectural practice and thought – historical, operational and empirical – and then surfacing them into a conceptual armature.

If it is difficult to cohere a 'school of thought' in architecture today, it may be because the 'body of knowledge' is no longer a useful model for understanding a transdisciplinary condition where the modern boundaries of design knowledges that were produced in relationship to their environment have not yet been succeeded by new formations. In such a period of transition neither normative nor avant-garde agendas can provide coherent pedagogies. There seem to be significant realignments and diffusion of boundaries, but without specificity and understanding of the historicity of contemporary problems; students are not 'liberated' from historical models of what constitutes architecture, its modes of practice and its objects so much as unable to construct meaningful alternatives. Once understood as not wedded to a specific ideological agenda, but as a means for the production of such agendas, design research can be usefully approached as a general pedagogical framework for every level of design education.

Bibliography

Allen, S. (1999) 'Infrastructural Urbanism', *Points + Lines*, New York: Princeton Architectural Press: 47–57.

Allen, S. (2000) 'Introduction: Practice vs. Project', *Essays Practice Architecture, Technique and Representation*, London: Routledge: xiii–xv.

Anderson, S. (1984) 'Architectural Design as a System of Research Programs', *Design Studies* 5, 3: 146–158.

Bateson, G. (1972) *Steps to an Ecology of Mind*, Chicago: University of Chicago Press.

Cross, N. (1999) 'Design Research: A Disciplined Conversation', *Design Issues* 15, 2: 5–10.

Deleuze, G. and Guattari, F. (1994) *What is Philosophy?*, New York/London: Verso Books.

Findeli, A. (1999) 'Introduction', *Design Issues* 15, 2: 1–3.

Frampton, K. (1983) 'Towards a Critical Regionalism: Six Points for and Architecture of Resistance', *The Anti-Aesthetic*, Port Townsend, WA: Bay Press: 16–30.

Frampton, K. (1994) 'Megaforms and Urban Landscape', *Columbia Documents* 4: 83–93.

Guattari, F. (2000) *The Three Ecologies*, London: Athlone Press.

Hensel, M. U. (2011) 'Type? What Type? Further Reflections on the Extended Threshold', *Typological Urbanism: Projective Cities, AD Architectural Design* 81, 1: 56–65.

Hensel, M. and Menges, A. (eds) (2006) *Morpho-Ecologies*, London: AA Publications.

Higgott, A. (2007) 'The Subject of Architecture: Alvin Boyarsky and the Architectural Association School', *Mediating Modernism: Architectural Cultures in Britain*, London/New York: Routledge: 153–188.

Hight, C. (2005) 'Oxymoronic Methods: The Incomplete Project of Design Research', *Corporate Fields*, London: Architectural Association: 198–203.

Hight, C. (2008) *Architectural Principles in the Age of Cybernetics*, London/New York: Routledge.

Ingraham, C. (1998) *Architecture and the Burdens of Linearity*, New Haven: Yale University Press.

Kipnis, J. (1991) '/Twisting the Separatrix/', *Assemblage* 14: 30–61.

Kipnis, J. (1993) 'Towards a New Architecture', *Folding in Architecture*, London: AD Wiley: 40–49.

Schumacher, P. (2000) 'The AA Design Research Lab – Premises, Agenda, Methods', *Research and Practice in Architecture Conference*, Alvar Aalto Academy, Helsinki, Finland.

Shannon, K. (2006) 'From Theory to Resistance: Landscape Urbanism in Europe', *Landscape Urbanism: A Reader*, Charles Waldheim (ed.), New York: Princeton Architectural Press: 141–162.

Somol, R. E. (2010) 'Less –ity, More –ism', Lecture at the Rice School of Architecture, April 12, 2010.

Somol, R. E. and Whiting, S. (2002) 'Notes Around the Doppler Effect and Other Moods of Modernism', *Perspecta* 33: 72–77.

Whiting, S. (2009) Lecture at the Future of Design Conference, University of Michigan, October 9–10.

Chapter 3

On the emergence of research by design and practice-based research approaches in architectural and urban design

Halina Dunin-Woyseth and Fredrik Nilsson

Introduction

The objective of this chapter is to delineate a picture of how research by design in architecture and urbanism has emerged and developed in the European and Scandinavian
scene, with a special focus on developments in the Netherlands, Norway, Sweden and
Belgium during the recent two decennia. This brief diachronic review will not provide a
single, 'complete', homogeneous account of this development process, as it will be
coloured by our own academic interests and experiences. For this historical review an
important statement of John Walker has been momentous:

> Although various histories exist, this does not mean that there is more than
> one material reality – as many worlds as there are individuals. One difficulty
> all historians experience is that the past can never be reconstructed in its
> totality and completeness; every history is, therefore, a partial or simplified
> representation of a past situation. Selection is inevitable in history-writing.
> Histories differ not only because scholars tackle different facts of design but
> also because one historian will select and emphasize certain facts and
> events while another will select and emphasize different facts and events
> … An analogy with map-making may be helpful: several maps do not contra-
> dict one another, instead they complement one another. Taken together
> they provide a more complete account of the terrain than taken singly.
>
> (Walker 1989: 2–3)

This chapter consists of three main parts. Its design has been inspired by another statement of John A. Walker about constituting new disciplines:

> The awareness that a distinct discipline exists occurs when a sufficient number of practitioners become self-conscious about their activities and begin to join together to discuss common problems and interests. It is usually at this critical point that a professional organization is formed … Once an organization exists, the trappings of an academic discipline soon follow: elected officers, a newsletter, a scholarly journal, an annual conference.
>
> (Walker 1989: 1–2)

We do not see Walker's use of 'trappings' in a negative sense, and we regard research by design not as a discipline in a strict sense, but as a field-specific research approach which is on its way to becoming a recognized way of studies in architecture and urban design.

We shall in Part I present what some seminal scholars have written about new modes of knowledge production and examine how research by design can be embedded in this mainstream of new epistemological developments. Part II will study how research by design manifested itself in various national settings of four countries, the Netherlands, Norway, Sweden and Belgium. The question of what happened in theses arenas will be addressed, having in mind the second part of Walker's description of how fields of inquiry emerge from fields of practice. The concluding Part III will consider how these issues presented in Part I and Part II can respond to Walker's outline of how new fields of inquiry develop parallel and in an interplay between the contents of the inquiry and the scenes this content has been developed within. The challenge is to provide a certain history of development of research by design as well as to assess how mature this development has become.

Part I – Research by design. What has been said about it?
'Post-academic science' and its relation to design

Philosophers of science talk about the advent of post-academic science parallel to more traditional developments: 'Post-academic science was born historically of academic science, overlaps with it, preserves many of its features, performs much of the same functions, and is located in much the same social space – typically universities, research institutes and other knowledge-producing institutions' (Ziman 2000: 68). But although the academic and the post-academic sciences merge into one another, their cultural and epistemic differences are sufficiently important to justify the new name. One of many terms addressing this post-academic science is Mode 2, as opposed to Mode 1 of traditional, established, academic knowledge production. Mode 2 is most often called transdisciplinary mode of knowledge production (Gibbons *et al.* 1994).

What the advent of post-academic science can mean for architectural and design research 'from within' the practice and for its modes of generating and communicating it within the context of an equal dialogue with other knowledge producers are interesting questions. Because when trying to explain and legitimize in a scientific context the way architectural practice generates knowledge, it becomes clear how immature our field is in relation to more traditional forms of research. The developments in relation to post-academic science can help to conceptualize other knowledge fields and use the potential of design in knowledge production.

For some years now, the term *transdisciplinarity* has been spreading around the world, appearing in different discussions and places, and giving rise to new insights, conceptualizations and perplexity. At the heart of the transdisciplinary approach is a quest for a deeper understanding of our present world, and with a palpable direction towards the future. The term *transdisciplinarity* was coined to give expression to a need to transgress disciplinary boundaries, and is interesting in relation to such a combinatory and inclusive discipline as architecture.

There is a long tradition of studying architecture 'from outside' by researchers from other disciplines. An example of such studies is the well-established discipline of art history. But even art historians themselves have recognized that a perspective 'from within' has been missing in their studies of artefacts and their production. E. H. Gombrich has been perhaps the one most preoccupied with the question of skill as a missing aspect in the discipline of art history. He believes that the focus of academic inquiry should be placed on the craft of art (Gombrich 1991: 68).

Ideas about disciplinarily viable design knowledge have been considered by several scholars. As early as 1969, Herbert A. Simon introduced the concept of 'the science of design' in his seminal book *The Sciences of the Artificial*. To the science disciplines, the exploration of natural things, he opposed the science of design, which deals with 'artificial things, how to make artefacts, that have desired properties, and how to design' (Simon 1969: 55).

Also the now widely discussed new form of knowledge production – Mode 2 – opens for a search for knowledge through design. The main feature of the new mode is that it operates within a context of application where problems are not set within a traditional disciplinary framework, and the approach is to focus on and follow research problems as they emerge in these contexts. The process is dynamic, and consists in specific clusterings and configurations of knowledge brought together on a temporary basis according to the specific problem at hand and context of application. There is an orientation towards problem solving, but it involves the strong feature of an experimental, innovative attitude (Gibbons *et al.* 1994; Nowotny *et al.* 2001).

Several concepts are now being used in the effort to delineate this specific kind of 'in practice model' of research, and especially in the field of architecture and design there are several concepts – e.g. practice-based, practice-led – related to the notion of 'research by design'. In the seminal report *Practice-based Doctorates in the Creative and Performing Arts and Design*, Christopher Frayling states that 'The practice-based doctorate advances knowledge partly by means of practice'. The relevance of this way of doing research is also argued for by saying that it is no longer possible to polarize research efforts as either conforming or not conforming to the 'scientific method', which previously was the guarantor of 'real research'. 'There is already a continuum from scientific research to creative practice' (Frayling *et al.* 1997: 15). Chris Rust *et al.* talk about 'practice-led research', which they define as 'research in which the professional and/or creative practices of art, design or architecture play an instrumental part in an inquiry' (Rust *et al.* 2007: 11).

The increasing number of doctoral projects within this research field also led to conceptual development in which notions like 'projective research' are used. 'Projective research' is design research that emphasizes 'the notion of project understood as "throwing ahead", as a reflexive conceptual action'. This conceptual action is made 'by means of spatial projections', that make prospective alternatives subject to anticipative reflection. Hence, 'the capacity of pre-figuration, which is native to design thinking, is central to projective research' (Janssens 2009: 48–49, 64).

It is especially during the last decades that we have seen an increasing discussion on the importance of knowledge through design and computational modelling which stresses the importance of information technology and communication (Gibbons *et al.* 1994: 44–45), forming research processes where visual simulation and dynamic imaging complement and develop scientific methods and language. 'The concrete/iconic modes of cognition are particularly relevant in design, whereas the formal/symbolic modes are more relevant in the sciences' (Cross 2007: 28). The particularly constructive, concrete thinking through different 'artefacts' can be seen as using the objects of the design thinking as modelling, communication and investigative devices.

Frayling and his group (Frayling *et al.* 1997) argue for a set of definitions of standards framed in such a way that they are sufficiently rigorous to secure the quality of research, but sufficiently inclusive to allow all subjects to find expression within them. This inclusive model would involve either demonstrating that the activities and outcomes could be seen as consistent with a traditional scientific model, or broadening the model so as to encompass the entire continuum from scientific to practice-based research.

Bryan Lawson has argued that the description of this new form of 'in practice model' of research, that emerges according to Gibbons *et al.*, has great similarities with design. Lawson states that it is possible that designers unknowingly 'are just ahead of the game rather than behind it after all' (Lawson 2002:114).

Part II – Research by design. What happened in its arenas?

Four national environments will be discussed in greater detail as examples of how new approaches have emerged and been integrated in academic and professional discussions. We shall examine how certain arenas in these countries have responded to the issue of research by design. These arenas, consistent with Walker's criteria for building fields of inquiry, are: innovative architectural and urban design practices, research conferences, design research journals, books, and innovative education of designers, doctoral research and research networks. The advantage of addressing these arenas is that it is not a unitary and homogeneous 'thing' that will emerge from these studies, but a set of cultural practices engaged in by a specific group of designers and design intellectuals.

The Dutch story

The development of research strategies at architectural offices in the Netherlands during the 1990s was palpable and also discussions on the need for research in architecture started spreading in the international debate (Lotsmaa 1999; Sigler and van Toorn 2003). Important in this context was Rem Koolhaas and OMA, who since his book *Delirious New York* in 1978 had presented alternative systematic approaches and research in strong relation to architectural design practice, and also in educational contexts (Koolhaas 1978, 1995; Koolhaas *et al.* 2001a, 2001b). Several architects and offices followed and published books in which they presented their work as research, and many developed working methods looking like systematic investigations of contemporary societies and urban situations (Maas *et al.* 1998, 1999, 2003; Hensel and Verebes 1999; Bunschoten *et al.* 2001; FOA *et al.* 2003). Even though criticism has been launched against the Dutch offices, the research approaches have also been described as part of the Dutch modernist tradition. The investigations by the architects Van Eesteren and van Lohuizen of city transformations during the 1920s, 1930s and 1940s formed a tradition of research for architects in the municipalities. When the building sector was deregulated in the 1980s the research in the municipalities was abandoned, but architectural offices continued investigating urban situations. Offices like MVRDV can therefore be seen as part of a longer tradition of systematic inquiries and research attitudes among architectural practices (Lootsma 2001), where design thinking in relation to research is used to investigate as well as to speculate and provoke discussion on contemporary and future possibilities.

In 1996 the Faculty of Architecture at the Technical University Delft organized the conference 'Doctorates in Design and Architecture' focusing the scientific status of design research as the fundamental framework for doctoral research in architecture. The conference presented a widespread, differentiated and specialized field of research areas and topics. Together with the awareness of lacking research tradition at several universities, initiatives were taken to establish a tradition of doctorate studies in design research. But it was also stressed that both the academic and professional worlds look upon design in very conventional ways with preconceptions of traditional divisions between science and art, at the same time as design methods and design approaches are becoming more important to deal with new challenges and complexities in cities and the built environment.

The Faculty of Architecture at TU Delft initiated a research project in 1998 called 'The Architectural Intervention', which had the objective to elucidate, develop and operationalize design research as a method of scientific research (Nieuwenhuis and Ouwerkerk 2000). The final event of the project was an international conference called 'Research by Design' organized in Delft in 2000, at which the main outcomes of the project were presented in preliminary versions of two books on the key themes of composition and methodology (Steenberger *et al.* 2000; Jong *et al.* 2000). The conference included presentations of both researchers and practitioners, where architects like Ben van Berkel and Wiel Arets made clear and confident contributions, while the researchers often seemed uncertain about their legitimacy in relation to the profession as well as to academia.

3.1
The cover of the book at the conference 'Research by Design' at Technical University Delft in 2000.

The conference 'Research by Design' was in many ways a milestone in the development of this direction in architectural design research, as it elucidated the issues of scientific research, design and research by design.

Another important institution in the Netherlands is the Berlage Institute in Rotterdam. Their post-graduate education for architects has had a strong focus on the advanced architectural practice, and in the development of relevant architectural research the importance of exploring specific architectural knowledge has been emphasized. Berlage publishes the periodical *Hunch* in which different aspects of architectural culture, research and criticism are discussed. The notion of transdisciplinarity is in one edition discussed as what happens at the edge, beyond, or when using your disciplinary skills and tools outside of one own's discipline; something that needs a clear disciplinary identity but must get rid of disciplinary control (Linder 2005). *Hunch* has also presented student and doctoral projects that are using architectural design tools to investigate knowledge fields and disciplines close to architecture and urbanism, but with a clear point of departure in the design projects.

The Norwegian story

Research education around the Doctoral Programme of the Oslo School of Architecture has been a primus motor for developing field-specific design scholarship since the beginning of the 1990s. The programme was primarily targeted towards architects, but professionals from other fields, such as landscape architecture, object design, visual arts and design education were admitted. The Doctoral Programme has played an active role as a hub within the national research education system called Norway Network (Norgesnettet). Its profile has been strongly formed by the recruited candidates being mainly from the 'making' professions, and affected further by research subjects being most often derived from the PhD students' own practice-related experience.

With the admission of various design professionals, a broader dialogue has been initiated. Various profession-related discourses, or even a lack thereof, have confronted one other, and a need has arisen for a common arena for scholarly discussion. Thus the concept of the 'making disciplines' has emerged and gradually consolidated as one of the epistemological premises for the design research education. The concept of the 'making disciplines' evolved from the need to establish a common intellectual platform for the doctoral students from various architecture, design and art fields. It also developed from the need to 'legitimize' the doctoral level in these professions within the system of the research education in traditional academic fields.

On the Nordic scene the research education initiative taken by the Oslo School of Architecture, titled 'The Millennium Programme' (1999–2001), seems to have been crucial for the further epistemological development at the Nordic schools of architecture and design. More than 50 doctoral students participated in this programme. At the conclusion of the courses, the participants agreed that the current status of the research education offered adequate training opportunities, but this seemed to apply mainly to traditional, academically initiated research. As the next phase of research education a new Nordic pilot study course was arranged in 2003, committed to the preparation of young researchers to meet the demands for new types of a broader research competence in problem and solution-oriented research. It resulted in a publication on transdisciplinarity and the 'making professions' (Dunin-Woyseth and Nielsen 2004).

One of the debates of recent years has arisen from the recognition on the part of the staff involved in the doctoral education that there already existed a 'continuum from scientific research to creative practice' in various fields of inquiry, even in the traditional academic fields. That recognition was shared with the external scholars who acted as 'gatekeepers' when assessing doctoral work. It resulted in the acceptance of some PhD theses in which the doctoral students integrated their own creative practice into the doctoral project, not only in an illustrative, but also in an argumentative way. This new academic stance within the institution can be dated to around 2004 when the first doctoral theses of this kind were conferred doctoral degrees (cf. Pedersen 2004; Sevaldson 2005). A new cohort of doctoral students was enrolled in 2008 of whom a part has chosen to pursue research by design in their doctoral work.

3.2
The doctoral thesis 'Developing Digital Design Techniques: Investigations on Creative Design Computing' by Birger Sevaldson at AHO 2005 focused on the early stages of the design process and investigated the use of generative design computing. Research by design was used as an approach to bind practice and reflexive, analytical activities together to reach new levels of insight and understandings.

Since 2007 courses have been offered at Master's level at the Oslo School of Architecture and Design (AHO). They have bridged on the one hand, design studio teaching and research by design, and on the other, the doctoral level of the novices of the Doctoral Programme. In 2008, a peer-reviewed journal *FormAkademisk* was established by a group of alumni and alumnae of the AHO's Doctoral Programme. The journal is devoted to research in design and design education, the most recent issue being dedicated to the theme of research by design.

The Swedish story

In Sweden there have since the 1990s been broad developments of research projects – on both doctoral and senior research levels – which can be considered as practice-based or 'by design', but the discussions on these issues have a longer history. 'Artistic development projects' have been pursued and discussed at universities in Sweden since the 1970s, but they were considered a parallel activity to and not on the same level as academic research. They can be seen as attempts to develop a clear academic identity and epistemological base for artistic and creative disciplines. Also in architecture, which has long since been influenced by and borrowed methods and theories from other academic disciplines, discussions started on developing an identity more founded on the specific knowledge modes of architecture. The Association for Architectural Research was founded in 1987 in Sweden, and it soon transformed into a Nordic Association and started publishing the journal *Nordic Journal of Architectural Research*. As for a long time the only peer-reviewed journal for architectural research in Scandinavia it played an important role for the developments. Even though the ambitions were to develop specific architectural research identities, the published papers in the journal have often continued to be based on traditional academic fields.

The three schools of architecture in Sweden all have long traditions of architectural research, and have been open to integrating different disciplines in the research approaches. In the late 1990s and beginning of the 2000s several doctoral projects started at the schools that had clear elements of a creative practice as a means in the inquiries (Grillner 2000; Zimm 2005; Akner-Koler 2007; Runberger 2008), and new approaches and research cultures began to develop.

In 2003 AKAD (the Academy for Practice-based Research in Architecture and Design) was founded with support from the National Research Council of Sweden. The Academy was a network collaboration between the KTH School of Architecture in Stockholm, the LTH School of Architecture in Lund and the Chalmers School of Architecture in Gothenburg. A point of departure for the Academy was the essential role of the architectural design project as the generative factor in research projects.

The AKAD can be considered to have strong connections to the arts and artistic research, but they chose to translate 'artistic research' to 'practice-based research' in their English name. Two of the founders, Katja Grillner and Lars-Henrik Ståhl, explain the main reason being that they find the term 'artistic research' problematic: 'The term 'practice-based research in the arts' is somehow less pretentious and therefore possibly more useful. 'Research by Architectural Design' is also more straightforward in its approach, focused as it is on what the researcher 'does', not

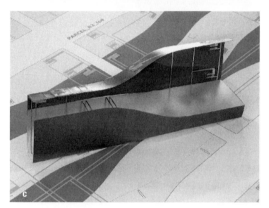

3.3
The licentiate thesis 'Architectural Prototypes' (Figure 3.3a) by the architect Jonas Runberger at KTH 2008 combines presentations of practical design work and projects with written analysis of both the processes and outcomes. The research is using design and construction of prototypes as investigative tools, and exhibitions as a means for communication. The project 'Parcel' (Figures 3.3b, 3.3c), developed together with Daniel Norell and Pablo Miranda, was exhibited at Stockholm Art+Science 2004 and the AKAD exhibition in Lund in 2006. The project 'Spline Graft' (Figure 3.3d), developed together with Pablo Miranda, was part of the travelling exhibition 'Open House: Intelligent Living by Design' which started in Essen in 2006.

on what he/she 'is' (i.e. 'artistic')' (Grillner and Ståhl 2003:16).

Grillner and Ståhl also presented a sketch to map the different sites where practice-based research in architecture may take place. They note that practice-based research in architecture may be related both to more conventional 'professional' practices as well as to alternative, 'academic' practices, meaning experimental practices based in academia and pursued through teaching, exhibitions and publications. The AKAD can be said to have especially emphasized and developed the academic practice in relation to practice-based and artistic research. They explicitly describe the research projects launched by AKAD during 2003 as 'all three may be positioned under the category of academic practices' (Grillner and Ståhl 2003: 20).

Experimental approaches were developed and implemented at all architectural schools. At Chalmers an integration of research within teaching has been a long tradition, and consciousness of research thinking in relation to design was

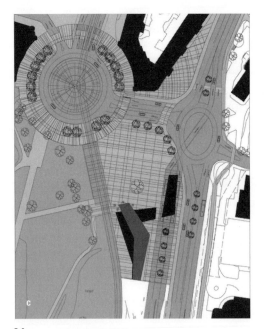

3.4

The project 'Den verkliga bytespunkten: Research by design kring kvaliteter i konflikt' (The real transfer point: Research by design on qualities in conflict) by Anna-Johanna Klasander and Lina Gudmundsson at White, Göteborg, Sweden, 2010, shows how new approaches to research are used in architectural practice. The research project together with stakeholders in the municipality had the objective to develop knowledge of spaces for public transport through the design process. Several competences and approaches were integrated, design solutions were systematically investigated, and in relation to a conventional process they revealed potentials both for new design and management of processes.

gradually being implemented in studio projects and student courses. Here experiments with methods, both from design and research, were staged and developed during several years (Dyrssen *et al.* 2009). Chalmers pursued a research project called 'Explorative Architecture', which involved architects, landscape architects and philosophers, and made contributions to the conceptualization of the field (Gromark and Nilsson 2006), and hosted the Nordic conference 'Architectural Inquiries' in 2008 focusing on contemporary theories, methods and strategies in architectural research.

The research projects done in relation to the AKAD platform show clear connections to what can be described as academic practices, but also strong relations to other creative disciplines than architecture. At the core of the projects and the developments are, for example, literature and creative writing, sound art and sonic space, film, video art visual culture, and computer art and technology. The elements and specificity of architectural design and the professional practice of architecture seem to play a less important role. Simultaneously there has been a growing interest for research from architectural offices. Large offices, like White and Sweco, have since long developed research strategies and collaboration with academia, but are increasingly using research in relation to innovation and creative design. The interest for research competence and methodologies closer to design now opens for fruitful developments.

The Belgian story

There are many schools of architecture and design in Belgium, but only one of them, the Sint-Lucas School of Architecture with campuses in Brussels and Ghent, has been the main locus for research by design and has consequently worked in order to establish this mode as the institution's research strategy.

The tradition of the Sint-Lucas School of Architecture is strongly embedded in the arts and humanities, and the school has always been at the forefront of developments in the fields of design and architecture. In September 2003, the Bologna-Berlin policies recognized doctoral studies as the third cycle in European higher education. For the Sint-Lucas School of Architecture, this meant developing a new culture, a culture of research and doctoral scholarship, and the idea was to develop experimental, practice-based concepts for this research, rather than to attempt to emulate the discipline-based research that is characteristic of the academic fields (Verbeke 2006: 9). The intention of this process was primarily to support younger teachers without any research experience in defining their research interests on the basis of their double practice as professionals and as teachers of architecture.

Sint-Lucas, together with the Network for Theory, History and Criticism of Architecture (NETHCA), organized an international conference in 2005: 'The Unthinkable Doctorate'. This conference was a step forward in the process of formulating the school's vision of research and setting up the Research Education Programme.

The formal scheme for the Research Education Programme at Sint-Lucas was first implemented in 2006 as a series of Research Training Session (RTS) modules (Verbeke 2008a; Janssens 2006). The RTSs are now described as a two-year programme, in which each year consists of four sessions led by various tutors with international academic experience or with an extensive design practice. The focus on research by and through design is emphasized in the curriculum. The programme was intentionally designed to foster a diversity of perspectives and opinions, and not to reflect the vision of a single person or methodology (Verbeke 2008b).

The intention of the session programme is to discuss fundamental issues of research by design in such a way that each participant can develop his/her own research ideas and research questions. The aim is that when the two-year RTS programme is finished, the participant should have developed a research project based in design practice that is mature enough to be formally started. Every year since 2006, the research education activities have been documented and discussed through the annual publications in the series of *Reflections+*, and the contributors consisted both of the participants and the tutors. Thus the process of maturing of the doctoral milieu has been recorded for ongoing debate.

Four years after the first conference at Sint-Lucas, the international conference 'Communicating (by) Design' was held. It turned out to be that many of those who had attended the RTS actively participated with papers and presentations, based on their ongoing doctoral research by design.

While comparing the proceedings of these two conferences, one can observe that the discourse on research by design has matured in Europe. It is interesting to notice that so many schools of architecture, especially those which had not been involved in traditional academic research in architecture previously, now engaged in research by design. These two conferences seem to have been momentous not only to the European community of architectural research by design, but first and foremost to the Sint-Lucas School of Architecture which during only these four years between the conferences has developed a strong milieu of young architects and teachers devoted to this new mode of research.

Part III – The research by design scene. New design scholarship?

The intention of this chapter has been to discuss some central concepts and theoretical frameworks as well as to show through various designerly and scholarly practices in four countries how research by design has emerged in different contexts and to map different approaches from more traditional disciplinary academic positions to those fully immersed in professional practices.

The discussions on 'post-academic science' and Mode-2 research have opened up new developments in research in the professional fields of architecture and design. A new conceptualization of the fields of knowledge, together with a more inclusive model of research, is developing, in which a more practice-based approach is possible. This new model is on the way to achieving academic recognition, as well as gaining significant interest among practitioners (Dunin-Woyseth and Nilsson 2008).

The Netherlands

We have noted there an early innovative explorative architectural practice, which often recognized itself as research-based, and, some years later, scholarly endeavours of the schools of architecture. The pressure of the prestigious academic institution, the Delft University of Technology, demanded scholarly legitimization of architecture and design. One of the field-specification ways of legitimization included conceptualization of research by design, as presented in the major publications of their School of Architecture, a collective work of the staff. The Dutch international contribution to the development of research by design has been the conferences on doctorates in 1996 and on research by design in 2000. The journal *Hunch* has continued this development further.

Norway

The Norwegian scene is highlighted by the case of one institution, the Oslo School of Architecture and Design, and the origins of research by design developed at its doctoral programme. A diachronic view of 20 years of this development process started from academically based doctoral research to an inclusive concept of architectural and design research with strong promotion of research by design. The Nordic network of research education, the Research Magazine series, documenting the development in the milieu's growing awareness of expanded understanding of design research, and the alumni-based Nordic peer-reviewed journal *FormAkademisk* indicate a growing arena for research by design, while the beginnings of this development can be attributed to endeavours of several cohorts of the doctoral students at one institution.

Sweden

There is a long tradition of architectural and design research, also research education. The schools of architecture have functioned as powerful vehicles in this development. A new angle, a more field-specific approach, research by design, was introduced through innovative education at the country's schools of architecture. The AKAD network, a cooperation of these schools, was a focused attempt to build up a broader awareness of the importance of field-specific architectural and design research. A growing interest of bigger architectural offices in this kind of research seems to be a result of this collective effort. There is also noted development of innovative, field-specific research in other creative fields in the country.

Belgium

New European guidelines of Bologna-Berlin of 2003 demanded that schools of architecture and design developed doctoral levels of education. Thirty years later than the first organized architectural research education in Scandinavia, the famous practice-based school of architecture, Sint-Lucas, needed to develop a new concept of research. Research by design seemed to be an answer as an explorative, innovative direction to comply with the new European policies, on the one hand, and with the school's practice-oriented tradition. An open attitude to developing various ways of defining what research by design could be has made this institution a laboratory for experiments and engagement among the staff and the students.

Brief conclusion

The four national 'stories' have showed that research by design has emerged as a new, practice-based, field-specific research mode in architecture and design. We can recognize in these 'stories' many of the components which according to Walker create new fields of inquiry: the growing critical mass of those interested in such a new mode, integrating of the mode into various levels of education in the field (at the Bachelor, Master and PhD level), international research conferences, books and academic journals. The 'stories' demonstrate also that the ways research by design has developed can vary in that sometimes the explorative research has been initiated by innovative practice (as in the Netherlands) and sometimes via (doctoral) research (as in Norway, Sweden and Belgium). The international discourse on research by design makes these ways known to and recognized by a growing audience of practitioners and design scholars.

Bibliography

Akner-Koler, C. (2007) *Form & Formlessness*, Stockholm: Axl Books.

Bunschoten, R., Hoshino, T. and Binet, H. (2001) *Urban Flotsam. Stirring the City*, Rotterdam: 010 Publishers.

Cross, N. (2007) *Designerly Ways of Knowing*, Basel: Birkhäuser.

Dunin-Woyseth, H. and Nielsen, M. L. (eds) (2004) *Discussing Transdisciplinarity: Making professions and the new mode of knowledge production*, Oslo: AHO.

Dunin-Woyseth, H. and Nilsson, F. (2008) 'Some notes on practice-based architectural design research: Four "arrows" of knowledge', *Reflections +7*, Brussels: Sint-Lucas Architectuur: 139–147.

Dyrssen, C., Rehal, S. and Strid, M. (2009) 'Dancing with Methods. Structuring Training in Research by Design Processes', *Communication (by) Design*, Brussels: School of Architecture Sint-Lucas: 385–395.

FOA, Ferré, A. and Kubo, M. (2003) *Phylogenesis FOA's ark*, Barcelona: Actar.

Frayling, C., Stead, V., Archer, B., Cook, N., Powel, J., Sage, V., Scrivener, S. and Tovey, M. (1997) *Practice-based Doctorates in the Creative and Performing Arts and Design*, Lichfield: UK Council for Graduate Education.

Gibbons, M., Limoges, C., Nowotny, H., Schwartzman, S., Scott, P. and Trow. M. (1994) *The New Production of Knowledge. The dynamics of science and research in contemporary societies*, London: Sage Publications.

Gombrich, E. H. J. (1991) 'Approaches to Art History: Three Points for Discussion', *Topics of Our Time. Twentieth-century issues in learning and in art*, London: Phaidon: 62–73.

Grillner, K. (2000) *Ramble, Linger, and Gaze: Dialogues from the landscape garden*, Stockholm: KTH.

Grillner, K. and Ståhl; L. H. (2003) 'Developing practice-based research in architecture and design', *Nordic Journal of Architectural Research* 1: 15–21.

Gromark, S. and Nilsson, F. (eds) (2006) *Utforskande arkitektur*, Stockholm: Axl Books.

Hensel, M. and Verebes, T. (1999) *Urbanisations*, London: Black Dog Publishing.

Janssens, N. (2006) 'The Sint-Lucas Research Training Sessions', *Reflections+3*, Brussels: Sint-Lucas Architectuur: 15–54.

Janssens, N. (2009) *Critical Design in Urbanism*, Göteborg: Chalmers University of Technology.

Jong, T., Voordt, T. and Cuperus, Y. (2000) *Ways to Study Architectural, Urban and Technical Design*, Congress version, Delft: Delft University Press.

Koolhaas, R. (1978) *Delirious New York. A Retroactive Manifesto for Manhattan*, Rotterdam: 010 Publishers.

Koolhaas, R. (1995) *S, M, L, XL*, New York: The Monacelli Press.

Koolhaas, R., Chung, J., Inaba, J. and Leong, S. (2001a) *Harvard Design School Guide to Shopping*, Köln: Taschen.

Koolhaas, R., Chung, J., Inaba, J. and Leong, S. (2001b) *Great Leap Forward*, Köln: Taschen.

Lawson, B. (2002) 'The subject that won't go away', *Architetural Research Quarterly* 2: 109–114.

Linder, M. (2005) 'TRANSdisciplinarity', *Hunch 9 – Disciplines*, Rotterdam: Episode publishers: 12–15.

Lootsma, B. (ed.) (1999) *The Need of Research*, *Daidalos* 69.

Lootsma, B. (ed.) (2001) *Research for Research*, Amsterdam: Berlage Institute.

Maas, W., van Rijs, J. and Koek, R. (eds) (1998) *FARMAX. Excursions on density*, Rotterdam: 010 Publishers.

Maas, W., van Rijs, J. and de Vries, N. (eds) (1999) *Metacity/Datatown*, Rotterdam: 010 Publishers.

Maas, W., Zaklanovic, P., de Rivero, M. and Ouwerkerk, P. (eds) (2003) *Five Minutes City*, Rotterdam: Episode Publishers.

Nieuwenhuis, A. and Ouwerkerk, M. (2000) *Research by Design*, Conference Proceedings, Delft: Delft University of Technology.

Nowotny, H., Scott, P. and Gibbons, M. (2001) *Re-thinking Science – Knowledge and the Public in an Age of Uncertainty*, Cambridge: Polity Press.

Pedersen, E. (2004) *Mellan tecken, teckning, teori och text* (*Between sign, drawing, theory and text*), Oslo: AHO.

Runberger, J. (2008) *Architectural Prototypes*, Stockholm: KTH.

Rust, C., Mottram, J. and Till, J. (2007) *Review of Practice-led Research in Art, Design & Architecture*, Bristol: Arts and Humanities Research Council.

Sevaldson, B. (2005) *Developing Digital Design Techniques – Investigations on creative design Computing*, Oslo: AHO.

Sigler, J. and Roemer van Toorn, R. (eds) (2003) '109 Provisional Attempts to Address Six Simple and Hard Questions About What Architects do Today and Where Their Profession might go Tomorrow', *Hunch 6/7*, Rotterdam: Episode Publishers.

Simon, H. A. (1969) *The Sciences of the Artificial*, Cambridge, Mass: The MIT Press.

Steenberger, C., Graafland, A., Mihl, H., Reh, W., Hauptmann, D. and Aerts, F. (2000) *Architectural Design and Research: Composition, education, analysis*, Bussum: Thoth Publishers.

Verbeke, J. (2006) 'The Sint-Lucas Research Training Sessions', *Reflections +3*, Brussel-Ghent: Sint-Lucas Architectuur: 9–12.

Verbeke, J. (2008a) 'Developing Architectural Research through Design. Experiences with Research Training Sessions'. Paper presented at the *Architectural Inquiries Conference – Theories, methods and strategies in contemporary Nordic architectural research*, Göteborg: Chalmers Arkitektur. Available online: http://tintin.arch.chalmers.se/aktuellt/PDFs/Verbeke_Developing%20Architectural%20research.pdf (accessed 25 September 2009).

Verbeke, J. (2008b) 'Research by Design in Architecture and in the Arts', *Reflections +7*, Brussels: Sint-Lucas Architectuur: 10–15.

Walker, J. A. (1989) *Design History and the History of Design*, London: Pluto Press.

Ziman, J. (2000) *Real Science – What it is, and what it means*, Cambridge: Cambridge University Press.

Zimm, M. (2005) *Losing the Plot*, Stockholm: Axl Books.

Chapter 4

Towards meeting the challenges of facilitating transdisciplinarity in design education, research and practice

Mark Burry

How do we move from focusing on the pursuit of excellence within individual design disciplines to asserting a wider role for design in helping tackle some of the world's most pressing issues? Few would disagree that in today's environment, *transdisciplinarity* is an essential ingredient to amplify the scope of design research to increase its relevance and application. As much as we need to research deeply into individual disciplines in order to add to their bodies of knowledge, we also need to look at combining knowledge from diverse disciplines in order to tackle the various wicked problems that beset contemporary society, and using design in a transdisciplinary framework offers an innovative platform for this new dialogue.

Such motherhood propositions are easy to make in writing, but in seeking to apply a transdisciplinary research framework are there sufficient polymaths who can ensure that team members remain appropriately wide-ranging yet focused – so-called 'T'-shaped people? In the manifest absence of sufficient numbers of polymaths, we therefore need to work more closely together in order to educate designers with the 'T'-shaped profile. This requires extra resources that design schools typically are unable to furnish, let alone the tools of persuasion to encourage design disciplines to leave their comfort zones. This chapter reports on the work at the Spatial Information Architecture Laboratory (SIAL) at RMIT University in Melbourne, Australia, where by targeting particular research funding opportunities and harnessing the enthusiasm of talented senior undergraduates and postgraduates, the learning and research environments are fused affording novel research across a wide range of design disciplines. No magic solution is offered but evidence of efficacy is in its place.

SIAL was established in 2001 within the School of Architecture and Design. Using spatial design thinking as its deep core focus its primary role was to bridge between spatial representations of the route from idea to physical outcome such as for designed artefacts, and spatial representations of systems and complex information for decision-making. In our overview we state that we offer:

> a facility for innovation in transdisciplinary design research and education. It embraces a broad range of investigative modes, involving both highly speculative and industry linked projects. SIAL is concerned with the integration of technical, theoretical and social concerns as part of its innovation agenda. High-end computing, modelling and communication tools associated with disparate disciplines are combined with traditional production techniques. Researchers are engaged in a wide variety of projects that collaboratively disturb artificial distinctions between the physical and virtual, digital and analogue, scientific and artistic, instrumental and philosophical.

Initially we had inordinate difficulty explaining who we were and what our mission was, eventually settling on the above as a hybrid mission–vision statement. Either it serves us sufficiently well now for we do not get the same level of requests for such explanation, or our purpose is now more universally understood and we are challenged less frequently. From the first we looked to include structural engineering and computer science and we were blessed with a surprising amount of interaction, but the normal competitive structures within universities – ours being no different – meant we failed to get the traction we needed with new media and communication. Much of the content of my chapter describes the impediments and identifies what needs to change for more fluid design research to occur.

After five years of successful operation with considerable support from the Australian Research Council the university sought to add another layer to the dialogue by establishing the Design Research Institute (DRI) mandated to work across the whole university and not just a single faculty (as it then was). This means that today SIAL (as a specialist group) and DRI reach across from hard-core technology, architecture and industrial design to applied arts: our design researchers exhibit interests and skills that range between jewellery to aeronautical engineering, applied art to architecture, graphic communication to creative writing, and from business to social science. The principal challenge has been reaching a consensus on the definition and dimensions for design with sufficient looseness that everyone can feel enfranchised yet tight enough to reach to the community beyond design – those we seek to influence through design.

Context and challenge

Worldwide 'design', 'innovation', and 'collaboration' are all words that have become heavily loaded politically, and Australia is no exception. In 2008 Dr Terry Cutler chaired the National Innovation System Review (NISR), a comprehensive review of all innovation activity within Australia: its funding and its impact (Burry 2008). A combination of over 700 entities and individuals responded to the call for submissions. Both SIAL and DRI contributed; DRI offered direct answers to the questions the review posed while SIAL provided more of a helicopter view and it is from this source that the bulk of the material here is drawn.

The definition of innovation provided in the NISR briefing is a useful one for our purposes here: 'innovation: creating value through doing something in a novel way'. For over a decade we had been contributing to the vital efforts made nationally to reposition creative thinking to the centre of the innovation agenda, especially design. But if design is so crucial to the innovation agenda, asks the classical researcher designer sceptic, how has it been so successful in remaining in the shadows of Australian nationally accredited research endeavour?

How designers work and what we do is poorly understood by non-designers, combining rather lethally with our tendency to over-intellectualize, self-obfuscate, fragment, and successfully reduce our status within the universities to one of brightly coloured baubles at the non-technology end of the spectrum adorning otherwise grey polytechnic institutions. There are a few exceptions such as the MIT MediaLab that are institutionally respectable through having commercially engaged with the wider world linking them to technology schools and departments. Lack of respectability leads to a correspondingly smaller pool of resources and with it, a 'back against the wall' attitude, which has proved singularly unhelpful in gaining sector recognition. Around the world, however, as global environmental and social challenges common to us all become more manifest and urgent, designers are assuming a collective impetus. The recent establishment of bold collective endeavours such as the D-School at Stanford, The Berkley Institute of Design, and the Industrial Design Engineering (IDE) programme offered by the Royal College for the Arts (RCA) in the UK with Imperial College help point other countries in new directions with regard to supporting the sector.

With insufficient encouragement to collectivize for the greater good, collaborative groups of designers quickly dysfunction. This dysfunction is often credited as helping foster the edginess and brilliance of the *designer-genius*, but this is hardly a sustainable argument in today's globally networked society relying on teams of deep practitioners from so many different disciplines, not only the creative ones.

There are six principal obstacles that we identified as major factors accounting for design's lack of prominence in our existing national innovation system, all of which are intimately connected. We used the opportunity of responding to the National Innovation System Review to articulate these distinctive obstacles as being the main causes preventing the design sector from working to its full potential. We were calling for enhanced national support structures, essential if we are to draw designers together as highly creative solution-seeking groups, as teams of key innovators.

Obstacles to collective creativity beyond individual disciplines
Obstacle 1: Wicked problem versus tame problem solving
The first reason for design's difficulty in being accommodated by the mainstream is the problem in defining design with comprehensive and universal agreement among designers themselves, commissioners of design, and end users.

Design was first identified as belonging to a class of *wicked problems*

Wicked problem

Tame problem

4.1
Wicked problem versus tame
problem solving.

by Horst Rittel (Rittel and Weber 1973). Wicked problems can be characterised as problems that spawn new problems in their solving, answers yes, but not black and white answers. Designers seek good solutions and cannot expect to come up with the right solutions as in 'right answers'. Six characteristics of wicked problems have been distilled by Jeffrey Conklin (2001; after Rittel's original 10) as the following:

1. You don't understand the problem until you have developed a solution.
2. Wicked problems have no stopping rule.
3. Solutions to wicked problems are not right or wrong, simply better, worse, good enough, or not good enough.
4. Every wicked problem is essentially unique and novel.
5. Every solution to a wicked problem is a 'one-shot operation'.
6. Wicked problems have no given alternative solutions.

All six characteristics have helped thwart tidy research funding processes which have been more oriented to that other class of problem identified first by Rittel as *benign problems*. Conklin (2001) simplified the list and describes them as *tame problems* with six defining characteristics.

1. Has a well-defined and stable problem statement.
2. Has a definite stopping point, i.e. when the solution is reached.
3. Has a solution which can be objectively evaluated as right or wrong.
4. Belongs to a class of similar problems which are all solved in the same similar way.
5. Has solutions which can be easily tried and abandoned.
6. Comes with a limited set of alternative solutions.

Grant-giving bodies find tame problems confidence-inspiring projects to fund, with far less risk of 'failure' than wicked problem-solving projects – like design.

Obstacle 2: Designers flock to form discrete discipline silos

The second obstacle that has helped alienate designers from being core to a highly regarded and financially supported research community is our signal failure to talk and act with one voice. At a prosaic level, since the commencement of professional delineations for craft, guilds have jealously guarded their own, and to an extent such proprietarily motivated distinction pervades contemporary life. Collaborating experimentally beyond immediate problem solving – an essential creative adjunct to pragmatic solution finding – has no ready source of funding in Australia.

There are practical reasons for this that extend well beyond the 'creative egos' and other unhelpful characterisations that non-designers make of designers. Hitherto, unique studio situations and sets of tools highly specific to each design discipline were natural separators. This is changing rapidly as we converge on similar work-spaces and tool sets (digital printers, 3D rapid prototyping, etc.). As a consequence in my university, for instance, when we talk about design research we are referring to a community that ranges across the whole spectrum of technology and art. The diversity is now signalled as being essential to making a bigger social contribution. It does not represent a dilution of expertise but is not easy to sustain internal energy and external credibility through many complex social factors, not least a pervading sense of the necessity to be useful to a particular end user, for example, 'car driver' and 'clothes wearer' as opposed to 'transport user' and 'climate adapter'.

4.2
Design discipline silos.

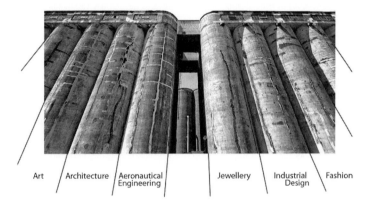

| Art | Architecture | Aeronautical Engineering | | Jewellery | Industrial Design | Fashion |

photo taken by aqui-ali. http://www.flickr.com/photos/aqui-ali/625171742/

Obstacle 3: Identifying 'design research' – multiple readings, but only one is project-based ...

> Design is a way of inquiring, a way of producing knowing and knowledge; this means it is a way of researching.
>
> (Downton 2003: 1)

The third obstacle preventing design from assuming a far more prominent and profitable role in innovation is its awkward relationship to research conventions. This is related to the two issues identified above: how can a diverse team not used to

4.3
Questions can arise from the answer.

Creative team   Emerging topic

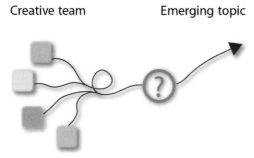

collaborating together research a topic whose redefinition only emerges as the research proceeds? This conundrum can be solved with a simple construct: *design is research* (Glanville 1999: 81). (Ranulph Glanville, adopting a cybernetic standpoint, argues that although research and design are separate activities and fields of operation, research is best understood 'to be a (restricted) design act, rather than design being inadequate research' (Glanville 1999).)

My experience supports the proposition that we research *through* design: 'as I design I reflect and this is an intimate part of my design process, and in doing so I add new knowledge through my design', which is Donald Schön's 'reflective practitioner' (Schön 1983). Research *for* design ('I research, and then I design with my newly acquired knowledge'), and research *about* design ('I'm an academic and I want to know all about design') seem less compelling as identifiers of design's intellectual value in this difficult domain.

Obstacle 4: Lack of cohesion between design disciplines

The fourth obstacle that helps us as designers to marginalise our research from the rest of society is fragmentation, as distinct from the deliberate creation of discipline silos, which we also do rather well. This issue is well understood in the design community, and is beautifully explained in the quote that follows, again by Jeff Conklin:

> Collective intelligence is a natural property of socially shared cognition, a natural enabler of collaboration. But there are also natural forces that challenge collective intelligence, forces that doom projects and make collaboration difficult or impossible. These are forces of fragmentation.
>
> The concept of fragmentation provides a name and an image for a phenomenon that pulls apart something which is potentially whole. Fragmentation suggests a condition in which the people involved see themselves as more separate than united, and in which information and knowledge are chaotic and scattered. The fragmented pieces are, in essence, the perspectives, understandings, and intentions of the collaborators. Fragmentation, for example, is when the stakeholders in a project are all convinced that their version of the problem is correct. Fragmentation can be hidden, as when stakeholders don't even realize

that there are incompatible tacit assumptions about the problem, and each believes that his or her understandings are complete and shared by all.

(Conklin 2006: 2)

4.4
Lack of cohesion.

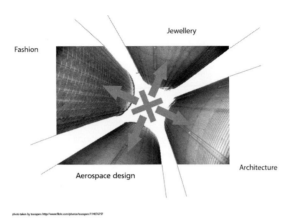

The 'natural forces of fragmentation' can be countered but probably not from within unaided. Societies with strong design cultures such as Finland and Denmark have succeeded through external agency, which actively assists a strong sense of collective strength and direction. In many cases the external agency can be industries that fully appreciate that a well-designed product will ultimately fare better than one that is not well produced.

Obstacle 5: Indistinct interdisciplinary/cross-disciplinary/multi-disciplinary relationships

Not knowing how best to generate and sustain synergies in inter-disciplinary/cross-disciplinary/multi-disciplinary design has also helped hold design back from the centre-stage of innovation. Designers and technologists form effective and productive working arrangements relatively easily whereas designers working across design disciplines often do not. Part of a recent Australian quest was to 'deal effectively' with cross-disciplinary research proposals. The issue was elaborated in an 18-page Expert Advisory Group Working Group Paper (EAG 2007). One of the two purposes of the Working Group Paper was to obtain agreement on 'approaches to assessing cross-disciplinary research for inclusion in the preferred model of the [now abandoned] Australian Research Quality Framework (RQF)', in response to the palpable increase in cross-disciplinary applications to the Australian Research Council for research funding – cross-disciplinary applications had risen to one-third of all those submitted between 2001 and 2004.

There are social impediments that limit the effective interaction and collaboration between design disciplines as noted above, except where necessity dictates otherwise: a mobile phone designer must collaborate with a signals engineer for a viable outcome just as an architect works alongside a civil engineer; these

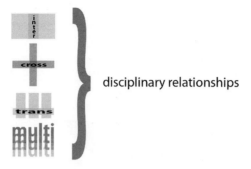

disciplinary relationships

4.5
Silos seem to actively resist cohesion.

are examples of necessity stimulating the formation of partnerships. What has been almost impossible to nurture in Australia are collaborations sponsored by mere speculation alone: what happens if a jeweller works with a mechanical engineer (kinetic jewellery beyond the watch), or a graphic designer with a nanotechnologist (inks with weird properties)? Not only are we not being encouraged to be more inventive in situations where the solution being sought is identified through the research itself, we are also hobbled by a research and training conceptual deficiency, which is 'obstacle 6'.

Obstacle 6: Conceptual denial of the vital relationship between skilling in design and design research

Pedagogues who attempt to separate design teaching and learning from design research will always be frustrated. Most design disciplines today have abandoned what used to be proscribed as 'design methodology' in favour of skill acquisition developed in tandem with creative exploration. Each supports and stimulates the other through mutual engagement and a smidgeon of creative antagonism.

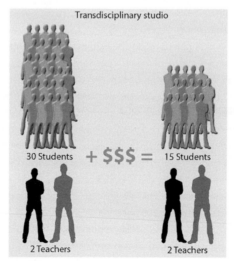

Skilling <> Research

4.6
There are several options for working across disciplines.

University structures and the origin of the disciplines preternaturally lead to the silo-ing of particular design disciplines. In current circumstances, to run a parallel studio with, say, civil engineers and architects means doubling the class size as two teach-ers will probably be required, and staff–student ratios will need to be maintained. This compromises the centuries-old studio teaching – the *atelier model* – by not maintain-ing the same number of students by doubling the input: simply there are insufficient polymaths available to lead cross/multi/interdisciplinary programmes unassisted, hence the need for a similar number of teachers as disciplines represented.

How best to support creativity as the core of innovation

That difficult nexus: research with links to external partners framed around projects

4.7
Academy, research and practice
The universities, practice and research groups all working with perfect synergy…
The recipe?
…indulgent clients in no real hurry, governments who believe in tax-funded research for public good, practices willing to share their knowledge, universities able to work with real-world constraints, postgraduate students willing to extend their architectural education by n years…

Many research-funding requests are framed around projects that include external partners. I believe that these should be bundled together as a single context, with variation in scale and importance. External partners can include industry, commerce, professional practice, the public sector, cultural organisations, NGOs and government – in Australia state and federal. By 'scale' I refer to the complexity of the problem being addressed, the size of the team who are contributing, and the range of disci-plines that they are drawn from. By 'importance' I refer to the beneficiaries (not impact) of the research, and long-term benefit rather than short-term expediency.

In most countries there is no real encouragement to initiate pilot projects that are wholly speculative in nature, small seeds that might grow if successful, nor is there an identified funding mechanism through which they might do so – patrons are more easily found to fund art, but not speculative design. Considerable efforts are required to start a Cooperative Research Centre (CRC) with an assumed scale and importance that is not echoed in the business start-up arena. Research teams need far more agility in generating funding than is currently available. This translates as a step-by-step process for complex and uncertain (but inspiring) projects. Why not institute a funding system that supports a pilot project with serious consideration promised from the outset for its extension in a planned series of iterative expansions? Similarly, as projects start to unwind, why not fund the research group to translate its work into new associated promising areas of enquiry rather than just turning the tap off as so often happens?

I believe that the design sector would benefit from an entirely different assessment process for grants involving external partners than currently instituted by nationally coordinated funding bodies. The two differences would be first having external sector assessors contribute directly to the process, and second a more concerted progress follow-up by the funders during the project – this maintains quality but also helps get the message beyond academic walls. In the spirit of more trust, progress reviews could be styled as mentoring sessions rather than grant policing. It seems to have missed the collective radar that the researchers' interests, their employers' and the grant-giving authorities' interests are all the same: success. No university wants to host a research team that was given more dollars than the research outcomes ended up being worth. A research team entering an annual 'research health check-up' would be far better disposed to get the most out of such a clinic than they are when facing yet another review.

Transdisciplinarity: towards the twenty-first-century polytechnic

There is ample evidence of the value of different disciplines solving problems together. At all the universities I have worked at beyond the initial animated and excited early discussions there has been opposition to working and teaching together once the true costs of the collaboration become identified. These additional costs of collaboration can be as trivial as the costs of travelling between campuses or sharing technical support, but they can be more fundamental. Let us consider the case of the architect and the engineer referred to in 'Obstacle 6' described above. At its best the architect–engineer is an example of a designer–designer collaboration. At its worst, the relationship is the engineer in the service of the architect, which limits the opportunities for a creative interchange of ideas.

Everyone knows that in professional practice architects and engineers work together on major buildings, but few outside the arena appreciate the reality of the distant relationship between the two. So remote are the collaborating design professions that engineers' 3D software cannot read architects' 3D digital models, for example, and vice versa. This represents a significant waste of time and effort. It is evidence of how far each office is from the other, intellectually, emotionally and practically. As a result university architecture and engineering departments reflect the same disengagement from one another. Only a handful of prominent schools around the world such as Bath in the UK have been able to show some success in solving this challenge.

The reasons for the separation in modes of practice are complex and extend back to the peculiar priorities of the craft guilds and subsequently, the birth of the professions as closed shops. The financial impediments to forming closer relationships and with it a closer *modus operandi*, however, are not so difficult to understand.

The studio learning method has historically been the richest possible environment for designers to first serve their apprenticeship and subsequently develop operational approaches. Universally architects and engineers' offices are organised internally as studios, not discrete worker's offices. This is because the unstructured sharing of ideas is an essential part of the creative process for any project.

To organise a studio that offers student architects and engineers at universities a chance to work together is simple to conceptualise but seemingly impossible to fund using current financial models. Studios typically rely on a staff–student ratio of 1:15. In a full working day each student can hold the floor in front of their peers in the presence of an expert for 30 minutes each. Combining classes of architectural and engineering students with the necessary two experts (teachers from both professions) helps narrow the divide between the two professions. Unless extra resources are found to pay for the necessary increase in numbers of expert staff that need to work together in a shared studio, combining architectural and engineering studios swells the staff–student ratio to an unmanageable 1:30. This is an acknowledged educational and practice conundrum that confounds the development of mutually supportive design skills across disciplines so vital to any nation:

> What, for example, would a transdisciplinary 'curriculum' look like? How would it be taught and by whom? How can the knowledge produced in the context of application be accessed by those who have not been part of that context, if it resides primarily in the collective memory of the problem solving teams? Will participation come to replace books? What are the skills required to participate in this mode of knowledge production? How are they to be acquired?
>
> (Gibbons 1997)

This model referred to here is *transdisciplinarity*, fundamentally different from cross-, inter- and multi-disciplinarity (O'Reilly 2004). The transdisciplinarian develops their own discipline through practice while enmeshed with others in shared design space, but they also redefine their discipline through project-based working association. They therefore protect the status of their discipline expertise but while doing so they transform it usefully through the ultra-awareness achieved designing mutually in the shared space. Rather than being a *Jack-of-all-trades* discipline dilution it might seem, it does quite the opposite: disciplines evolve far more richly than they can if they remain sequestered in their silos.

Transdisciplinarity is the twenty-first-century equivalent of the former polytechnic spirit, institutions where designer technologists came together with pride and revelled in their mutual expertise and entrepreneurship. With the Internet facilitating a rich diversity that can transcend physical boundaries there is no need to revert to that model necessarily, but if we are to celebrate the advantages of transdisciplinary flux we will need to provide more meaningful support than currently possible with our existing perceived funding priorities.

Embedded practice

The principal means by which we have steered a route out of this long-standing morass has been through 'embedded practice'. Embedded practice embeds our doctoral candidates within a leading design practice such that for the two years that stretch between the middle of their first and third years, 90 per cent of their time is spent in the partner design practice's studios engaged in research that the practice is less likely to undertake without the collaboration of us in SIAL. Senior partners co-supervise the candidates.

This can hardly be claimed as an original idea when medicine and sciences have operated aspects of this model for decades, but it is nevertheless a model that design researchers have yet to take advantage of more fully. By having cohorts of several candidates located in different design offices at the same time, significant new opportunities are created to forge relationships between practices that would otherwise not occur, and for the sharing of what previously has been jealously guarded know-how. At SIAL we are now on our fourth iteration, but each year we have to find new industry partners and write new applications essentially for this tried and tested programme (different projects obviously), simply to ensure continuity. In Australia there is no long-term programme offering sequential postgraduate funding stability.

The programme works best if the postgraduates have three to five years' prior experience in practice, with stipends competitive with the salaries of top young designers. In design, postgraduates most likely to excel in the programme are very likely to be the top designers of their age group.

Figure 4.8 contrasts the typical fragmented design school (top) with the *Embedded Practice* model (bottom).

Conclusion: radical rethink of postgraduate design programmes required

In this chapter I have outlined the creation first of the Spatial Information Architecture Laboratory (SIAL) in 2001, and the Design Research Institute (DRI) in 2006, specifically to look for opportunities for collaborative design research crossing discipline boundaries. I then looked at the general condition of design research lacking respectability in a country where the scientific model of research is dominant and I contrasted this with what should be emerging opportunities for design researchers to engage with the ever more urgent wicked problems besetting society. Six obstacles to getting traction in the sector were identified that are peculiar to Australia as a combination perhaps, but by no means geographically unique.

Our embedded practice programme seems to have the most prospects for influencing positive change whereby design research contributes more fully to tackling world-scale problems beyond the concerns and constraints of particular design disciplines. We have not found a way to make this entirely self-funding, but with nationally competitive funding support to date we have at least been making headway. Our emerging PhDs are finding positions of influence globally, offering evidence at least of some limited success through direct engagement of practice, industry and research groups with the academic community. Through this approach we are able to peep over the parapet at unexpected opportunities for design research.

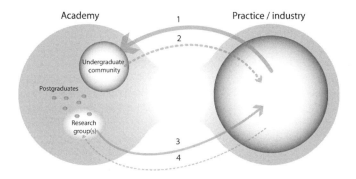

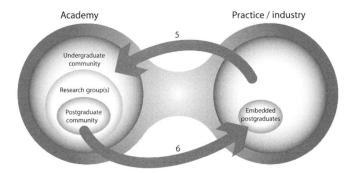

4.8

Top: Typical relationship between the academy and practice. The practice's primary contribution to schools of architecture is through substantial support to the undergraduate teaching programme (stream 1), principally design studios. Talented students might be invited back into practices as 'interns' while still studying (stream 2). Postgraduates often find themselves as individuals, possibly associated with established research centres, but often somewhat remote from the school's core business (teaching). On occasions practices will consult research groups, typically for technical input (stream 3). At the same time, practices might provide useful 'problematisation' – contextual support for the research groups – if the practice has time to communicate in this way (stream 4).

Bottom: Strengthening the 'academy-practice nexus' by ensuring that research is the common denominator for all interaction including design studio contributions. Postgraduates form a community embedded within the research group(s), which are conspicuously embedded within the school in such a way to be relevant to the undergraduate community. Practice supports the school's education through tutoring and adjunct professorships (stream 5) while hosting full time 'embedded' postgraduates for the duration of their candidature (stream 6) thereby providing a formal research link back to the school's research group(s).

Bibliography

Burry, M. (2008) *Submission to the National Innovation System Review, made on behalf of the RMIT University's Spatial Information Architecture Laboratory (SIAL)*, RMIT University.

Conklin, J. (2001) 'Wicked Problems and Social Complexity'. CogNexus Institute [online] http://cognexus.org/wpf/wickedproblems.pdf (accessed 1 August 2011).

Conklin, J. (2006) 'Wicked Problems and Social Complexity'. [online] http://academic.evergreen.edu/curricular/atpsmpa/Conklin%201.pdf (accessed 1 August 2011).

Downton, P. (2003) *Design Research*, Melbourne: RMIT University Press.

EAG Working Group (2007) Mechanism of Assessment – Panels/Cross-disciplinary Research. [online] http://www.dest.gov.au/NR/rdonlyres/F6368EE8-6F45-4286-94C96C4A3011526A/7864/MechanismsofAssessmentPaper1.pdf (accessed 1 February 2008).

Gibbons, M. (1997) 'What kind of university? Research and teaching in the 21st century',Victoria University of Technology 1997 Beanland Lecture, Melbourne.

Glanville, R. (1999) 'Researching design and designing research', *Design Issues* 15 (2): 81.

O'Reilly, M. (2004) 'Educational design as transdisciplinary partnership: Supporting assessment design for online'. In R. Atkinson, C. McBeath, D. Jonas-Dwyer and R. Phillips (eds), *Beyond the comfort zone: Proceedings of the 21st ASCILITE Conference* (pp. 724–733), Perth, 5–8 December (for a broad discussion on the parameters of transdisciplinarity). [online] http://www.ascilite.org.au/conferences/perth04/procs/oreilly.html (accessed 1 August 2011).

Rittel, H. and Weber, M. (1973) 'Dilemmas in a general Theory of Planning', *Policy Science* 4: 155–169.

Schön, D. (1983) *The Reflective Practitioner: How professionals think in action.* London: Temple Smith.

Chapter 5

Beyond Kenkyushitsu and atelier – towards a new professional education and practice

Hidetoshi Ohno and Bruno Peeters

The urban landscape, education, or designers' operational conditions are quite distinct in Japan and Europe, yet both entities, often described as 'soft' powers, share similar challenges. This article situates an extended 'East & West' dialogue between Hidetoshi Ohno and Bruno Peeters on the issue of design and research, our respective trials and experiments, joint research and educational endeavours.

The authors teach respectively at the University of Tokyo and St.-Lucas Brussels. Representing two distinct educational traditions, both departments have a long history and are currently undergoing fundamental reorganizations.

At the University of Tokyo, established in 1877, architecture traditionally is organized within the Faculty of Engineering. At the time a novel field, its historic focus was rather technological, engineering oriented. The first modern university in the Far East – founded only a few years after the Meiji Reformation in 1868, Japan's transition from the feudal to modern era – from its inception the university took on the role as the leading academic institution of Japan. Being a key strategic instrument within the overall Japanese modernization process and education of the new elite, academic research was to become the core of the university's performance.

Today, the University of Tokyo counts 22 faculties at the undergraduate level, and 35 faculties including Graduate Schools and Research Institutes at the graduate level accommodating more than 28,000 students. It is the highest ranked, non-Anglo-Saxon institution on the Shanghai Jiao Tong Academic Ranking of World Universities. Education is organized following a four-two-three years' module, with an undergraduate professional program of four years leading to a full degree. Continued education is organized under the form of a research-oriented Master course of two years, and a subsequent PhD course of another three years.

In 1998 a new Faculty of Frontier Sciences (GSFS) was established, that also incorporated design. GSFS consists of three divisions, Trans-Disciplinary

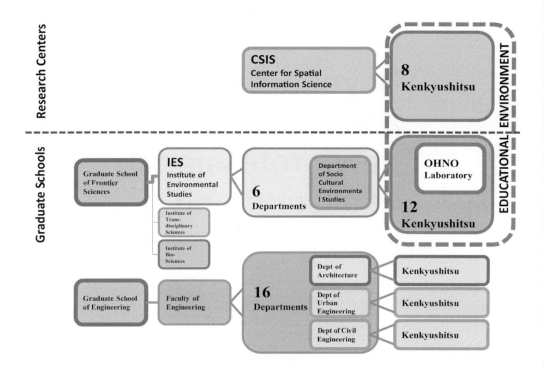

Sciences, Biosciences and Environmental Studies. The aim is to develop innovative fields of research through restructuring disciplines.

5.1
Graduate School of Frontier Sciences (GSFS) in its educational framework at the University of Tokyo.

St.-Lucas, founded in 1862, is the oldest, largest and leading school of architecture in Belgium, established at the height of the neo-gothic movement, design pedagogy related closely to the arts and crafts movement, resulting in a strong, 'atelier'-based design and conceptual orientation.

Traditionally adhering to a 'Beaux-Arts' apprenticeship-style education, a substantial part of the academic and teaching staff still combines high-profile practices and education. St.-Lucas incorporates the departments of Architecture, Urban Planning, Interior Architecture, and Interior Design, totaling 1,720 students, counting many of the most renowned Belgian architects among its alumni.

Following common EU standards, the St.-Lucas' Graduate School of Architecture is organized into a three-year Bachelor program, allowing access to either the two-year Master course of Architecture or Urban Planning, leading to the degree of an Architect or Urban Planner. A PhD program was only recently established, focusing primarily on tutors and teaching staff. Completing a long transition process, recently St.-Lucas became a partner in association with the University of Leuven, into which it will be fully incorporated from 2013 in the new Faculty of Architecture and the Arts (FAA).

Backgrounds

In the past decade, both Japan and Europe experienced a multitude of Higher Education reforms, which set in motion an almost permanent transformation process at both departments. Reforms, while still going on, generated interesting

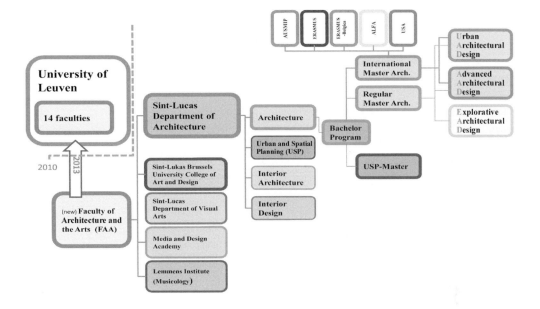

5.2
Faculty of Architecture and the Arts (FAA) in its educational framework at St.-Lucas' Graduate School of Architecture.

potentials for experiments beyond established educational practice within an increasingly international and competitive environment.

The common denominator at both departments, as to how to integrate research, design, and education, remains open to many discussions, trials and adjustments.

As such this chapter is an interim report, reflecting a difficult age in which our understanding is changing, and once set values are shifting. In a stable age, there are few doubts as to its value system; purpose and methods applied to design become self-evident. All architects must do is to devote themselves to the refinement of their techniques and methodology. However, within any value system reaching a point of apparent permanence there usually exists already a movement towards the creation of a new value system. Natural sciences may have brought tremendous advancements in the past 200 years, few today would applaud whole-heartedly the inherent possibilities of technology without reserve, and the recent collapse of socialist ideology, and ensuing consensus about liberalism, being the most desired political-economic system, seems to have been short-lived. It is thus self-apparent that 10 years into the twenty-first century we have approached the end of modernism and that the age-without-scepticism is no longer.

Preparing future generations, education is rooted within tradition, and the œuvre of past generations provides us with the knowledge to define and teach guidelines and ideas to future designers. However, teaching such basic knowledge, tested over time, tends to resist change.

Compared to exact sciences, architectural design focuses on the production of space, defying linear scientific progress. Similar to the humanities, many issues concerning architecture or urban planning extend over the ages. For example, whereas modern techniques did not exist during the Roman era, its buildings continue to be appreciated today, requiring only little technology to allow for a contemporary use. However, education must also be constantly on the lookout towards new frontiers, and within our field avant-garde ideas equally exist. Similar to philosophy the same issues are continually being challenged, yet the means to address those issues permanently changes.

Fulfilling certain functions at any given time, architecture and cities re-generate continuously. Simultaneously, architecture is also a representative medium; when design values or user awareness change, content and representation will inevitable change as well.

The reason why architecture needs to look both towards the traditional and new frontiers, is that when teaching present trends, students will eventually realize that their knowledge has soon become outdated.

Education therefore needs both a diligent instruction of the classics, or certified knowledge, while simultaneously exploring new frontiers, questioning established knowledge. Architectural design, and the way it communicates tends to make it lean towards solutions and representations which are highly susceptible to trends, so one must be especially aware of our proximity to such trends.

Introducing new frontiers into education necessitates an avant-garde attitude, exploring beyond established knowledge. In our opinion this can only be achieved through research. Architectural research then, much like any other research, is endowed with the task of discovering and charting new frontiers. This aspect is crucial and its incorporation into design pedagogy profoundly changes our education.

Now exceeding 6.4 billion people, mankind's continuous expansion has put ever more strain on the planet, and the recent rise of former developing coun-tries is leading to an unprecedented environmental crisis. Such an incessant quest for growth cannot be sustained; thus we must now begin to include shrinkage in our field of vision. This is a new condition, unknown in human history.

Many developed nations are now facing rapidly aging populations, and in the case of Japan, a fast shrinking of the population. Japanese life expectancy, the highest in the world, further aggravates conditions. Investment in construction, still featuring a disproportionate share within the overall economy, is already shrivelling. The 'standard-cure' Keynesian policies of the successive Japanese governments, applied for decades to stimulate the economy through investment in construction, became untenable. This unilateral focus on growth, combined with a very liberal planning instrument left Japan with a legacy of vast urban sprawl and anomic subur-ban areas, defying traditional urban planning.

Sharing some of the peculiarities of Japan's suburban landscape, Belgian sprawl, equally characterized by decades of intentional liberal policies, led us to the common question as how to respond to such urbanity from the position of the designer.

Within this perspective, the issue of 'shrinkage' is not necessarily related to an immediate population decrease, but concerns the much wider global environmental crisis. No longer able to rely on expansionist scenarios, the authors are convinced that a mere classic education of our future planners and architects, hitherto 'growth' based, has lost its relevance.

Shrinking becoming a principal theme, redefining the role of the designer requires an approach and education beyond the conventional. However, connecting research and design is not a given fact, as in any field we need hypotheses and the testing hereof, verified through a process of exposure and availability of outcomes to a wider audience. Yet, such a method is very difficult to attain in architecture or planning, as no conditions or criteria exist, as, for instance, in STM-research and publishing. To put it narrowly, even if you have an exciting hypothesis, its validity can be verified only when you get a design commission, which suits your hypothesis. It is hard to imagine such an optimal situation becoming a reality, and within this regard, our graduate design studios came to function as experimental test-grounds and students' proposals are the result of experiments, cooperating with professors in creating new value within an uncertain context.

Needless to say, attaining an optimal balance and integration between education, research, and ultimately its relevance posed a major challenge to both departments. Establishing integrative research and design platforms required the development of new formats, often presenting a clear break with our institutions' traditions. Reforms ran parallel with an ever-increasing internationalization and in our specific case the AUSMIP program; a first Japanese–European pilot-exchange of architecture and planning faculties at the Master level, AUSMIP substantially accelerated innovations. Recently extended, it had a considerable impact on both our departments, instigating a regular exchange framework.

Contrary to some other EU-funded intercontinental programs, the AUSMIP consortium did not seek to develop joint curricula, but stressed the diversity of its partners, allowing students to enhance and broaden their skills at faculties with very different foci.

5.3
AUSMIP program, a first Japanese-European pilot-exchange of architecture and planning faculties at the Master level connecting the University of Tokyo and the University of Leuven.

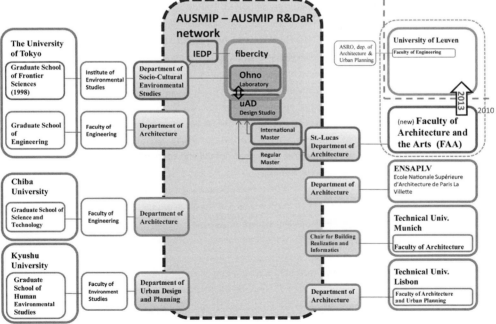

Research platforms
IEDP

Since the 1990s Japanese education has experienced a continuous series of reor-ganizations, culminating in the 2004 and 2009 reforms; the new faculty of Frontier Sciences (GSFS) is a key exponent of these transformations. At the GSFS, one of the main pedagogical challenges was to integrate design studios covering those areas of research relevant to the new faculty.

This led to the set-up of the Integrated Environmental Design Program (IEDP), a conglomeration of six design studios, Man-Made Environment, Architecture, Urban Planning, Urban-Agriculture, Farming and Forest Management, among which students can choose freely. Even though the University of Tokyo accommodates many different design studios, often leading to highly specialized professions, these are confined to their respective faculties. Exceptionally, within the IEDP design studios are located and co-organized at one location, allowing a permanent interaction with neighbouring disciplines. This process involved the tran-sition of entire units and laboratories into the new faculty, hence the Ohno Laboratory moved from the Department of Architecture, graduate school of Engineering, into the GSFS's Socio-Cultural Environmental Studies Department coalescing humanities, civil engineering, architecture and urban planning.

uAD

In Europe, the 1999 Bologna agreement spurred a structural transformation towards a common three-cycle academic module, coercing St.-Lucas to integrate research within its core activities in order to meet academic criteria, and as such the reorientation towards research at St.-Lucas was initially triggered externally. Comprised of design-related departments only, the core of St.-Lucas, be it in terms of education, pedagogy or recently research, is formed by the design studios, or 'ateliers'; subsequently it was considered obvious that research and research output would ideally coincide as much as possible with the design studios. This required first of all an overhaul of the ateliers' organization and methodology, involv-ing the creation of three 'tracks' at the Master level; advanced Architectural Design (aAD), focusing on the architect as a builder, explorative Architectural Design (eAD), emphasizing artistic research and design, and urban Architectural Design (uAD), specializing in transitional urban processes, positioning the designer in between urban planning and architecture. These tracks altered substantially the design studio concept, which tended to be the exclusive domain of the design tutors and for the first time it was possible to develop themes and incorporate research within a longer timeframe.

Though these reforms set the conditions at both departments to reor-ganize design studios, integrating research and design, implementation itself was certainly not an even process, revealing fully the traditional strengths and weak-nesses of our departments.

At the University of Tokyo research is a long-established competence, design education gradually becoming more independent, less subservient to tech-nology and engineering tradition. However, at St.-Lucas research needed to be introduced almost from scratch not just into the design studios but also within the department itself, leading to a protracted process of trials and errors. In Tokyo, integration could be organized from the beginning within the existing format of the 'Kenkyushitsu', or laboratories.

Kenkyushitsu, or design by research

An established tradition, the Kenkyushitsu is typically a research unit, supporting research and education at the Graduate Schools in Japan. It usually consists of a leading professor, assistants, researchers as well as graduate students. Even for students with a major in design, writing a thesis is mandatory and concludes their research, tutored by the professor and assisted by senior students. Students' involvement in the Kenkyushitsu is very extensive but not exclusive, as they can take other lectures or design studios by other professors. Apart from being a collective research platform, the Kenkyushitsu also serves as an important social bond, and identification with the laboratory is quite strong.

In fields with a strong tradition in scientific research, Kenkyushitsu usually develop their own research themes similar to research institutes, and students are assigned some part of the research work.

Pursuing such a collective process requires a different attitude as to the pedagogic role of the design project, as it is known within conventional architectural education. Hence the focus has shifted from individual design, determined by collective design assignments, to individual assignments and research, steering and co-determining a broader research project.

Tracks, or research by design

In Brussels, design studios were previously allocated on the basis of tutors' assignment proposals, requiring a redefinition of assignments each year. Such competition resulted often in very original assignments; however this quasi-permanent rotation did not allow much research or accumulation of knowledge beyond the interaction of student and tutor. The tracks therefore were to integrate design, theory and research at the level of the design studio through a fixed interaction for each assignment between two different theory clusters and design. These theory clusters, either providing specific theoretical frameworks, or participation of theory professors in the design studio, gradually generated a specific track content.

Apart from the issue of research itself, output generated by the department changed as well, and this is perhaps best exemplified by the status of the diploma-project. Preceding recent reforms, diploma-projects were an important means to profile the department to the outside world, defining its image and reputation. The diploma-project focused almost exclusively on design, highly stressing individuality and originality, with students defining their own topic and assignment. This turned out to be a crucial weak point, as it encouraged many students to engage in projects far beyond their capacities. Often resulting in spectacular presentations, many projects failed to generate any relevance beyond this point. Great emphasis was put on a student's maturity and autonomy, yet coaching projects was an intensive one-to-one exchange, and these individual apprenticeships put a substantial strain on resources, actually increasing dependency of students.

The tracks attempted to curb this dependency, reducing the weight of the diploma-project, emphasizing the overall formation of students. However, implementation was strenuous, as it directly affected the autonomy of the 'atelier', and also the ultimate symbol of designer autonomy, the diploma-project. The rather forced collaboration between theory and design did not help much to overcome resistance at the level of the design tutors either. The resulting collapse of the diploma-project system, with dramatic percentages of failed students, led to a second reform, trying to improve the match between tracks, research and diploma-project, still considered the pinnacle of education.

Thus, the pilot-module developed for AUSMIP students, required to develop their diploma-project in Japan, including a research dissertation, became a standard procedure for all students, and a system of 'labs', parallel to the tracks was set up, pooling research themes and assignments, coordinated by professors engaged actively in research relevant to the tracks orientation. Hence, gradually diploma-project, research and tracks became better integrated.

Compared to traditional design education, primarily project based, the specificity of the design studios, in combination with long-term research and educational projects carries an innate risk, in the sense that the leading professor becomes the ultimate reference and authority, inclined to confirm his own research hypothesis or model. It is therefore crucial to reach out, allowing external verification beyond faculty borders. Here too, both departments followed entirely different paths.

uAD international exposure

In Brussels, research-oriented reforms went hand in hand with a rapid internationalization of the department resulting in the organization of two full English language tracks, uAD and aAD, preceding the later International Master's programme. Newly established, these international tracks had the advantage to be able to streamline design studio, theory and research more coherently.

Since there is no dominant nationality, a very wide and stimulating variety of educational and cultural backgrounds coexists. Most international students only complete their first Master year at St.-Lucas, being mainly exchanged through programmes such as Erasmus or AUSMIP, and this high fluctuation, in addition to the still embryonic link between research and studio, somehow restrains the possibility to develop longer term research within the design studio. However, the high mixture of nationalities does allow the exposure of research to a multitude of interpretations.

RTS

Beyond the issue of the design studios, fostering a research culture was crucial at St.-Lucas, and the choice to focus on design-related research, accommodating to St.-Lucas's historic strength, led to the creation of the RTS (Research Training Sessions) programme in 2006, a two-year postgraduate programme for established designers, stimulating the development of PhD-oriented research based on their own practice. The programme resulted in a veritable mushrooming of artistic 'research by design' projects, which, very similar to the previously 'flat' system of design assignments allocation, each excel within their own very personalized research. To curb the development of a too self-contained research output, and to ensure research quality and relevance, the programme is run in close cooperation with external international experts. Originally focusing on 'in-house' training only, the programme was recently opened up to external participants.

UDCK

At the GSFS an entirely different, equally innovative formula was established. Being a new faculty, it is located in the town of Kashiwa-No-Ha, the new and third campus of the University of Tokyo, which is part of a series of important public, commercial and housing developments along the recent Tsukuba Express commuter line. This led to the University of Tokyo, Chiba University, the municipality of Kashiwa and Mitsui Real Estate Company doing the urban development in the area, to establish the Urban Design Center Kashiwa, or UDCK. Addressing issues of common concern, consulting city authorities, while supporting citizens active in the promotion of their neighbourhood, the UDCK developed into a unique exchange platform. Remarkably, the UDCK has its own building and this venue not only serves as a meeting place to foster local neighbourhood culture, but also became a place for education as well; IEDP design studios are organized here, and are permanently accessible to the local public. Juries and presentations are attended by citizens, experts and city officials all expressing their opinions about students' works.

5.4
IEDP design studio presentation.

Such high-level participation vitalizes the interdisciplinary concept of the IEDP, and professors and researchers are provided with opportunities to test their hypotheses, materialized and enriched by the graduate students, at the same time exposing their proposals to third parties, generating a permanent triangular relationship between academia, students and stakeholders.

Fibercity

In 2001, a first experimental joint Tokyo-Brussels urban design studio assignment was organized titled 'Addition once, Subtraction once', which was presented at the 'Chronopolis' symposium in Tokyo that year. Students were asked to remove before adding, suggesting a possible intervention in a shrinking society preceding a more extensive collaboration and adherence to the theme of shrinking later on.

This experimental studio, characterized by many trials and errors, was a first in recognizing how to improve our environment within a shrinking society, eventually leading to the development of Fibercity by the Ohno laboratory within the Kenkyushitsu system and IEDP studios.

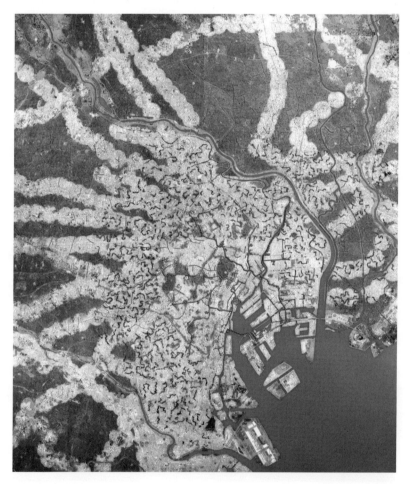

5.5
Fibercity research in the laboratory run by Prof. Ohno within the Kenkyushitsu system and the IEDP studios.

In Brussels, the concept of the Fibercity was introduced within the uAD International Track in 2005. Deeply rooted within the authors' interpretation of today's large-scale transformations in terms of a change 'from growth to shrinkage', Fibercity came to serve as the main research incubator and our design assignments' principal hypothesis.

Developed at both of our faculties, the ongoing Fibercity experiment provides interesting comparative insights as to how research has been incorporated into the education and is greatly enhanced through the AUSMIP programme. The common AUSMIP theme, of which Fibercity is a main exponent, is developed exclusively within the design studios, and approaching Fibercity from both a design by research, as well as a research by design methodology not only enriched students, but also enabled participating departments to learn from each other, at the same time enforcing their specificity.

At the University of Tokyo, conventionally applying research as an exclusive scientific tool, design itself needed to be introduced into research. Finding their origin at the time of Japan's industrial revolution, the Kenkyushitsu's design pedagogy traditionally adheres strongly to an industrial and technology-oriented laboratory system. As students in the Kenkyushitsu have diverse capabilities and interests, the collective result of their different research enables a steady development of the Fibercity model, which would be impossible if their design and/or research were organized through more traditional given assignments, setting the same (design) parameters for all students. For example, one student, strong in design, conceived a new type of bus as part of a mobility study for the Fibercity. Another student, excelling in statistics and mathematics, configured the bus routes using a cost-benefit analysis. More analytical yet, one research project calculated the effect of urban compactness on the CO_2 emissions.

The GSFS's introduction and integration of design into research, from an established research tradition, could be summarized as a 'design by research' approach. Capacitating the ability of design through analysis is indispensable for any designer/architect in an age of change, and is still a weak point within the uAD studio.

At St.-Lucas, which since its establishment has stressed design as an art, research itself needed to be introduced. The resulting 'research by design' approach highly values designers' capacity to explore potentialities and advance solutions through design, and is still underdeveloped within the GSFS. Team based and composed in such way that there is a maximum diversity in terms of nationality, expertise but also preceding education and affinities, the (so to speak) 'total' internationalization of the uAD studio generated a dynamic design environment.

Though still very much focused on assignments, these are split up into different phases, results being rotated. For instance, an urban planning hypothesis developed by one team will be transferred to another team, which will then develop the planning proposals from the viewpoint of the designer/architect. Results, potential conflicts or discrepancies arising out of any of the preceding phases are solved and discussed among teams, with tutors acting as mediators. This way, students take on different roles within the process, but must also negotiate permanently within and externally to their team, allowing a permanent, critical attitude and a check and balance on obtained design output.

Though evidently each department maintained its own distinctive approach as to how to integrate research and design, the grand experiment of the Fibercity resulted in a common ground in regard to the image of the architect/urban planner in an age of shrinkage and the crystallization of the contours within which such professionals would have to operate:

1   the ability to manage shrinkage and minimize the negative impact on the mate-
    rial environment, as well as maximize the possibilities within the existing
    situation (skills of a landscape architect);
2   the ability to maximize the inherent value of existing objects and to make good
    use of them in relation to the existing environment (skills of an editor);
3   removing the boundary between the professions of architect and urban planner
    – the ability to choose not to build, or to make corrections to a master plan (the
    skills of a profession between architect and urban planner).

The complexity of our age and reversive relation of shrinkage in regard to conventional design and planning convinced us that there is no unique desirable solution as
to how to integrate design and research, highlighting the importance of an equal
international exchange, as shown through the dynamic interaction and integration of
Fibercity within both the Graduate School of Frontier Sciences and St.-Lucas.

Chapter 6

Reality Studio – a search for design tools to meet complexity

Inger-Lise Syversen

Globalization is conceptually a consolidating phenomenon, but it proves on the contrary to be fragmented and complex and generates the need for a search for new operative tools. Due to the 'shrinking' of the globe, everyday life on an enormous scale is turning into something right outside our windows. A global reality is coming steadily closer and more readily visible, independent of longitude or latitude.

These and other unforeseen and complex situations that seemingly occur globally and independently necessitate new forms of interventions, new tools and actions demanding transdisciplinary and exploratory approaches requiring open minds which exclude prejudice and preconceptions. In the demand for meeting globalization, chaos, hyper-capitalism, flow of information, 'same same but different', a search for ways of bridging and linking the findings in a meaningful way is emerging. This chapter introduces the Reality Studio, a master studio at Chalmers Architecture (Chalmers University of Technology, Goteborg, Sweden), which attempts to meet these challenges by using an explorative approach to design complexity.

The Reality Studio has its geographical focus in East Africa, studying development in small and mid-sized cities. The Studio utilizes a pedagogical approach, systems thinking and an explorative avenue in dealing with complex and unforeseen situations. This chapter discusses the Reality Studio, its approach to knowledge production, as illustrated by the cultural aspects studied in the context of its focus on sustainable architectural heritage conservation and transformation and the complex impact of migration and change. The chapter will also illustrate how this explorative approach through research by design can construct the foundation for PhDs and Doctoral theses.

REALITY STUDIO

The Studio operates in close cooperation with international and local organizations and institutions. Reality Studio is not an aid project; rather it is a capacity-building project for the students and local partners who are involved. Mutual learning is the key concern. However, the experience from this approach to urban and product design education in cooperation with UN-HABITAT and local people has revealed potentials in a broader sense of capacity building. Students from higher levels of education constitute an important target group for capacity building. First, they are a great resource in data collection, idea generation and communication with locals. Second, student projects have proven to be useful 'neutral' tools for communication between researchers and practitioners, experts and laymen.

The late Professor Thorvald Åkesson at the Department of Architecture, Lund University of Technology (LTH) in Sweden, introduced the philosophy and the teaching approach of the Reality Studio through the first field study in Bagamoyo, Tanzania, in 1967. Since then the Studio has been run in many regions in East Africa, following in the historic footsteps of the slavery, spice and ivory trade to Lake Nyanza in inland Tanzania and along the East African coastline from Bagamoyo in Tanzania to Lamu in Kenya up to Kisumu at Lake Victoria in Kenya. Professor Lars Reuterswärd and Professor Maria Nyström brought the concept further and have since 2006 run Reality Studio through Chalmers Architecture in Sweden. The Studio integrates students of different disciplines (design, architecture, planning, industrial design, water and sanitation, engineering and landscape architecture) from several nations worldwide. Through the Studio's exploratory approach to design its output has over the years resulted in innovation manifested in an array of prototypes, projects, publications and project documents.

6.1
A number of Reality Studio design projects and research based on an explorative approach.

Pedagogical approach

The pedagogical approach in the Reality Studio is based upon the student's ability to observe, reflect and to be critical. Critical thinking is an essential aspect of design education that spawns new knowledge – advanced knowledge based on experiences gained from perceptive deliberations in which the physicality of making and designing something is ever present. The Reality Studio is one means of teaching in this context of complexity where the students (and the teachers) must constantly maintain a focus and simultaneously remain open for a continual change of directions: 'tiptoeing with a high degree of openness and humbleness' (Reality Studio 2007). The tool used is based upon systems thinking as is described in *Leverage Points – Places to intervene in a system*: 'The rules of the systems define its scope, its boundaries, and its degree of freedom' (Meadows 1999). The pedagogical goal is to make the students aware of the social and cultural context of their future work and capable of analysing that context as a necessary point of departure in their design efforts. The students are gradually trained to use research methods for systematic investigations, to formulate questions and define problems needing a solution, instead of starting with answers. Project design is central and the students are expected to gradually become capable of developing and designing their own projects.

Accordingly, the field studies contain the main stages: 1: Read and Discover which is a systems analytic survey of the local situation and context from micro to macro levels, 2: Project Area Definition (PAD) including strategy and programme design, 3: Project Design, formulating the issues of study and their boundaries, and 4: Exhibition and Communication, where the design projects, being process or object related, are exhibited and disseminated, leading to the fifth stage; Design Proposal.

6.2
Design process proceeding from the phase of observation (1) to investigation (2), testing (3), reading and discovering, to reinvestigation and retesting before a design proposal (4) and dissemination (5) takes place.

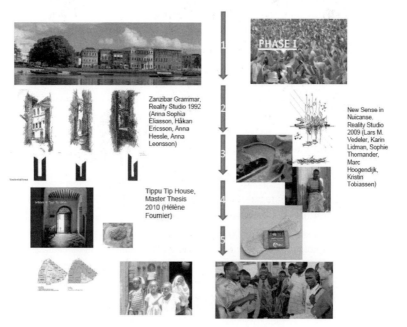

Zanzibar Grammar, Reality Studio 1992 (Anna Sophia Eliasson, Håkan Ericsson, Anna Hessle, Anna Leonsson)

Tippu Tip House, Master Thesis 2010 (Hélène Fournier)

New Sense in Nuicanse. Reality Studio 2009 (Lars M. Vedeler, Karin Lidman, Sophie Thornander, Marc Hoogendijk, Kristin Tobiassen)

The design project should in some way support and improve the everyday lives of local people. However, the project/product should be locally rooted and based on local preconditions, culture, materials, skills and environment. The concluding exhibition and communication (4) with local people serve as an input to the final Stage 5: Design Proposal. The design proposals include design criteria, i.e. the design before the actual design. The projects presented in this chapter are the synthesis of all stages and the result of this last stage of elaboration.

The Reality Studio is locally grounded (e.g. in the form of experience-based learning). In such approaches students may play important roles as designers for the development and implementation of locally grounded vision, policies, strategies and action plans for sustainable urban development. Moreover, through increased options for continuing education and support of networking activities these young future practitioners also play significant roles in a longer term perspective regarding urban development.

Research by design

As is discussed globally among architectural teaching institutions, the discipline of teaching architecture today is undergoing a major reconsideration and transformation. J. Muntanola (2008) argues in his introduction to *Changes of Paradigms in the basic understanding of architectural research* by referring to the 'group of theories' of Jaan Valsiner (2003), S. Gottlieb (2003), Joseph Muntanola (2006) and the dialogical theory by Mikhail Bakhtin (1981), that: 'The analysis of the feedback between brain and machine throughout the design process is, in my opinion, the best way to apply these *new theories.'* At the same time as Muntanola (2006) discusses the interaction between the brain and the machine Bill Hillier (1999) discusses the interaction between the process of design and the buildings. Maybe the most obvious transformation is seen within the means by which the projects are developed and designed moving between augmented and virtual reality. To prepare students coming from 'the making disciplines' where augmented reality and computer-based design are obvious and normal design tools, and to meet the demands of sustainability, Reality Studio takes the notion of bringing the design process out of the studio and into the field in East Africa where sustainable urban development is one of the greatest challenges facing the societies. In The Oslo Millennium Reader *Towards a Disciplinary Identity of the Making Professions* (2001), Halina Dunin-Woyseth and Jan Michel discuss who are 'the so-called making professions' and elaborate on which position these professions are taking in the scholarly criticism and knowledge production.

As a further development of the Reality Studio and the cooperation between Chalmers Architecture in Goteborg, Maseno and Bondo universities in Kisumu, Kenya, Chalmers Architecture launched the idea of establishing the East African Urban Academy in 2009 (Nyström 2010).

The concept of borderless is reflected in education and teaching as well as in the profession and among professionals. Methods and means become more and more sophisticated, new materials develop, new production methods and new digital capabilities emerge. This complex and at the same time heterogeneous production of knowledge demands a transdisciplinary approach to design. A new body of knowledge is evolving in the making disciplines, which reflect behaviours and patterns, systemic relations and sustainability. In turn these help to place the physical built environment in the context of culture and time. Fredrik Nilsson argues in his article in *The Nordic Reader* (2004: 30–43) that a new form of knowledge production (Mode 2) is emerging alongside the interdisciplinary knowledge production (Mode 1), which is specific to the making disciplines and architectural design. In this same *Reader* Helga Nowotny (2004) claims the demand for a development of a robust representative knowledge within a transdisciplinary approach.

By using the Reality Studio as an example of the new knowledge production we see that the interdisciplinary production of knowledge in Mode 1 is forced by the sake of complexity towards a transdisciplinary production of knowledge: Mode 2. Recently we also recognized that the Reality Studio approach, which is design oriented, also goes beyond Mode 2 towards a new mode, Mode 3: the design production of artefacts.

The Hogeschool voor Wetenschap & Kunst, School of Architects Sint-Lucas organized an international conference, *The Unthinkable Doctorate*, in 2005, unifying academics and practitioners aiming at discussing the advancement of knowledge. Kevin McCartney presented a paper in this conference: *Professional Doctorates in the UK – An Appropriate Model for the Design Disciplines*, in which he concluded that the documentation and evaluation of the rich variety of approaches to research in the design disciplines will be of key importance.

6.3
Transition from interdisciplinary to transdisciplinary knowledge production based on research by design.

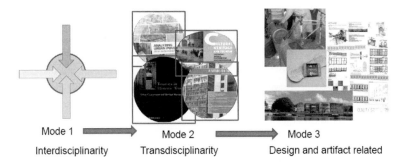

Mode 1 ➡ Mode 2 ➡ Mode 3
Interdisciplinarity　　Transdisciplinarity　　Design and artifact related

To handle this complexity we see a need for a paradigm for urban design and planning that can meet challenges and is capable of handling complexity. It involves an integrated systems design approach to urban development, taking into account various pre-conditions in different parts of the world and including a long-term perspective on resource-efficient urban management. We need to mobilize expertise from different sectors of society in innovative, transdisciplinary knowledge development processes placed in real world urban development efforts of cities where points of departure are social-cultural transformation in the everyday lives of people. Such processes have to be understood, designed and facilitated, in ways that promote the integration of relevant scientific knowledge at the forefront with place-specific experience-based knowledge. The design disciplines, like architecture and design, have a problem-oriented and synthesizing approach, which addresses the increasing complexity that planners, politicians and others must cope with in society. The design approach communicates between disciplines and levels – from micro to macro studies. The paradigm philosophy is centred on what architecture and design do, over time, rather than what they are. This dynamic systems design includes an emphasis on how we can contribute to development and research-based design.

Concept of sustainability in the context of the Reality Studio

Sustainable development is a political vision and a social construct of the United Nations, with roots in the 1972 Stockholm Conference on environment and development. This was developed further through the Brundtland Commission's *Our Common Future* (1987), and manifested at Rio de Janeiro in 1992 and more recently at the fifth World Urban Forum in Rio de Janeiro in 2010, bridging public and private sector, professionals and academics, civil society and non-governmental organizations. The latter document refers to the potential capacity of urban processes for necessary knowledge development leading to socio-economic development. However, urban practices in rich societies are unsustainable because of their huge energy and resource dependency. Such practices are neither applicable nor recommendable in developing countries. Thus, there is a crucial need for social and technical innovation based on a combination of local traditional culture, skills and knowledge based on future-oriented high-tech thinking. In this way, developing countries can become the forerunners of an urban development that the old industrial countries have to learn from or risk being left behind in an increasingly resource-sensitive global metabolism. Reality Studio therefore likes to transform the old connotation of 'Third World' to third option.

The complexity of architectural conservation and transformation

Built environments, sites and landscapes defined as heritage of cultural importance are being threatened by large-scale or uncontrolled development where architectural heritage becomes marginal and irrelevant. The recent demand for ecology and sustainability, transformation and reuse of the built environment sets an agenda with regard to teaching the subject of conservation and transformation. This raises the questions: How to ensure the development of a creative engagement as a foundation for professional life? How can conservation and transformation contribute to the ability of architects to address the future?

Recent research shows that more than 80 per cent of the building stock needed for the next decade is already constructed. This fact is not reflected in the pedagogy of architectural education. Thus teaching conservation and transformation ought to focus on morphological determinants, universal access, topography, climate, ecology, resources and creativity as well as history, attitudes, habits, seeing, recording, analysing, construction and materiality. All in all this entails a need for being future oriented as problem solving and space forming deal with tectonics and with a built environment as a living organism. Saskia Sassen (2008) argues for 'a more diffuse urban landscape of opportunities for "making" in urban landscapes dominated by massive structures and powerful actors'.

Reflecting the notion of the diversity of cultural heritage in the Venice Charter (1964), the Washington Charter (1987), the Nara Document (1994), the Burra Charter (1999) and the San Antonio declaration (1996), the complexity of 'globalization of values', integrity and authenticity calls for an interdisciplinary collaboration that is now broadly accepted. The escalating demand for transformation of settlement patterns and habitation, global development and sustainability extends the concept of conservation/restoration to include landscapes of cultural significance, urbanized areas, contemporary as well as historical.

The Reality Studio in the East African Swahili context

Chaos and system are two factors that are both in contradiction and mutually supportive. Simple non-linear dynamic systems and even piece-wise linear systems like bubbles of happenings can reveal completely unpredictable activities and results that initially might seem to be random. An example is the recent global economic meltdown starting in the United States coinciding soon after with similar situations all over the world, which have again triggered a chain of closely connected economic happenings that far from being random are interrelated through a domino effect.

In 2001 this complexity became the stepping-stone for the PhD *Intentions and Reality in Sustainable Architectural Heritage Management* (Syversen 2007) to Zanzibar Stone Town as well as Reality Studio in 1992, 2003 and 2008 focusing on architectural conservation and transformation in a historic urban context (Reality Studio 2008). Ungudja Island in the Indian Ocean is the largest island in the Zanzibar Archipelago outside mainland Tanzania. In this context of architectural and cultural heritage Reality Studio had already run similar Master courses on the mainland Tanzania and at Lamu in Kenya following the history of the slave routes and the transcultural Swahili culture (Helsing and Räiim 2004).

Mode 1 – Interdisciplinary approach

Architectural conservation has traditionally been regarded as a discipline of its own but is in contemporary times also closely linked to planning, tourism, economy, climate change, social coherency and pollution, and is today better conceptualized as an interdisciplinary field of action which demands factual knowledge of a range of other activities and at the same time a profound understanding of conservation theory and practices on international as well as on national and local levels (Syversen 2007).

Mode 2 – Transdisciplinary approach

Thanks to support from the Water, Sanitation and Infrastructure Branch (WSIB) of UN-HABITAT, cooperation with Maseno and Nairobi University in Kenya, Ardhi University in Tanzania and STCDA (Stone Town Conservations and Development Authority, Zanzibar), Reality Studio has been able to execute student field studies and studio work in Mji Mkongwe – the Old Stone Town at Ungudja Island in the Zanzibar Archipelago outside Tanzania in the years between 1991 and 2008.

Mode 3 – Design and artefact-oriented proposal

This chapter presents a selected number of the resulting student projects from spring 2003, 2008 and 2009. They have been selected to represent the variety of topics chosen by the students in close contact with local authorities and inhabitants. The projects are selected with regard to cultural heritage challenges in the Old Stone Town of Zanzibar, Pangani village, Tanzania, the Slave Route and Kisumu in Kenya.

Research by design

The PhDs *Intentions and Reality in Sustainable Architectural Heritage Management – Case: Zanzibar Stone Town* (Syversen 2007), *Healing Architecture – How local climate is able to bring forward a feeling of wellbeing in medical treatment* (Mkony 2010) and *Ordering Chaos – a case study of water and sanitation in Dar es Salaam* (Mwaiselage 2002) are all based on a research by design concept in which they are augmented by each other's knowledge and illustrate how Reality Studio functions as a stepping stone for research by design.

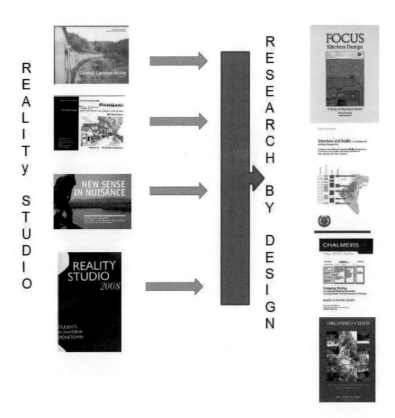

6.4
Reality Studio work as the basis for research by design.

Reality Studio design projects

The project *Central Caravan Route* (Helsing and Räiim 2004) took a meta-mapping approach to the subject by physically travelling the trade route from inland Ujiji to the coastal town of Bagamoyo, Tanzania with the aim of documenting architectural foot-prints from the slave trade period left by Arabs, Indians and Europeans.

The study served as a starting point for further discussions about listing the history of slave and trade routes as a case on the World Heritage List of

UNESCO. During the reconnaissance the students documented a profound amount of architectural reminiscences from the period investigated. The historic event of the slave trade is now nominated but still not included in the World Heritage List.

Pangani is one of the oldest Swahili towns on the East African coast, although today almost no architectural traces remain from the trade period between the fourteenth century and the early 1960s.

6.5
In 2001 and 2003 the Reality Studio used Pangani in Tanzania as a case study, searching for Swahili influences in the built environment in the context of the African East Coast.

Through phase two in the approach – reading the site – the students realized that the Swahili content of Pangani was stronger than expected both on national and local levels which brought a strong cultural awareness to the local people.

Kisumu is situated on the Kenyan shore of Lake Victoria. The city was formally established in 1901 as a node in the hinterland Tanganyika colonial trade, which is architecturally expressed through the richness of buildings from the Colonial and Functionalistic periods.

6.6
Left: Kisumu in post-colonial times. Right: The colonial building for the Province Secretary in Kisumu (from the Reality Studio 2009).

The Passage project in Kisumu 2009 (Reality Studio 2009) took its foothold in the fact decided by the National Authorities that the recent use of the building was to be changed. After serving as the Province Secretary's head office the aim was to transform the building into a museum. Through an open approach, the registration and documentation period, the potentials of the building were revealed and the design proposal suggested developing the building as an art centre for musicians, sculptors and painters based on local and international inspirations.

Although Kisumu consists mainly of buildings from the Colonial and Functionalistic period, even today there are some reminders from an earlier trading period that bear witness to the widespread Swahili culture (Reality Studio 2010).

Through observing, reading, investigating and analysing, the students obtain a profound understanding of the content and context which lead them to their design proposal.

The PhD thesis *Intentions and Reality in Architectural Heritage Management* (Syversen 2007) is based upon the Reality Studio project by using previous studies and design projects as the stepping stone for empiricism.

6.7
The last trace of Swahili influence in the streetscape of Kisumu (from the Reality Studio 2009).

Common attributes   Recommendable common attributes

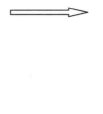
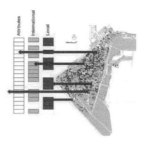

The analytical process moves between mapping and text analyses and ends by testing the findings on the built environment, moving from Mode 1 to Mode 2, resulting in a design proposal for sustainable conservation management: Mode 3.

Through a systemic approach based on an applied Geographical Information System (Hillier 1999) method and Grounded Theory (Strauss and Corbin 1998) the thesis executes the analysis through a synthesis of the relation between built form and documents. Through the analysis and testing of the findings the research recommends a design proposal for a sustainable architectural conservation that is first and foremost locally rooted but internationally respondent.

6.8
Illustration from the PhD thesis *Intentions and Reality* (2007) by the author was based on two main lines of inquiry: first, the physical structure of Zanzibar Stone Town, and, second, international and local policy documents on heritage conservation.

Conclusion

As the concept of architectural conservation has taken new shapes according to time and challenges and changed from being protective and related to historical objects to heritage allied, the connotation of conservation today is being associated with national entity and identity of place whereas the actions taken with regard to conservation are pro-active and action minded. The major challenges of conservation/transformation are complex due to: globalization, sustainability and fragmentation. To embrace these challenges teaching conservation and transformation need to embrace creativity and provide for a reorientation of the discipline, making the students able to redefine their way of investigation and understand built environment with regard to the complexity of knowledge and to face innovation versus tradition, to understand the relation between materials, morphologies, structural principles and ways of connecting and characterize the different parts of architecture (Syversen 2010).

The discipline urgently requires a fundamental expansion being able to bridge the gap between the architect responsible for new building work and the architect responsible for conservation: taking care of the existing built environment. The discipline of conservation/restoration and transformation needs new, comprehensive research embracing all levels from the mortar used to the changing landscape and the silhouettes of towns and villages, or as Prof. Jo Coenen (2007), Delft, says, 'handling the "art of blending" through: modification, intervention and transformation'.

Bibliography

Bakhtin, Mikhael (1981) *The Dialogic Imagination: Four Essays,* ed. Michael Holquist, University of Texas Press, Austin.

Brundtland, Gro Harlem (1987) *Our Common Future,* UN World Commission.

Coenen, Jo (2007) Paper presented at the EAAE Conference; *Teaching Conservation/Restoration of Architectural Heritage,* EAAE proceedings No 38, ed. Musso and DeMarco, EAAE Be.

Dunin-Woyseth, Halina and Michel, Jahn (2001) *Towards a Disciplinary Identity of the Making Professions,* Oslo Millennium Reader, AHO, Oslo.

Gottlieb, S. (2003) *Theories of Globalization,* Worchester Polytechnic Institute, Massachusetts, USA.

Helsing, Cecilia and Räiim, Elonor (2004), *Central Caravan Route Tanzania,* Ark3 LTH, Sweden.

Hillier, Bill (1999) *The Space is the Machine,* Cambridge University Press, Cambridge, UK.

McCartney, Kevin (2005) *Professional Doctorates in the UK – An Appropriate Model for the Design Disciplines,* Paper presented at the seminar, *The Unthinkable Doctorate,* Sint-Lucas, Belgium.

Meadows, Donella (1999) *Leverage Points – Places to intervene in a system*, The Sustainability Institute, Harland VT, USA.

Mkony, Moses (2010) *Healing Architecture – How local architecture is able to bring forward a feeling of wellbeing in medical treatment,* Chalmers Architecture, Sweden.

Muntanola, Joseph (2006) *Architecture and Dialogics,* Arquitectonics Review No 13, Barcelona, UPC.

Muntanola, Joseph (2008) *Changes of Paradigms in the basic understanding of architectural research,* Paper presented at EAAE (European Association for Architectural Education) Conference, vol 42, Copenhagen.

Mwaiselage, Agnes (2002) *Ordering Chaos – a case study of water and sanitation in Dar es Salaam,* Department of Architecture, Lund University, Sweden.

Nilsson, Fredrik (2004) *Transdisciplinarity and Architectural Design – On knowledge production through practice,* Nordic Reader, AHO, Norway.

Nowotny, Helga (2004) *The Potential of Transdisciplinarity,* Nordic Reader, AHO, Trondheim, Norway.

Nyström, Maria (2010) *East African Urban Academy, preliminary study,* Chalmers University of Technology, Sweden.

Reality Studio *Pocketbook* (2007, 2008, 2009 and 2010) Chalmers Architecture, Chalmers University of Technology, Sweden.

Sassen, Saskia (2008) *Why Cities Matter,* Paper published at the Conference *Changes of Paradigms,* EAAE, Copenhagen.

Strauss, Anselm and Corbin, Juliet (1998) *Basic of Qualitative Research; Techniques and Procedures for Developing Grounded Theory,* Sage Publications, London.

Syversen, Inger-Lise (2007) *Intentions and Reality in Sustainable Architectural Heritage Management,* Chalmers Architecture, Sweden.

Syversen, Inger-Lise (2010) *Complexity and Challenge of Architectural Heritage and Transformation,* Lecture given at Goteborg University, Dept Of Cultural Management and Chalmers Architecture, Sweden.

Valsiner, Jaan (2003) *Beyond social representation, a theory of enablement*, Papers on social representations, JKU, Linz, Austria.

Chapter 7

Research by design in the context of the OCEAN Design Research Association

Michael U. Hensel, Defne Sunguroğlu Hensel and Jeffrey P. Turko

This chapter describes the OCEAN Design Research Association's specific approach to transdisciplinary research by design, from its first manifestation as OCEAN net in 1994 until today. This commences with a short introduction to the structure and history of the Association and an elaboration of the disciplinary backgrounds and expertise of the currently active members and their individual and collective research interests. Furthermore, four examples of work are discussed that exemplify key aspects of particular research areas within the Association. It is important, however, to mention that the scope of current research areas in the Association is wider than the range represented by these four projects. The selected projects form the basis for discussing the conceptual and methodological approaches that underlie the respective approach to research by design.

Preceding and current structure and mode of operation of the OCEAN Design Research Association

In 1994 OCEAN was founded in London by Michael Hensel, Ulrich Königs, Tom Verebes and Bostjan Vuga – all graduates of the AAGDG Graduate Design Programme at the Architectural Association School of Architecture in London – as a collaborative network of young architects, with the aim to advance the production of knowledge, expertise and skills as well as to advance the shared portfolio in order to achieve a high level of competitiveness. Due to two of the founding members moving to different locations and the growth in the number of involved individuals as per the newly established different locations, OCEAN was restructured in 1995 into a network of collaborating groups located in Cologne, Helsinki, Ljubljana, London and Oslo (Hensel 1997). What followed was an initial period of intense research by design activities carried out through competition projects and commissioned works and related dissemination via various publication channels (see e.g. Hensel and Verebes 1999). In the phase between 1995 and 1998 OCEAN received wide interest from various research by design-related colleagues, academic institutions and practices in The Netherlands due primarily to the original design processes and methods that were being developed and pursued within the group at the time. OCEAN's specific operational structure, modus operandi and the work originating from it were published widely in The Netherlands in particular (see e.g. Möystad 1998). Collaborations with Ludo Grooteman, as well as with Ben Van Berkel cemented this link and served the exchange between OCEAN's Pan-European research by design set-up with strong links to the global Anglo-Saxon context and the very specific efforts shaping up through the numerous collaborations in The Netherlands

In the following time period, some of the local groups turned into successful practices in fulfilment of the initial aim of the network when it was first founded. These practices left the network to focus on their own specific brands of commercial work (i.e. Sadar and Vuga Architects in Ljubljana). The groups that remained within the network decided against a commercial practice profile due to the specific research constraints this format and mode of operation entailed. In 1998, the three remaining groups in Cologne, Helsinki and Oslo fused into OCEAN NORTH, now with even greater focus on research by design and with a strengthened link to the Scandinavian research by design context, with focus on the relation between architecture, urbanism and landscape design, leading eventually to an integral design approach that linked small-scale to large-scale designs and increasingly emphasised a systems approach to design.

7.1
Since its formation OCEAN has focused on sharing its research by design findings with the architectural, urban and industrial design communities. Different types of publications were produced, including catalogues of works (examples: left 1997 and right 2008), as well as publications that involved broader networking efforts such as the do-Group initiated by members of OCEAN to serve as platforms for critical debate and exchange (centre do-Group Hensel, M. and Sevaldson, B. Eds. (2002). *do-Group – The Space of Extremes*. Oslo: Oslo School of Architecture and Design).

In 2008 the name was changed back to OCEAN and the network was registered as a Design Research Association in Norway with formal membership and membership duties. At the time of the production of this chapter the Association has six active members: Dr. Natasha Barrett, Prof. Michael U. Hensel, Defne Sunguroğlu Hensel, Dr. Pavel Hladik, Prof. Dr. Birger Sevaldson and Jeffrey Turko, as well as a number of support members. In order to gain an experienced advisory committee the network invited Prof. Mark Burry and Prof. Dr. George Jeronimidis in 2008 as honorary members.

Although OCEAN started initially as a network of architects, its transdisciplinary character was soon established and strengthened due to the realisation that most design problems and research by design inquiries are often too complex to be addressed or even formulated from within one discipline. It soon became obvious that these design problems required a methodological approach based on elements from different disciplines and their related research modes and methods. As a result, the backgrounds of members began to reflect the necessary disciplinary exchange and collaboration. The backgrounds of the current members include architecture and urban design, interior architecture, industrial and furniture design, agricultural research and musical composition with many of the active members holding doctoral degrees in their respective disciplines. The scope of activities of many members combines practice and education with particular emphasis on research and production of knowledge. In addition, the field of activities of members includes inherently interdisciplinary areas such as systems thinking and biomimetics.

The various approaches draw to different extents from both the humanities and sciences and enable the production of a cohesive relation between seemingly lesser related areas of expertise, which can be seen, for instance, in the series of sound-related projects by Natasha Barrett and Birger Sevaldson. Realised in the form of installations within public and gallery settings, projects like *Agora* and *Barely* tested the correlation of sound spatialisation and material interventions towards synergetic spatial effects.

Operating as an association inspired by the format of learned societies in England and with an emphasis on interdisciplinary collaboration and collective self-improvement made it possible to adhere to practice without necessarily being constrained by it. Moreover, the format of an association facilitates financial resourcing through a broad scope of research grant applications. By removing financial profit as the primary motivation, the focus could then be shifted to a broad and holistic mode of production of knowledge and aspects of the renovation of practice that is unlikely to originate from within practice. The affiliation to academic institutions makes it possible to develop research themes through teaching on Master, PhD and post-doctoral levels. This enables transdisciplinary research activities, which are closely linked to education, research, practice and the industry.

Since its onset, OCEAN has been a dynamic entity made up of individuals with dedicated research interests and areas of investigation and the strong intent to pursue collective research agendas. The various disciplinary backgrounds are intersected by individual areas of interest that are more generally applicable across disciplinary boundaries forming the current areas of research such as *Systems-oriented Design* directed by Birger Sevaldson, *Performance-oriented Design* directed by Michael U. Hensel and Defne Sunguroğlu Hensel, *Digital Morphogenesis* directed by Pavel Hladik, *Heterogeneous Envelopes and Grounds* directed by Jeffrey Turko and Michael Hensel, and the sound-related research directed by Natasha Barrett and Birger Sevaldson.

Initially the design and research interests of the first group members were formed in the Graduate Design Programme (AAGDG) at the Architectural Association in London. This included a strong emphasis on instrumental and rigorous design methods with significant consequences for the development of the particular take on research by design in OCEAN.

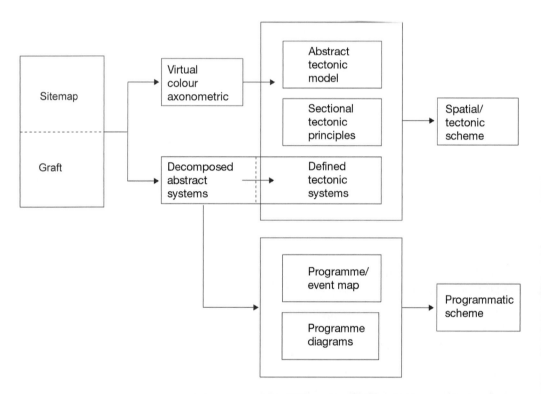

7.2
In the early 1990s several future members of OCEAN studied in the Graduate Design Programme at the Architectural Association in London (AAGDG) under the tutelage of Jeffrey Kipnis, Bahram Shirdel and Donald Bates. In this context major emphasis was placed on sequential and parallel translational design processes described in this diagram. This was done with the aim to derive rigorous and instrumental design processes that make the design process intelligible and, significantly, also available for design research. Following this development instrumental design processes became key to the work of OCEAN.

Four research by design examples in the context of OCEAN
In the following part four different research by design projects and three themes are discussed that benefited from the particular scope of research interests and skill-sets that were present in the network at the time when those researches took place.

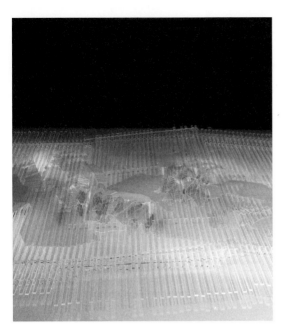

7.3
A Thousand Grounds:Tectonic Landscape – Spreebogen, A New Governmental Center for Berlin Urban Design Study, 1992–93.
By Johan Bettum, Michael Hensel, Nopadol Limwatankul, Chul Kong under supervision by Jeffrey Kipins and Don Bates at the Architectural Association in London.
Left: Conceptual Model indicated the folding of landscape and built mass into one another. Top right: Program and Event map showing all systems that organise the site and its potential for use over time. Bottom right: Axonometric indicating spatial transitions and degrees of interiority in conjunction with landscape surfaces and other spatial elements such as plantation fields and densities.

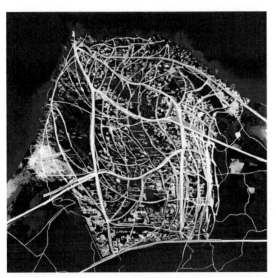

7.4
Changliu Grouing Area Masterplan, Haikou, Hanian island, Peoples Republic of China, 1993–94. By the AA Graduate Design Group 93–94 under supervision by Jeffrey Kipnis, Bahram Shirdel and Michael Hensel at the Architectural Association in London. Left: 1/5000 model of the masterplan for a new city for 600,000 inhabitants at 70 per cent of the final density. The model indicates building volumes and densities, road and harbour infrastructure, green and reserved areas, and in the centre the Central Business District. Right: 1/ 20.000 masterplan showing single, mixed, multiple and differential use areas, road, rail and harbour infrastructure, parks and landscape elements, 40 integrated farmer and fisher villages, and reserved land for future development.

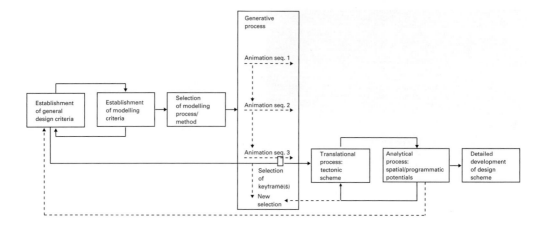

7.5
From the mid-1990s onwards OCEAN began to work with generative design processes, employing, for instance, animation techniques in the form generation of projects. The broader movement of architects employing such generative design methods included most notably Greg Lynn, Mark Goulthorpe, Markos Novak *et al*.

The *Synthetic Landscape* project consisted of three phases of research and a fourth phase that was outlined and initiated but not executed. The first two phases were directed by Johan Bettum and focused on research questions that are not elaborated further in this chapter. Phase 3 (1998) and the beginning phase 4 (1999–2000) was a broader research that involved numerous members of OCEAN in the research outline and pursuit (Bettum and Hensel 2000). The research aspect that emerged in phase 3 focused on the relation between planned design interventions on an urban and architectural scale, their effect within a specific context and the question of how to address contingencies that cannot be foreseen and planned for. On the methodological level, this involved the relation between analytical and generative processes and the feedback between them. For analytical purposes, a computational mapping method was developed that registered a number of dynamic site-specific conditions, such as climate, economic factors and human activities. These maps served as an underlay and were linked with digital animation techniques that served the purpose of adding selectively specific data-streams into the map to continually disturb it and to keep it from settling into a steady state. The purpose of this was to maintain a dynamic aspect in the map to which an intervention would need to adhere. This would lead to projects with a looser fit in relation to the generating information originating from a site analysis and a design brief, thus avoiding the pitfalls of arriving directly to a material object, but, instead, delineating a more diagrammatic and indexed 'performance envelope' that the project can then develop within. Much of the following research in OCEAN and research undertaken by individual OCEAN members is directly rooted in these realisations, which had arisen from the specific research intentions that were informed by the design experiments undertaken. In this way parts of the specific research interests that originated in the third phase of the *Synthetic Landscape* research project had rapidly evolved into a variety of detailed research inquires precisely due to the fact that urban and architectural design problems and design experiments served as the means of pursuit of research. The fourth phase was intended to address specific methodological questions such as how to solve the relation between analytical and generative data from a computational perspective. While on the one hand phase four was not pursued directly due to a key member of the project leaving the group, the questions at hand did remain and continued to be addressed in a number of other OCEAN projects.

The *A_Drift-Time Capsule* project in 1998, for instance, took some aspects of the *Synthetic Landscape* project further. The project was initiated by an invited competition to design a time capsule for the lobby of the planned New York Times building to contain selected items that embody the technical and design sensibility of the twentieth century and to preserve them for one thousand years for future generations. Instead of selecting specific items to be contained in the capsule and to design one time capsule only, OCEAN pursued a radically different path. A state-of-the-art digital animation technique was utilised to wrap any number and shape of selected objects into an intricate envelope. The proposal was to produce nine different yet similar capsules, all with different content and therefore all with a different geometry. This was meant to address in a succinct manner the shift from mass-produced to mass-customised objects, a tendency that clearly characterises the related changes in design and technical sensibility at the end of the twentieth century.

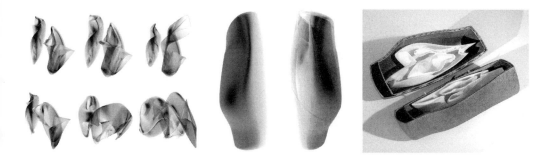

7.6
OCEAN's invited competition entry for the New York Times *Time Capsule* project (1998) utilised animation techniques in the form-generation of the design. The method was deployed to derive capsules that negotiate the shape of their content as an internal resistance with the performance criteria related to the aquatic environment the capsules were to be placed in as an extrinsic input. (Left: Sample animation sequence. Middle: Digital model of one time capsule. Right: Rapid-prototype model of one time capsule.) This and similar projects in OCEAN also initiated an interest in multiple envelopes as a means of addressing a manifold of intrinsic and extrinsic design context-related criteria.

It was proposed to place the capsules in different locations in the Antarctic ice shelf. If the ice shelf were to melt due to global climate change, the capsules would be released into the ocean currents at different times and in different locations, increasing the chances that some capsules would survive the dramatic changes that a millennium might witness. For this purpose the material form of the capsules had to withstand the ice pressure and be aqua-dynamic. Shaping the capsules therefore crossed two generative data-streams: the shape of the objects contained and their spatial organisation within the capsule on the one hand with the external context and the resulting performative requirements on the other. The material solution required expertise in metallurgy for the outer titanium layer of the capsule and in advanced ceramics for the inner layer and coupled with expert knowledge in climatology and oceanology. This proposal was possible precisely because winning the competition was not the primary objective, which made it possible to subvert a much greater number of competition requirements than seemed sensible for the purpose of winning. This, in turn, enabled a radical design experiment.

7.7
The research into multiple envelopes characterised the work of OCEAN since 1998 in a significant manner. This included, for instance, the design for an apartment block in Cologne, Germany (1998) that investigated the potential of heterogeneous interior conditions that arise from utilising envelopes with different characteristics (opaque, transparent and scree-walls) to substitute commonplace programming of spaces. The design study for a hotel in Sandefjord, Norway (1998) pursued similar aims that were adjusted to a much colder climate.

This approach was further developed for an architectural design in 2001, a few months after the tragic events of September 11. Fifty selected architects, including OCEAN, were invited by Max Protetch to develop designs for a new World Trade Center for an exhibition at his New York-based gallery. OCEAN proposed a *World Center for Human Concerns* that would provide forms of representation for all peoples, not only those represented by nation states. This required a formal approach that was not already associated with existing forms of representation and institutional forms and arrangements (Hensel 2004). OCEAN opted for wrapping a new volume around the void of the former twin towers. This would also be extendable as a research agenda of arranging new volumes around existing volumes in places where high densification is required. This was achieved by deploying a similar method to the one used in the *Time Capsule* project and resulted in a very large volume that produced an extreme deep plan condition.

Instead of attempting to bring daylight into the deep plan arrangement, the possibility emerged to organise a 24-hour programming with constant night areas in the portions of the deep plan that are the darkest. In other words, a gradient

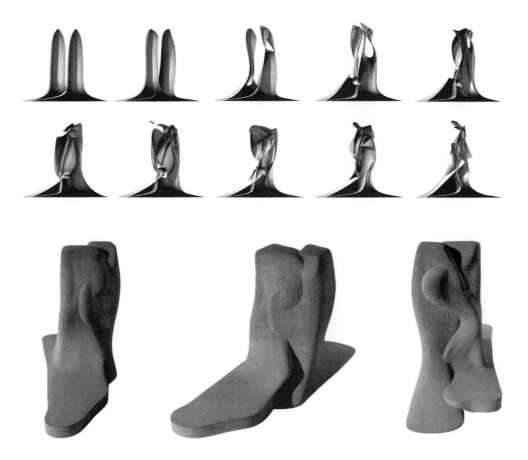

7.8
The design of the *World Center for Human Concerns* was OCEAN's answer to the call by the Max Protetch Gallery to design a new World Trade Center for New York (2001–02). The interest in multiple envelopes was examined at a much larger scale, aiming to provide a richly differentiated interior environment that can serve a 24-hour programming scheme. While the tools employed are very similar to the *Time Capsule* project the criteria for the development of the form and the related input data for the process were obviously different. Top: Sample Animation Sequence. Bottom: Rapid-steel model of the final volume of the *World Center for Human Concerns*.

of conditions was utilised as the precondition of developing ideas for inhabiting such a space. An additional possibility that had arisen from the intersection of various volumes in the animation that generated the design was to let different architects design different spatial pockets of the very large building, thus opening the project to another scale of design speculation and possibly expanding the collaborative expertise of this research by design process. This project demonstrates how conditions that result from design experiments can be used as opportunities for radically rethinking some of the entrenched dogmas and canonical solutions of contemporary architectural design, as well as the policies and regulations associated with it.

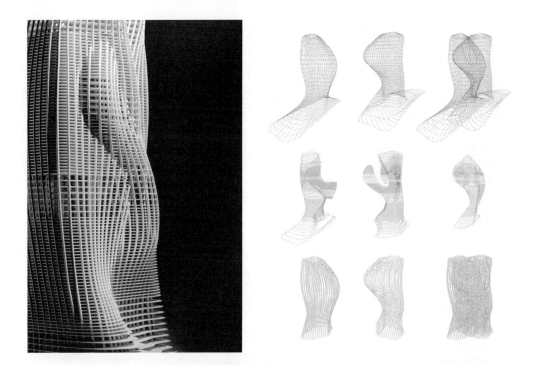

The *Deichmanske Media-stations* project was a commission by the Deichmankse Library for the design of media-stations that provide access to the Norwegian film archive. The project was conducted as an OCEAN-led collaboration with AHO Oslo School of Architecture and Design and HfG Offenbach, the Deichmanske Library as both client and collaborator and YNOR for production. The Deichmanske Library was represented by Reinert Mithassel, OCEAN was represented by Michael Hensel, AHO by Birger Sevaldson, HfG Offenbach by Achim Menges and YNOR in Kragerø, Norway, by Ronny Andresen. This arrangement made it possible to conduct a live project with all requirements of practice and a related research and development aspect within an educational environment with Master-level students from product design and architecture. The challenge was to conduct a research and design project resulting in fully developed media stations to be used in context in the time span of one semester and within the constraints of a small budget. The research inquiries included the architectural potential of objects placed within a given space and its resultant transformation, the functional aspects of the media stations and their integration into library-related processes, activities and circulation, a specific interest in material and material performance, as well as interface and search-and-browse-related innovation. The architectural inquiry was based on the related notion of vast space and a box-in-a-box section as elaborated by Jeffrey Kipnis (Kipnis 1993), with the aim to approach a closer relation between the given architecture of the library and the stations as objects set within. The study of the integration of the media stations was based on a systems-oriented analytical approach deploying methods of inquiry originating from within Birger Sevaldson's approach to systems-oriented design. The material research was directly coupled

7.9
The design for the *World Center for Human Concerns* was further developed by means of articulating the principal tectonic elements (envelopes, floor slabs, combined structural and circulation elements). The spatial pockets generated by the intersecting envelopes enable conceiving of the large vertical volume as an urban block that can be designed by different architects, with the provision that the principal tectonic elements are not to be changed.

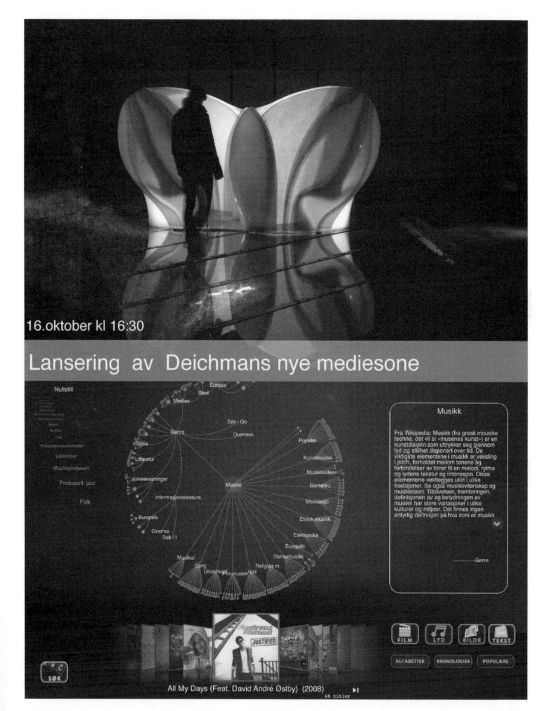

7.10
Invitation card for the launch of the *Media-stations* at the Deichmanske Library in Oslo, Norway. This project constituted an experiment in carrying out a life project in the educational project of two schools (AHO – Oslo School of Architecture and Design and HfG – Hochschule für Gestaltung in Offenbach, Germany) under the guidance of the OCEAN Association.

with consideration of production and undertaken at the HfG in Offenbach in tight collaboration with YNOR in Norway. In parallel, the digital interface was undertaken and developed by a team led by Reinert Mithassel at the Deichmanske Library. Integrating the required technology into the design and the makeup of the material envelope required close collaboration between the involved teams. The collaboration was based on working concurrently between two schools, the library and the production facility and required a well working communication. Frequent internet meetings and reviews and file share were utilised for this purpose. In addition, Michael Hensel travelled extensively between the two locations to facilitate the communication and project responsibility of OCEAN. All this helped to ensure that this high-risk project could be delivered in time and to budget while at the same time fulfilling the various research agendas. Research by design led in this case to an integrated and novel product for direct use and the development of the related methods of knowledge production into a model case for other research by design-oriented Master-level studios based on the combination between research-driven life projects. Currently a detailed analysis of the use pattern of the media stations is underway in order to obtain information on the specific interaction of library visitors with the stations.

While the selected examples above may all be discussed as individual research by design projects, they also share specific interests that can be stated as overarching themes of inquiry, including, among others:

7.11
The media stations in context at the Deichmanske Library in Oslo, Norway.

1   the production of new institutional form and social arrangements (Kipnis 1993);
2   the relation between spatial organisation, ambient conditions and potentials for inhabitation or use;
3   the interrelated spatialisation of material effects and ambient conditions such as sound (see e.g. the collaborative works of Natasha Barrett and Birger Sevaldson);
4   methodological approaches to context-specific feedback-driven design and digital morphogenesis.

7.12
From the early 2000s onwards OCEAN gradually began to develop and deploy recursive design processes with the aim to further develop notions and methods related to performance-oriented design. The design methods are characterised by multiple feedback loops and iterative processes that evolve designs within a set of defined control parameters. In so doing this kind of process overcomes the arbitrariness involved in selecting randomly frames of animations for the development of a design scheme.

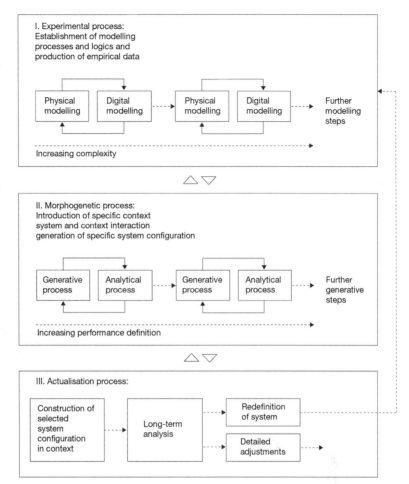

Such areas of inquiry characterise the individual and collective interests in OCEAN. At present, these themes prevail in different aspects of the larger research areas outlined above and also serve to distil more specific areas of research related to application, such as the theme of extended architectural thresholds with various sub-themes entitled Multiple Ground Arrangements, Articulated Envelopes, and Auxiliary Architectures (Hensel and Sunguroğlu Hensel 2010a, b and c).

Characteristics of research by design approaches in OCEAN

How can practice question and renovate itself if not by subverting its entrenched dogmas and canonical solutions to design problems? Can the renovation of practice be accomplished in the established modus operandi of practice? The selected examples above suggest that in order to challenge design problems at a deeper level it is necessary to subvert a larger number of requirements and expectations than is commonly done in practice. This can be accomplished through design experiments that lead to unexpected results, which in turn require reflection and post-rationalisation in order to be turned into tangible alternatives that are outside the

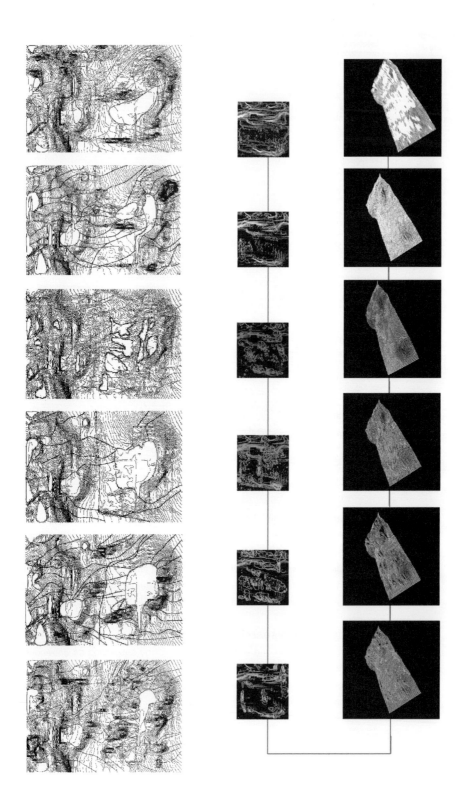

7.13

An early project by OCEAN began to develop recursive and iterative methods. The third phase of the Synthetic Landscape projects departed from the data-scape projects of the 1990s in that much more complex data-sets were deployed for mapping diverse conditions of interest that were in the process embedded in the articulation of a richly differentiated ground condition before any architectural design takes place. In so doing the project constitutes an early contribution to the development of contemporary parametric design, as well as the convergence of landscape design and urbanism.

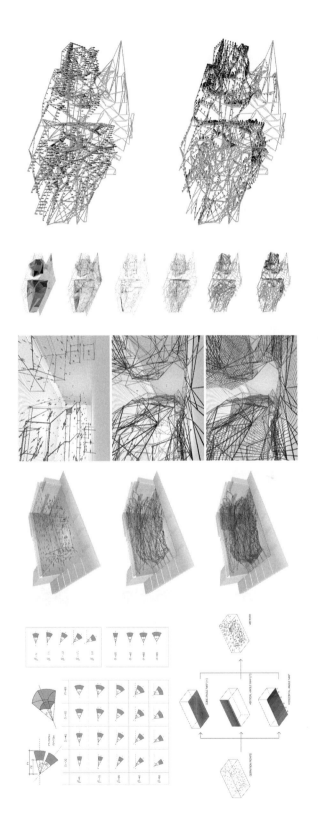

7.14

Performance-related recursive and evolutionary design methods were developed and utilised in numerous projects by OCEAN. The second phase for the Music and Art Centre in Jyväskylä, Finland, for instance, demonstrates this endeavour. The rule-based design process combines a generative method with an analytical one in a feedback loop that can produce numerous iterations of a design. The thus generated designs can subsequently be rated with regard to the extent to which these meet defined performance criteria and the highest-ranking design\s can then be further developed.

established canon. By being unexpected these alternatives require creative thinking and elaboration in further design experiments to become instrumental to the extent that practice, especially critical practice, can begin to deploy the findings. Alternatively, or in addition, a transdisciplinary approach offsets the constraints that arise from thinking limited to the context of any singular discipline. While it may be of interest to inquire, as some theoreticians do, into what might constitute disciplinary specificity in architecture and more broadly speaking in design, it is nevertheless clear that a transdisciplinarity is a key characteristic of current research by design approaches. While OCEAN started as a collaborative network of architects, there is key significance in the fact that only one year after its founding, the network had acquired a much greater scope of expertise. While this may be inherently related to the specific character of architecture as a discipline it was a novel approach characteristic of OCEAN to flatten hierarchies between disciplines and collaborating individuals, and, in so doing, to enable the challenge to core values and modus operandi specific to each discipline. In effect, this amounted to redesigning the various disciplines as a core project of collective self-development. While numerous other networks assumed OCEAN's structure and modus operandi and perhaps even had similar aims and visions, the temptation to snap back into a practice modus at the first sign of success prevailed. Persistence is indispensable where research is involved as both research projects and agendas are developed alongside over time. The challenge is to avoid settling into fixed patterns of operation when potentials for innovation may arise at any time and at any level of operation through diversifying disciplinary exchange. Taking this into consideration, perhaps OCEAN in itself can then be seen as a research by design project.

Bibliography

Bettum, J. and Hensel, M. (2000) 'Channelling Systems: Dynamic Processes and Digital Time-based Methods in Urban Design', *Contemporary Processes in Architecture*, AD *Architectural Design* 70, 3: 36–41.

Hensel, M. (1997) 'OCEAN Net – Networking: The Practice of Interchange', *Operativity*, AB *Architect's Bulletin* 135–136: 22–29.

Hensel, M. (2004) 'Finding Exotic Form: An Evolution of Form-finding as a Design Method', *Emergence: Morphogenetic Design Strategies*, AD Architectural Design 74, 3: 26–33.

Hensel, M. and Sunguroğlu Hensel, D. (2010a) 'The Extended Threshold I: Nomadism, Settlements and the Defiance of Figure-ground', *Turkey – At the Threshold. AD Architectural Design* 80, 1: 14–19.

Hensel, M. and Sunguroğlu Hensel, D. (2010b) 'The Extended Threshold II: The Articulated Envelope', *Turkey – At the Threshold. AD Architectural Design* 80, 1: 20–25.

Hensel, M. and Sunguroğlu Hensel, D. (2010c) 'The Extended Threshold III: Auxiliary Architectures', *Turkey – At the Threshold. AD Architectural Design* 80, 1: 76–83.

Hensel, M. and Verebes, T. (1999) *Urbanisations*, London: Black Dog.

Kipnis, J. (1993) 'Towards a New Architecture', *Folding in Architecture, AD Architectural Design* 102: 40–49.

Möystad, O. (1998) 'Architektuurpraktijk in de vorm van een network – Een beschouwing over de werkijze van de groep OCEAN' (Architectural Practice in the Form of a Network – An Overview Over the Work of the OCEAN Group'), *De Architect* 6: 52–59.

Chapter 8

Systems-oriented design for the built environment

Birger Sevaldson

This chapter revisits the way we look at the built environment from the perspective of systems-oriented design. To meet the challenges of sustainability and globalisation for our cities and rural environments we need to get to grips with the interconnectedness and interdependencies that make up the super-complex weave of our built environment. We need to think deeper and wider into how different processes influence each other and what the consequences of our interventions would be. The chapter describes relations to earlier research, and presents recent research regarding this challenge.

Models of the built environment

The typologies we use for the built environment sometimes stand in the way of innovation. One talks of houses, apartment blocks, roads, churches, bridges, factories, shopping malls and warehouses. When one addresses infrastructure within the built environment one talks of transportation, access, parking, roads, power lines, internet, etc. The limitations of a typology-based approach to the analysis of the built environment has recently been re-addressed by Michael Hensel (Hensel 2011). Looking at the built environment as a collage of accumulated types does not help us to place sufficient attention on interdependencies and relations between the built environment and its inhabitants, the processes of production and consumption, and the environment at large.

Several writers have suggested models for a more synthetic understanding of the built environment. Christopher Alexander (Alexander 1965) argued that the city is similar to a semi-lattice, a cross-referenced structure that has a point of departure and a hierarchy. Deleuze and Guattari (1988) compared the city to a rhizome as a more appropriate model for understanding the growth of human civilisation. Also worth mentioning is Manuel Castells' notion of the Network Society emphasising the growing importance of the immaterial aspects of our built environment (2010).

These models indicate the need for a holistic and inclusive view of the built environment as composed of myriad interconnected immaterial and material flows and processes, spanning from superfast transmission of energy and information to the flow of goods related to the everyday material needs, slow-moving flows of building materials, earth masses and the cultivation of artificial landscapes. The different time scales involved are intimately related to the environment, micro, local and regional climates, daily weather changes, seasonal changes and ultimately to cosmic and geological processes.

It is this interchange much more than simply the entities (types) and their boundaries that is of significance. The interchanges may be seen as forming part of a larger organism. The urban areas are dependent on rural areas where raw materials are produced. In urban areas the refinement of materials and the immaterial institutional and cultural production is more apparent, including institutional levels such as political, jurisdictional and financial forces.

The global material exchange resulting in exploitation and unjust trade, peak resources and the destruction of the biosphere are serious challenges to this organism. Such global conditions combined with local suppression and cultural contradictions are leading to global conflict and latently to large-scale structural changes, the rise and fall of civilisations.

From models to generative methods

However clever such descriptive models are, the complexity of the issue at hand makes such models very hard to use in planning. Reaching beyond descriptive representations, generative methods are potentially powerful ways of approaching super-complexity. Such an approach would allow for us to seamlessly integrate multiple readings and modes of analyses with generative design.

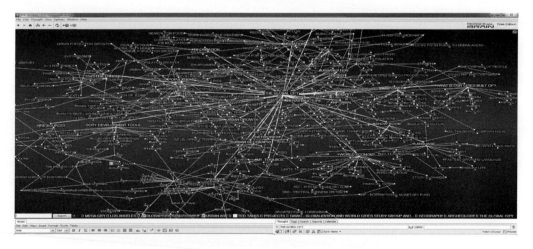

8.1
A dynamic diagrammatic model of the global city understanding and depicting the urban as highly interconnected. The Personal Brain™ software rearranges large mappings (GIGA mapping) according to the selected points of focus in animated and self-generating manner. This creates many different readings and enables an intuitive grasp of the vibrant complexity of the mapping.
Tanja Berquist's Master's project, Oslo School of Architecture and design, 2009, supervised by Birger Sevaldson.

In design and architecture some such generative and synthesising strategies for designing for super-complexity and unforeseen futures of dynamic and partly self-organising systems have been suggested. Michael Hensel (2011) revisits the method of grafting suggested by Jeffrey Kipnis (1993) *et al.* This approach includes both a way of resisting and reaching beyond the typologies of the city and a way of working with the city as a dynamic entity. The concept of grafting implies the use of rich colour maps, or abstract diagrams that are graphic structures, and uses them as global spatial organisers on the same level as one would use a grid as an extensive organisational system, a generic abstract spatial organiser with no particular programme or function. A more differentiated and richer device, such as the colour map, would arguably result in a more diversified and flexible approach to the organisation of space, indicating localisations, interrelations and developments of different programmes and activities over time. This move to a new mode of generative design was a radical step away from descriptive models of the city that attempted to create a base for rational intervention and involved in this case an understanding of the city as a self-organising and in parts unpredictable organisation.

8.2
Changliu Grouping Area
Master Plan, Hanian Island,
People's Republic of China.
The architects developed and
deployed a graphic technique
that made it possible to show
concurrently single, mixed,
multiple and differential-use
areas, including infrastructure,
as well as the interrelations
between the different items.
AA Graduate Design Group
1993–94 at the Architectural
Association School of
Architecture in London
supervised by Jeffrey Kipnis,
Bahram Shirdel, and Michael
Hensel.

This approach was further developed in a research project by OCEAN NORTH entitled *Synthetic Landscape*. This research resulted in the definition of Channelling Systems, a concept for digital time-based urban design (Bettum and Hensel 2000). The research associated with Channelling Systems examined many of the issues that are important for a systems-oriented design approach to the built environment: the contours of a planning process that takes into account dynamic change over time, the need for a planning mode that operates between hard planning, soft planning and emergence, suggestions of how to cope with real time change of information while planning, how to cope with future changes and the fusion of analytical, synthetic and generative design processes and the extensive implementation of diagrammatic visualisation. Moreover, the concept of Channelling Systems was a means to interrelate categorically separated systems, like, in the case of *Synthetic Landscape*, geographic, biological, economic, and sociological and other locally specific parameters. These and additional channels form the *ecology* of the system.

New knowledge fields

In the same period new fields of knowledge emerged from ecological science. Ecology is the ultimate systems-science crossing many scales and disciplines. Ecology was applied to the urban environment and to industrial production processes. Examples are the science of Urban Ecology (Marzluff *et al*. 2008), and the science of Industrial Ecology (Frostell *et al*. 2008). These new knowledge fields pose new challenges to designing for complexity. We need to base design projects on substantial knowledge, both quantitative and qualitative, while maintaining the integrated and generative way of approaching complexity as described above. Links are needed between theoretical and practice-based inquiry. Earlier systems approaches to design have failed regarding the application of multiple types of inquires and in shaping and being shaped dynamically in and by such complex knowledge ecology. Some have got lost in systems ideologies forming utopias like that suggested by Ackoff and Sheldon (2003), where self-organisation and emergence and the larger networks of production are addressed in an insufficient way. These examples strongly suggest that systems thinking needs design thinking. The intention of systems-oriented design (Sevaldson 2008) is to develop such synthetic processes that are imaginative and innovative, yet also very closely derived from and connected to the total ecology of the system at hand and that are able to act as incitements for systems interventions in self-organising and emergent processes with uncertain futures.

Towards systems practice for the built environment

One early attempt at systems-oriented design was the author's redesign of a production plant in 1986. The project started with an investigation into economical futures, social aspects, cultural issues, negotiating contradictions, facilitating collaborations, negotiating control, rearranging and streamlining production, looking into space management to free rental space, enriching the milieu, implementing flexible and adaptive structures and many more issues. After a period of incubation of this complex 'cloud', synergetic solutions started to emerge. This information-heavy and simultaneously intuitive process formed the foundation of the method that was later developed into systems-oriented design (Sevaldson 2008). This project indicated the possibility of a pragmatic and operational perspective to a generative and systems-oriented approach where design practice and a highly informed intuition and scenario thinking played a central role as method simultaneous and iterative analyses and synthesis.

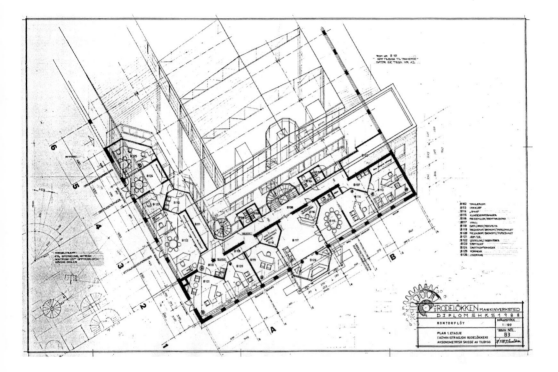

8.3
Rodeløkken Maskinverksted (1986) was an early systems-oriented design project by the author. It negotiated many different scales and dimensions across the production facility from production floor to offices, and addressed technological, social, territorial, communicative, collaborative and economical dimensions. The drawing shows the office section with the suggested structural system layout designed for differentiation and flexibility that together with a custom-made furniture layout could cater for individual adaptations and future change.

The *Ambient Amplifiers* project (Sevaldson and Duong 2000) continued the specific line of research of the aforementioned *Synthetic Landscape* project, building on the same generative diagramming techniques, but combining it with the high information density and intuitive synthesis as found in the Rodeløkka project. Referring to Eisenman (1999) the dynamic generative diagram generated by the computer was used as a tool to resist the planning intentions, schemata and clichés coming out of the framework of building typologies (Figure 8.4). In *Ambient Amplifiers* three defined main actors, the science museums, the art galleries and the sports facilities at the site, were coordinated to intensify and revitalise the central areas of the site. The main device to achieve this was the flexible 'islands'-scheme that was used for softly programming the area and to amplify the collaboration between the actors. Flexibility was built into the islands applying two principles. First, the articulated surface geometries where presenting options for usage without typologically prescribing and locking future use; and, second, a system for optional up- and down-grading was pre-planned according to four stages of development, spanning from footprint, foundation, framework to fully developed pavilions.

It was proposed that the islands would be administrated by the three main actors in collaboration. Territories were challenged and an ambience for inter-action and collaboration was created by intermixing the location and responsibilities for the different islands. The project's value was that it reached a higher level of specificity when integrating an extensive research and reading of the site, designing the interrelations of a selection of actors operating in a complex field, addressing the fluctuations of these relations over time and taking into account a high tolerance for unforeseen futures.

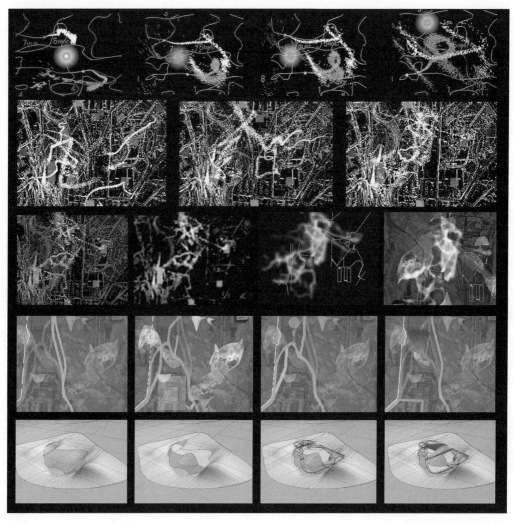

8.4

The *Ambient Amplifiers* commenced with un-programmed spatial structures generated from an intricate set-up of particle animations derived from the Channelling Systems and the topographic model of the site (top row). Through several translational graphic stages (second row) the generative diagrams were gradually programmed to inform the design interventions for the site (third row). The design interventions combined a circulatory and play surface (fourth row), a programmable road system, a flexible fence to the botanical gardens and a system of 'islands' as architectural devices for negotiation and collaboration between different stakeholders and the site (bottom row). The 'Islands' are a system of surface articulation to provide added value and usability to the site. They are shown in four stages of development and can be developed from one stage to another, either upgrading or downgrading their articulation according to needs.

From 2001 onwards, time-based aspects of such processes were further investigated in a series of master studios at the Oslo School of Architecture and Design called 'Designing Time' (Sevaldson 2004). Here the analyses were focusing on time lines sequences and how systems played out over time. This started a deeper research into ways of understanding relations and interactions, something that ultimately led to the development of systems-oriented design.

Systems perspectives

Systems-oriented design draws from the above introduced ideas and skills in design and merges them with systems theories. Systems theories span a large field, from hard theories to soft theories and approaches that apparently contradict each other. In this context only the most important sources for systems-oriented design will be mentioned. Amongst these are Soft Systems Methodology (Checkland 2000), Systems Architecting (Maier and Rechtin 2000; Rechtin 1999) and Critical Systems Thinking (Midgley 2000; Ulrich 1983). Amongst writers from the field of design we find Christopher Alexander (1964), Ranulph Glanville (1994) and Wolfgang Jonas (1996).

Although there are a number of people referring to and applying systems theories and practices in design, these approaches are most often based on established systems thinking from other fields. Furthermore, there is a lack of adaptation and further development to make systems thinking and systems practice more suitable for the field of design. These attempts of importing systems approaches from other fields have not been very successful in combination with design thinking and design practice. Typically the approaches are too technical and 'mechanistic' or too 'anthropological'; they leave little space for design thinking.

Systems-oriented design

Systems-oriented design is an approach to systems thinking especially developed by the author and colleagues at the Oslo School of Architecture and Design, and now demarcated as a design research domain. The main goal of systems-oriented design is to build the designer's version of systems thinking and systems practice so that systems thinking can benefit from design thinking and practice and so that design thinking and practice will be better armed to deal with super-complexity.

This does not prevent systems-oriented design from finding useful theoretical and methodological input from other fields and theories as mentioned before. In some of these approaches, intuition and an artistic approach are described as important. The notion of intuition is understood here as an ability of the expert, as described in Dreyfus and Dreyfus' skill-acquisition model (Dreyfus and Dreyfus 1980). A soft approach to systems practice will allow for the holistic expert intuition to be developed through observation, participation, intensive research, analytic and synthetic thinking, and design practice. Design cuts across soft and hard approaches and often benefits from quantitative and hard systems models as a supplement to the soft approach. Critical Systems Thinking forms the theoretical basis that allows different systems approaches and methods to be 'triangulated'.

Crossing scales and categories

Systems-oriented design implies understanding the relations between different scales and categorically separated items. Here we will look at three such levels:

1 From a very large perspective we can discuss cities and the built environment as a combination of multitudes of processes and temporary storage of material (Bettum & Hensel 2000).

2 Seen in a semi-large perspective the transformation of the built environment is a continuous process involving maintenance, refurbishment and change of ownerships. This involves large-scale economic fluctuations, regarding property as investment, cultural, political and social changes like gentrification and the change of Western society from industrial to service industries. The significance of this systemic level of our built environment became apparent in the recent financial crises.

3 On the other end of the scale, the everyday operation within singular buildings also renders a super-complex network of interrelated activities and operations. The building is inseparable from its operation, its inhabitants and their life and activities during the day. The building seen from this perspective is a living machine, a dynamic interface that has multiple interpretations according to the individual access and usage and the complexly layered systems and interconnections that play out over time.

All these levels might well have impact on the design of buildings. To understand the built environment from the perspective of systems-oriented design we need to cross scales and categories to find how they are interrelated. This demands attention to systems practice with emphasis on skills and techniques.

Skills and techniques in systems-oriented design

Systems-oriented design is based on systems thinking and practice that needs to be learned as skills and techniques. The most important characteristic of these techniques is that they are based on design practice in general and information visualisation and diagramming in particular. Information visualisation is generally thought of as a communication tool. In systems-oriented design it is central to use information visualisation as a process tool. The most important concept within visualisation in systems-oriented design is GIGA-mapping.

GIGA-mapping

A GIGA-map is any type of information visualisation for design process purposes that is very extensive both in the number of elements, the horizon of fields and the number of categories that are mapped out and related. The general aim of the GIGA-map is ultimately to develop a 'feel' for the overall complexity, an overview and expert intuition of the theme explored and to develop the detailed knowledge of the entities, filaments and interconnections in the field where needed and to reach a state of generative design, finding points of interventions and potentials for innovation. The maps can have the following functions:

- Mapping and coordinating pre-existing knowledge
- Including and organising knowledge gained from targeted research
- Building expert networks and communicating with them
- Mapping a field involving stakeholders
- Defining the boundaries of a system in an informed manner
- Defining areas and points for intervention and innovation
- Visualising and communicating of the final projects.

In GIGA-mapping more width and depth is reached iteratively. The first mapping should be inclusive and serves as a first very extensive unfolding of the field of investigation. Several proceeding maps are drawn from that point of departure. Such further developments are typically mapping of boundaries, zooming into certain points of interest and defining white spots and areas for potential interventions. GIGA-mapping helps in addressing the well-known boundary problem in an informed way. Instead of drawing the systems boundaries based on typology, tradition, prejudices or schematic considerations, GIGA-mapping helps to frame the systems in a more relevant and critical manner. While traditional systems theories are dependent on defining systems through their boundaries, recent developments have realised that this is problematic. Soft systems methodology regards both the notion of systems and their boundaries as artefacts. A pragmatic definition of the boundaries based on deep knowledge is most relevant when looking at the super-complexity that is at stake here. Boundary critique is central in modern systems thinking (Midgley 2000).

The mapping technique is combined with fieldwork and contributions from building up of expert networks and other modes of research to understand the subject for investigation. Observation and involvement techniques span from distant observation to participation observation and action research.

Applications of GIGA-mapping

In the following we will show two different ways of applied systems-oriented design and GIGA-mapping for innovation in the built environment. The cases are chosen to give examples of different applications of systems-oriented design that might be generalised and applied to other situations. The first case involves dynamic event planning and the second the negotiation and utilisation of territories through an innovative material system for auxiliary architecture.

The case of the 'Miniøya' music festival for children demonstrates a planning process for emergent phenomena, in this case the patterns of densification in a big crowd. The case shows how an event can be planned in a dynamic manner, where time is of the essence. In fact time appears to be the main 'design material'. This principle can be translated to many other situations and it also provides a valuable contribution to crowd management.

The two central issues in the project were the design of the event over time and the security aspect where crowding was the most serious potential problem. The project uses events as attractors. A very popular band would form a strong attractor at a certain moment in time with a certain duration, while smaller events would form weaker but differently distributed and timed attractors. The smaller events were planned and timed so that they would dampen the crowding

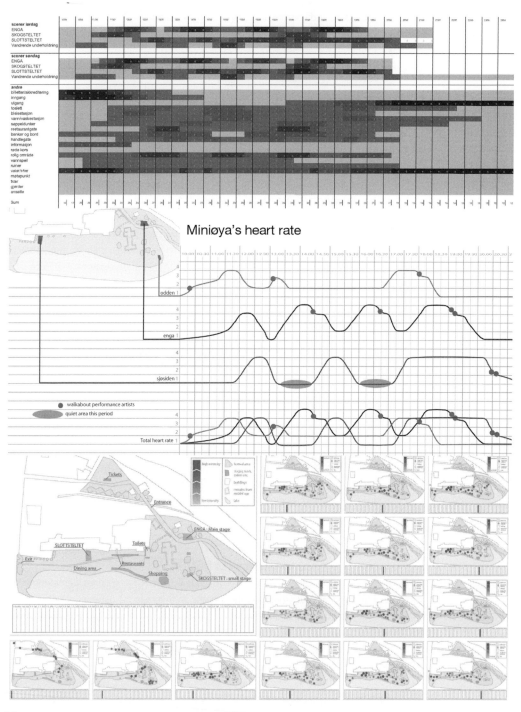

8.5
Example of time-based maps for the Miniøya music festival for children: from the top: time line with activities, time line with the three most important stationary attractors with addition and timing of mobile attractor the wandering performance artist, and 'key frame scenarios' of crowding patterns during the festival. Systems Oriented Design Studio at the Oslo School of Architecture and Design, Master student Ingunn Hesselberg, Supervisor: Birger Sevaldson, 2010.

tendencies instigated by big and powerful attractors. The strategy was to activate a series of smaller events when bigger events were coming up so that they would 'stretch' the field a bit and thin out the density of the spectactors. This was combined with the activation of other actors. Security would be especially aware of the patterns of events and would be present where needed just in time. Also a mobile entertainer class was suggested to modify the intensity in space in a dynamic way. These could also be responsive on a tactical level whenever needed. They would also have a double role of entertainers and informants to gather important information on the intensity and density of the crowd and to report irregularities to the proper people. GIGA-mapping in this case was done in the form of 'key frames'. The key frames indicated special scenarios that were regarded as possible. The driving engine in the design was the programme of the festival and the scenarios were built around that programme. The programme was altered according to the information produced by the scenarios. 'Minioya' was designed by Ingunn Hesselberg under the supervision of Birger Sevaldson in the context of the systems-oriented design research at AHO – the Oslo School of Architecture and Design.

The *Auxiliary Architectures* research addresses opportunities to generate spatial transitions and intermediary spaces in an already built-up context. This involves juridical, territorial, social, cultural, pedestrian, microclimatic and commercial questions and ultimately questions of sustainability in the widest sense. New buildings can be built according to updated standards like 'Energy +'. These standards are addressing solely the consumption of energy while leaving out other aspects like those mentioned above. Even more critical is the fact that the large part of the building environment will take years to replace or upgrade to more adequate standards of social and ecological sustainability. Therefore modifications of the existing buildings will play a crucial role in the future to come. In fact the refurbishment of buildings requires a new and more flexible approach to the concept of building.

The GIGA-map from one of the projects shows how auxiliary architecture can play a role on many levels. It crosses territorial, microclimatic, social, economic and juridical discussions of the site and addresses the chosen material system for an imagined intervention relative to these aspects. Challenging the accessibility of the site by referring to the Scandinavian All Mans Right, an old right of access for everybody to the farmer's outlands, the project suggests an expansion of the accessibility to the backyards. From this follows the negotiation of many different uses and a dynamic negotiation of the territories. The project demonstrates the use of a flexible material system with multiple aspects and functionalities that would cater for a multiplicity of the mentioned issues. The material system, in this case wood shingles and their dynamic performance according to microclimatic change, is activated to be a means to negotiate all those scales. Hence the project constructs an intimate logic between large-scale considerations and micro-scale material performance. Such thinking forecasts a more advanced approach to the built environment that has a great potential to reach synergetic solutions. The research was conducted in the context of the Auxiliary Architectures Studio at AHO – the Oslo School of Architecture and Design by Master students Daniela Puga and Eva Johansson under the supervision of Professor Michael Hensel, Defne Sunguroğlu Hensel and the author.

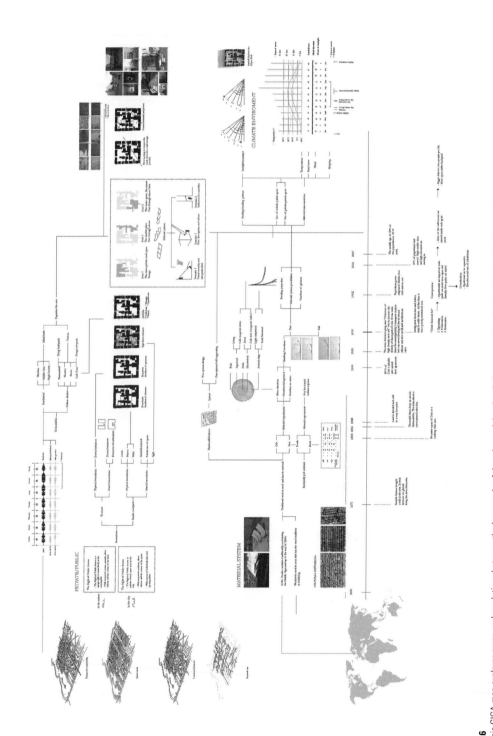

8.6

This GIGA-map explores cross-scalar relations between the large scale of the urban neighbourhood, the meso-scales of urban block and building and the micro-scale of detailed material systems and their performance. Auxiliary Architectures Studio at the Oslo School of Architecture and Design, Master students Daniela Puga and Eva Johansson, Supervisors: Michael Hensel, Defne Sunguroğlu Hensel and Birger Sevaldson, 2010.

Conclusions

The examples shown are all dependent on a systems approach to draw out their scope and boundaries. The projects go beyond considerations that are normally included in a design project brief. Obviously there have been many cases of design projects that have been so well briefed that they tend to reach a complexity that could be mistaken for systems thinking. The author has first-hand experience with such very well-briefed architectural projects. But normally such projects lack the hallmark of systems-oriented design, the flexibility and the connectedness to a dynamic context, the reading of the interrelations in the systems, the development of synergies and the resilience to adapt to unforeseen future changes.

All the shown examples demonstrate a high level of innovation resulting from the systems approach. Typically these innovations are found in-between scales, fields and disciplines in the cross-section between, for example, social space, economy and technology as in Rodeløkken, between planning, emergence and dynamic events as in Ambient Amplifiers and Miniøya, or between social activity, juridical territory and material systems as in the auxiliary architecture research.

True innovation for the built environment is clearly needed but to achieve it we need to investigate further and better forecast the consequences of our interventions. The biggest potential for innovation is no longer found on the singular technological invention but at the systemic level where such inventions are contextualised and where systems synergies are exploited.

Bibliography

Ackoff, R. and Sheldon, R. (2003) *Redesigning Society*, Stanford, CA, Stanford University Press.

Alexander, C. (1964) *Notes on the Synthesis of Form*, Cambridge, MA, Harvard University Press.

Alexander, C. (1965) 'A City is not a Tree' (Part I and Part II), *Architectural Forum* 122: 58–62 (Part I), 58–62 (Part II).

Bettum, J. and Hensel, M. (2000) 'Channelling Systems: Dynamic Processes and Digital Time-based Methods in Urban Design', *Contemporary Processes in Architecture*, AD Architectural Design 70, 3: 36–41.

Castells, M. (2010) *The Rise of the Network Society*, Chichester, West Sussex; Malden, MA, Wiley-Blackwell.

Checkland, P. (2000) *Systems Thinking, Systems Practice*, Chichester, West Sussex, John Wiley & Sons.

Deleuze, G. and Guatari, F. (1988) *A Thousand Plateaus: Capitalism and Schizophrenia*, London, Athlone Press.

Dreyfus, S. E. and Dreyfus, H. L. (1980) *A Five-stage Model of the Mental Activities Involved in Directed Skill Acquisition*, Report, Operations Research Center, University of California Berkeley.

Eisenman, P. (1999) *Diagram Diaries*, New York, Universe.

Glanville, R. (1994) *A Ship without a Rudder* [Online]. Southsea: CybernEthics Research, http://citeseerx.ist.psu.edu/viewdoc/download?doi=10.1.1.37.7453&rep=rep1&type=pdf.

Hensel, M. U. (2011) 'Type? What Type? Further Reflections on the Extended Threshold', *Typological Urbanism: Projective Cities, AD Architectural Design* 81, 1: 56–65.

Jonas, W. (1996) 'Systems Thinking in Industrial Design', Paper presented at the *Systems Dynamics 96*, Cambridge, MA.

Kipnis, J. (1993) 'Towards a New Architecture', *Folding in Architecture, AD Architectural Design* 102: 40–49.

Maier, M. W. and Rechtin, E. (2000) *The Art of Systems Architecture*, Boca Raton, FL, CRC Press.

Marzluff, M., Shulenberger, E., Endlicher, W., Alberti, M., Bradley, G., Ryan, C., ZumBrunnen, C. and Simon, U. (eds) (2008) *Urban Ecology – An International Perspective on the Interaction between Humans and Nature*, New York, Springer.

Midgley, G. (2000) *Systems Intervention: Philosophy, Methodology, and Practice*, New York, Kluver Academic/Plenum Publishers.

Rechtin, E. (1999) *Systems Architecting of Organisations: Why Eagles Can't Swim*, Boca Raton, FL, CRC Press LLC.

Sevaldson, B. (2004) 'Designing Time: A Laboratory for Time Based Design', *Future Ground*, Melbourne, DRS, http://www.futureground.monash.edu.au/.

Sevaldson, B. (2008) 'A System Approach to Design Learning', *Systemisches Denken und Integrales Entwerfen/System Thinking and Integral Design*, Offenbach, Präsident der Hochschule für Gestaltung Offenbach am Main: 22–33.

Sevaldson, B. and Duong, P. (2000) *Ambient Amplifiers*, http://www.birger-sevaldson.no/ambient_amplifiers/competition/.

Ulrich, W. (1983) *Critical Heuristics of Social Planning*, Berne, Haupt.

Chapter 9

Performance-oriented design as a framework for renovating architectural practice and innovating research by design

Michael U. Hensel

*Technology is epistemologically prior to science because when techno-
logy is conceived of as humanity at work, action precedes theorizing ...
The need to know derives from the need to act better.*

(Pitt 2000: 104)

*The gradual penetration of scientific research into every aspect of
human activity is inevitable. It's happening. This doesn't mean the take-
over of science, it simply means the involvement of science in every
activity.*

(Ackoff 1967: 151)

Initial thoughts on the relation between architecture and research

This chapter commences by examining the particular relation between architecture
and research and proceeds to discuss a theoretical and methodological framework
for an instrumental approach to research by design in architecture entitled *performance-oriented architecture*. Generally attempts to examine the relation between
architecture and research face two problems, first the difficulty to pin down the
disciplinary specificity of architecture and, therefore, second the struggle to assign
appropriate forms of research to architecture. Moreover, the presently central

question is whether architects can actually claim to undertake research and, correspondingly, what may or may not count as such. This question addresses not only the type of activity that may be considered as research but also the degree of clarity, focus and depth to which it is undertaken. In order to not be immediately entangled in questions regarding degree it is of use, instead, to consider different types of research, or, in other words, forms of structured and systematic investigation, that are relevant to architecture. It can be argued that relevant forms of research in architecture include basic and exploratory research aiming to identify new problems and opportunities, constructive and applied research seeking to find solutions to problems, as well as empirical research testing the feasibility of a solution by means of observation and experience.

A fundamental difficulty resides in the fact that architecture inherently and concomitantly relates to and borrows from the humanities, as well as the empirical (social and natural), interdisciplinary, applied and also the formal sciences. Efforts to reduce this scope of relations would lead to an insufficient description of the subject matter of architecture. This apparent predicament can be addressed through the notion of *transdisciplinarity*. At the *First World Congress of Trandisciplinarity, Convento da Arrábida,* in Portugal, in November 1994, the 'Charter of Transdisciplinarity' was launched that laid out the fundamental traits of transdisciplinarity. Article 3 of the charter is of particular interest in addressing the problem at hand in that it states that:

> Transdisciplinarity complements disciplinary approaches. It occasions the emergence of new data and new interactions from out of the encounter between disciplines. It offers us a new vision of nature and reality. Transdisciplinarity does not strive for mastery of several disciplines but aims to open all disciplines to that which they share and to that which lies beyond them.
>
> (CIRET 1994)

Given the particular characteristics of architecture as a sphere of knowledge that inherently and concomitantly relates to various other spheres, it may initially be argued that the demand for reintegration of various spheres of knowledge stated in article 5 of the charter offers a suitable way forward. If this is acceptable it may the further argued that architecture is intrinsically transdisciplinary.

What often complicates the examination of the relation between architecture and research is the fact that architects are typically not necessarily sufficiently thorough in distinguishing between various modes and methods of production of knowledge, let alone a careful treatment of the integration of modes of knowledge production, which renders detailed inspection often rather difficult if not impossible. Whenever closer and more rigorous attention is given to the matter at hand this entails frequently a shift to a meta-level of critical reflection that is often difficult to tie back into general practice. The opportunity to remain in contact with the actual process of knowledge production is thus often lost and consequentially reinforces the perceived, yet entirely artificial dichotomy between theory and practice. In reinforcing this dichotomy a second opportunity is missed, namely the production of knowledge based on a continual bidirectional flow of information between experimentation and reflection from and towards an overarching perspective. There are certainly a number of different ways in which one may undertake to remedy this. Research by design offers indeed a prospective opportunity, as it requires an instrumental and rigorous approach in the modes and methods that underlie and drive it. However, research by design also requires an overarching theoretical framework to ground the experimentation and to give it purpose and direction in relation to the production of a relevant architectural discourse and equally relevant improvements in practice and, by extension, the making of the built environment. This necessity is often overlooked or at least underestimated and undervalued in spite of all declarations to the contrary. This indicates that considerable effort has to be made regarding the simultaneous advancement of research by design and the formulation of overarching theoretical frameworks that can feed into an intelligible and relevant production of knowledge in the field of architecture. It is of course entirely possible to criticise such attempts as being too closely aligned with the sciences in a manner that seems inappropriate to the field of architecture. However, fewer would refute that architecture is actually inherently related to various spheres and forms of knowledge production, and thus it would seem reasonable to continue this line of argumentation towards the formulation of a suitable theoretical and methodological framework that can underpin and ground research by design in architecture.

Architecture and performance

A number of developments outside and within the field of architecture have taken place since the mid-twentieth century which in their wake have together contributed to ushering in discourses on performance in architecture. These include on the one hand the rise of systems theory, thinking and analysis and, on the other, the rise of an instrumental notion of performance across a wide scope of disciplines.

In the 1940s and 1950s an intellectual effort took shape that is known as the 'performative turn', which constituted a paradigm shift in the humanities and social sciences, with focus on theorising 'performance' as a social and cultural category. This paradigm shift comprised two key developments. The first development had arisen from efforts that pursued the development of a specific take on a dramaturgical paradigm to be applied to culture at large, that opened the concept of performance to a significantly larger public arena and enabled a dramaturgical paradigm in which all culture can be viewed as performance (see Kenneth Duva Burke, Victor Wittner Turner, Erving Goffman *et al.*). The second development commenced with the efforts of the British philosopher of language John Langshaw Austin, who posited that speech constitutes an active practice that can affect and transform realities (Austin 1962). As a result of these developments, performance is today frequently referred to as a concept that serves as a heuristic approach to understanding human behaviour. It is rooted in the hypothesis that all human practices are 'performed' as an act of public staging of the self.

Subsequently the concept of 'performativity' also began to hold sway in science and technology studies, as well as in economic science. Andrew Pickering charted a shift within the sciences away from a 'representational idiom' and towards 'performative idiom'. He argued that 'within an expanded conception of scientific culture … – one that goes beyond science-as-knowledge, to include material, social and temporal dimensions of science – it becomes possible to imagine that science is not just about representation' (Pickering 1995: 5–6). Pickering argued that:

> One can start from the idea that the world is filled not, in the first instance, with facts and observations, but with agency. The world, I want to say, is continually doing things, things that bear upon us not as observation statements upon disembodied intellects but as forces upon material beings.
>
> (Pickering 1995: 6)

Pickering's proposition that 'practice effects associations between multiple and often heterogeneous cultural elements' (Pickering 1995: 95) resonates in some ways with specific aspects of transdiciplinarity. Article 5 of the 'Charter of Transdisciplinarity' states that:

> The transdisciplinary vision is resolutely open insofar as it goes beyond the field of the exact sciences and demands their dialogue and their reconciliation with the humanities and the social sciences, as well as with art, literature, poetry and spiritual experience.
>
> (CIRET 1994)

Pickering argued that through this practice there operates the production of knowledge and scientific practice as a means of 'doing things', which has a transformative impact on multiple and heterogeneous contexts, for instance, through potential paradigms through which other disciplines, activities and agencies are transformed.

9.1
Cover page of the *Progressive Architecture* journal from August 1967, which focuses on the theme of *Performance Design*.

While the 'performative turn' held sway across the humanities and the 'performative idiom' offered a different take on science, another concurrent development was of key importance. In the wake of the development of systems theory, systems engineering and systems analysis, architecture began to adopt key aspects of these approaches in the late 1960s. The US-American *Progressive Architecture* Journal (P/A) dedicated in August 1967 an entire issue to the topic coined for the purpose as 'Performance Design'. The journal traced a development that commenced in the 1940s culminating in the notion of systems engineering, a holistic interdisciplinary approach to engineering that focuses on very complex engineering problems. NASA's Apollo programme is often cited as a key example of systems engineering. Great emphasis was placed on methods of addressing and modelling complex engineering problems. P/A listed as points of origin systems analysis, systems engineering and operations research. Each of those entails mathematical modelling towards some notion of efficiency, and more generally the application of scientific method. The latter involved, according to P/A:

1   the formulation of a theory to account for a set of isolated facts, or observations of the environment;
2   checking to see whether the theory actually explains the known facts, which involves formulating and reformulating (and re-reformulating) the facts in terms of the theory;
3   testing the theory's validity by seeing whether or not it accurately predicts events (i.e. gives the correct result).

While the relation of the portrayed approach to performance to questions outside of the scope of efficiency such as aesthetics, etc. was discussed and concerns of balancing quantitative and qualitative measures and measurements were voiced, the shortcoming of this approach was the somewhat exclusive alignment of the approach with the hard sciences only. This required that design problems had to be clearly and sufficiently described a priori and that the approach itself was therefore mainly one of problem solving via hard systems methods that cannot easily account for unquantifiable criteria and variables. In consequence such mathematical hard systems methods leave the active agency of the human subject largely out of consideration, although the importance of environment was clearly identified and integrated. What was needed then was an approach that combined hard, soft and evolutionary systems approaches to cope with complex dynamic systems. While a cybernetics approach already featured in some way or another in P/A's version of performance design it was the rise of interdisciplinary efforts such as complexity theory and systems ecology, and eventually also systems biology that helped to shape a more inclusive approach than the hard systems take on performance in the late 1960s. However, the repercussions of this approach and its critique carried on as some recent publications on performance in architecture attest (i.e. Kolarevic and Malkawi 2005; Hensel and Menges 2008). These publications evidenced the continued divide between hard and soft approaches, and also some calls for integration and inclusiveness. Yet, exactly how the latter is to be accomplished was not elaborated at any level of detail. This is only now beginning to take shape (Hensel 2010 and 2011) and will require a considerable effort over the next few decades. It is clear that there is no quick fix to the problem at hand, since it requires the formulation of an overarching theoretical and methodological framework alongside ongoing research by design efforts.

'Performance' as a paradigm enables the study of four interrelated domains of active agency: the human subject, the environment (in the broadest sense), and the spatial and material organisation complex (Hensel 2010). Yet, already now it is beginning to show that this approach may be in general too anthropocentric to accommodate a much more ecological approach to sustainability and that a more inclusive and nuanced version may be required. At any rate a number of key concepts have begun to take shape that may form the basis for the necessary development of a performance-oriented architecture. These concepts, considerations and criteria are introduced and discussed below.

Auxiliarity as a key concept for performance-oriented design

A systems-based approach to architecture will foreground the importance of the manifold systems an architecture participates within, that it affects and is affected by. On the road to an instrumental understanding, the criteria for a research paradigm for sustainable development as outlined by Professor Pim Martens, Chair of Sustainable Development at Maastricht University, are of use:

> a new research paradigm is needed that is better able to reflect the complexity and the multidimensional character of sustainable development. The new paradigm, referred to as sustainability science, must be able to encompass different magnitudes of scales (of time, space, and function), multiple balances (dynamics), multiple actors (interests) and multiple failures (systemic faults).
>
> (Martens 2006: 38)

Many interdisciplinary efforts combining the fields of environmental science, integrated science and economics, among others, have tackled the task of developing conceptual and methodological tools for such a new research paradigm related to questions of sustainability. This includes, for instance, multi-scale and multi-criteria analysis of sustainability (see e.g. Giampietro, Mayumi and Munda 2006 and also Giampietro, Mayumi and Ramos-Martin 2008). Key features of this paradigm can be found in urban and regional planning practice, such as, for instance, the field of *Urban Ecology* (Marzluff *et al.* 2008). In addition, more general systems thinking-related approaches to design such as systems-oriented design (Sevaldson 2009 and 2010) are beginning to take shape. Only the field of architecture has not adequately repositioned itself vis-à-vis these developments. This problem may well originate in the fact that architectural design operates on notions of *discreteness* of buildings that seem to preclude a more complex understanding of how buildings may arise from and engages in more complex relations over time. From this realisation arises the need to formulate alternative notions rooted in approaches that promote complexity.

The distinguished German architect and researcher Frei Otto posited that 'constructions are auxiliary means, not an end in themselves' (Songel 2010: 11). Likewise, the US-American theorist David Leatherbarrow stated that architecture 'participates in numerous authored and un-authored conditions' (Leatherbarrow 2011) including man-made, man-influenced and natural conditions. This realisation presents a vital opportunity for overcoming the continual predisposition of considering and designing buildings as discrete objects and processes, and may also prompt a more careful rethinking of architecture from an *auxiliarity* perspective. Clearly architectures always engage in this way whether intentionally or accidentally. Yet, to place these realisations at the very core of design considerations may constitute a promising way forward. The particular combination of auxiliary relations to conditions, systems and processes across scales gives a project its context-specific character and a high level of robustness. It is therefore of vital importance that *auxiliarity* criteria are developed on a project-by-project basis relative to context- and project-specific conditions. For this a new approach is needed that might arise out of carefully conducted analytical and research by design efforts. Auxiliarity as a key concept and an instrumental approach also needs to be developed in much greater detail. For now it is useful to distinguish between two different kinds of auxiliarity, for now termed first- and second-degree auxiliarity.

First-degree auxiliarity

An interesting example of a first-degree auxiliary architecture is the Khaju Bridge built around 1650 in Isfahan, a city located on the Zayandeh river plain in Iran. The two-storey bridge was and still is part of the circulation system, while also participating in

9.2

Auxiliary Architectures Research: The two-storey Khaju Bridge built around 1650 in Isfahan, a city located on the Zayandeh river plain in Iran was and still is both part of the circulation system of Isfahan, as well as the large water management system that served multiple purposes including irrigation of fields, drinking water supplies, the cooling of houses, and so on. By functioning as a weir with sluice gates, the role of the bridge in the regional and local water management was of vital importance. Moreover, the need to construct the bridge was tackled in an opportunistic manner: its spatial organisation facilitates the cooling of air by way of its contact with the water surface, and distributes it in such a manner that the spaces on the lower floor are comfortably cooled during the hot season. By utilising local conditions and climate the bridge provides both a well-calibrated and heterogeneous microclimate by means of a careful arrangement of the spatial and material organisation in interaction with the environment. The microclimatic conditions, together with the spatial layout provide spaces for appropriation and add to the civic project suitable provisions as an environmental comfort-oriented social space.

a large water management system that serves multiple purposes including irrigation of fields, drinking water supplies, the cooling of houses, and so on. By functioning as a weir with sluice gates, the role of the bridge in the regional and local water management was of vital importance. Moreover, the need to construct the bridge was tackled in an opportunistic manner that is of interest for the argument at hand: its spatial organisation facilitates the cooling of air by means of contact with the water body as a heat sink, and distributes the airflow in such a manner that the spaces on the lower floor are comfortably cooled during the hot season. By utilising local conditions and climate the bridge provides both a well-calibrated and heterogeneous microclimate, yet not by means of electrical-mechanical equipment, but by means of a careful arrangement of the spatial and material organisation in interaction with the environment. The microclimatic conditions, together with the spatial layout provide ample spaces for appropriation and add to the civic project suitable provisions facilitating it to be used as a social space.

Auxiliarity is clearly not an attribute exclusive to representational or civic architectures. Pre-industrial vernacular architecture is abundantly rich in such examples and ample research efforts have been invested to gain insights into integrated environmental and economic consideration given expression to local context-specific solutions. In principle almost all architectural projects place the main focus on anthropocentric provisions.

In order to derive an alternative approach to questions of sustainability emphasis needs to be placed on a much less anthropocentric and more broad and inclusive ecological paradigm in which humans clearly participate, but may not be prioritised in the same manner it has been done until today. This constitutes a major demand for the reskilling and retooling of architects. At the Research Centre for Architecture and Tectonics at the Oslo School of Architecture a research project on this subject has commenced and will be developed into the above-mentioned broader ecological model through research by design efforts in dedicated Master studios, as well as PhD and post-doc-level research.

Second-degree auxiliarity

There exists also an obvious need for supplementary designs to the built environment in cases where the latter cannot be changed in the short term. This necessitates research regarding designs that are supplementary to those already existing. Such supplementary designs constitute what might be called second-degree auxiliarity, and provide powerful ways to design more differentiated heterogeneous spaces and modulate microclimatic environments in situations and contexts in which it is not possible to modify the urban fabric or buildings. Architectural history is rich in such supplementary interventions that can provide varying degrees of shelter and exposure. However, research and publications on this topic are rather sparse. Some useful examples include the related research undertaken by Frei Otto and his team at the Institute for Lightweight Structures in Stuttgart and current research at the Research Centre for Architecture and Tectonics at the Oslo School for Architecture and Design. The latter entails further research into historical examples, as well as research by design that focuses on design criteria and methods and the development of suitable material systems for the purpose at hand.

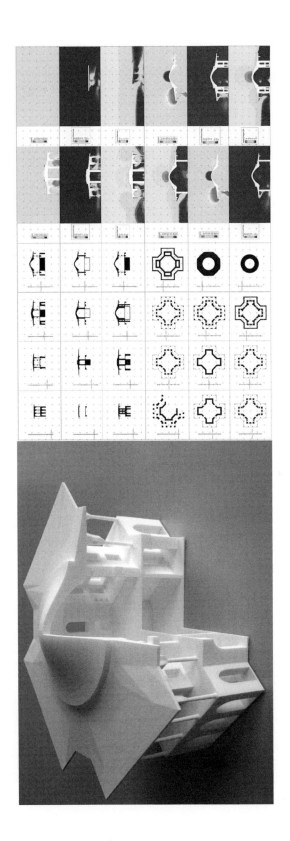

9.3

Extended Threshold research 2010 by Defne Sunguroğlu Hensel at the Oslo School of Architecture and Design in collaboration with Øyvind Andreassen and Emma M. M. Wingstedt at FFI – the Norwegian Defence Research Establishment.

Focus of the detailed analysis is the spatial and material threshold articulation and environmental performance analysis of the Baghdad kiosk (*Bağdad Köşkü*) (1638–39) at the Topkapı Palace in Istanbul, Turkey. Centre: vertical and horizontal sectional sequences indicating the intricate articulation and variation of the combined spatial and material deep threshold of the kiosk. Right: Computational Fluid Dynamics (CFD) analysis of airflow velocities, pressure zones, and turbulent kinetic energy indicating the environmental effects and interaction of the kiosk. For further elaboration see: Hensel, M. and Sunguroğlu Hensel, D. (2010) 'Extended Thresholds II: The Articulated Threshold'. *Turkey: At the Threshold, AD Architectural Design* 80, 1: 20–25.

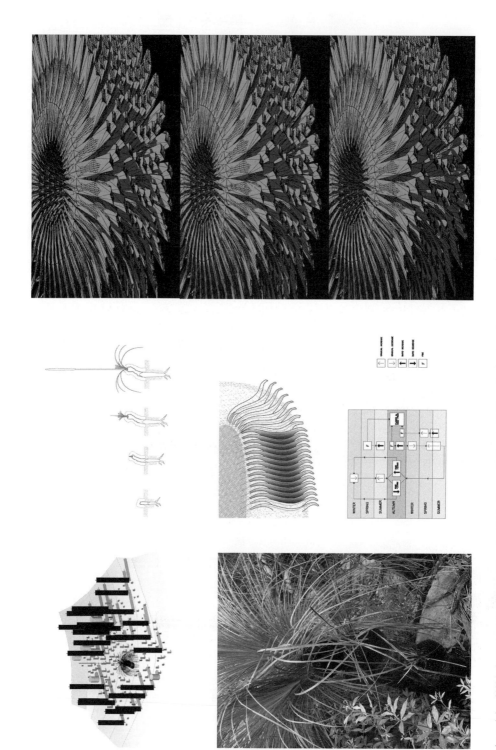

9.4

Ecologies workshop 2008 by innovation fellows Michael Hensel and Defne Sunguroğlu Hensel with Master-level students from the University of Technology in Sydney, Australia. The workshop focused on mapping a small area of an extensive ecosystem with focus on biodiversity, organism and environment relations and a particular plants species set with these relations, examining its various morphological and physiological aspects in relation to environmental and microclimatic conditions.

9.5
Auxiliary Architectures – Membrane Spaces 2009 workshop at IEU Izmir University of Economy directed by Michael Hensel and Defne Sunguroğlu Hensel. The workshop focuses on the empirical production of reliable knowledge and data for the design of differentiated membrane structures. These second-degree auxiliary systems can serve to improve the performance capacity and habitational provisions of already entirely built-up contexts. Views of the various types of experiments ranging from physical and computational form-finding, to environmental performance tests to the construction-scale installations as a means to experiment directly in the intended scale and context.

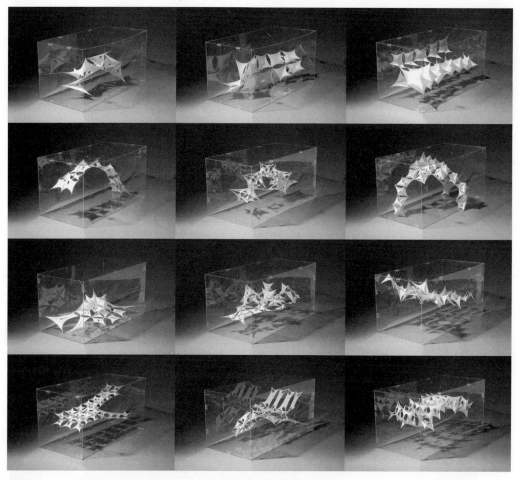

9.6
Auxiliary Architectures – Membrane Spaces 2009 workshop at IEU Izmir University of Economy directed by Michael Hensel and Defne Sunguroğlu Hensel. The structured and systematic research by design efforts leads to results that can serve a comparative performance analysis. Physical models of 12 of the 20 differentiated membrane systems produced in the workshop.

Of critical importance for this undertaking is the empirical production of reliable data and performance capacities of such supplementary architectures, and, in so doing, this requires systematic research by design, in particular since such designs are required to be highly context-specific and are sought to provide a related scope of combined spatial and environmental differentiation and heterogeneity.

Desegregation of form and function

As part of his research into the environmental modulation capacity of vernacular architecture in hot, arid climates the late Hassan Fathy analysed Islamic screenwalls, so called *mashrabīyas* (Fathy 1986). These consist of wooden latticeworks and are characterised by a scope of integrated functions: *mashrabīyas* regulate in a finely

9.7
*Auxiliary Architectures –
Membrane Spaces* 2009
workshop at IEU Izmir
University of Economy directed
by Michael Hensel and Defne
Sunguroğlu Hensel.
Computational analysis of the
shading and self-shading
pattern of a specific
membrane system. For further
elaboration see: Hensel, M.
and Sunguroğlu Hensel, D.
(2010) 'Extended Thresholds III:
Auxiliary Architectures'.
*Turkey: At the Threshold, AD
Architectural Design* Vol. 80, 1:
76–83.

9.8
*Auxiliary Architectures –
Membrane Spaces* 2009
workshop at IEU Izmir
University of Economy directed
by Michael Hensel and Defne
Sunguroğlu Hensel. A full-
scale installation was
designed to shade a corridor
during morning and midday,
while reflecting and amplifying
the low-angle sunlight in the
corridor in the evening.

nuanced and differentiated manner the passage of light, airflow, temperature and humidity of the air current, as well as visual penetration from the inside and the outside. All this is accomplished by the careful calibration of the sizes of the balusters that make up the latticework and the interstices between them. Different parts of these screen-walls cater for different hierarchies of the integrated functions. If, for instance, interstices need to be smaller at seating or standing height to reduce glare, the resultant reduction in airflow would be compensated for by larger interstices higher up in the latticework. While fulfilling their various functions in a nuanced and interrelated manner, the actual formal articulation of the pattern of the balusters can absorb very different aesthetic preferences. Examples include expressive floral pattern and abstract geometric pattern. These screen-walls are compelling demonstrations as to how formal and multi-functional criteria can be merged instead of the familiar division into separate single-function building elements. The question of multi-functionality is also directly related to the notion of auxiliarity. When building parts and more so buildings are to obtain multi-functional capacity this can arise from participation in multiple systems across scales of magnitude and time.

Extended thresholds/microclimatic modulation

Another interesting aspect is demonstrated by *mashrabīyas*, namely the understanding of the material threshold or boundary as an active and extended zone. The American scholars Addington and Schodek explained that:

> For physicists … the boundary is not a thing, but an action. Environments are understood as energy fields, and the boundary operates as a transitional zone between different states of an energy field. As such it is a place of change as an environment's energy field transitions from a high-energy to low-energy state or from one form of energy to another. Boundaries are therefore, by definition, active zones of mediation rather than of delineation.
>
> (Addington and Schodek 2005: 7)

Undoubtedly such architectural elements as the Islamic screen-walls can be understood in this manner. They provide a microclimatic environment that extends clearly beyond the physical extent of the object. Just how sophisticated the environmental performance of such screen-walls is can be seen from Hassan Fathy's elaboration:

> Its cooling and humidifying functions are closely related. All organic fibres, such as the wood of the *mashrabīya*, readily absorb, retain and release considerable quantities of water … Wind passing through the interstices of the porous-wooden *mashrabīya* will give up some of its humidity to the wooden balusters if they are cool at night. When the *mashrabīya* is directly heated by sunlight, this humidity is released into any air that may be flowing through the interstices … The balusters and interstices of the *mashrabīya* have optimal absolute and relative sizes that are based on the area of the surfaces exposed to the air and the rate at which the air passes through. Thus if the surface area is increased by

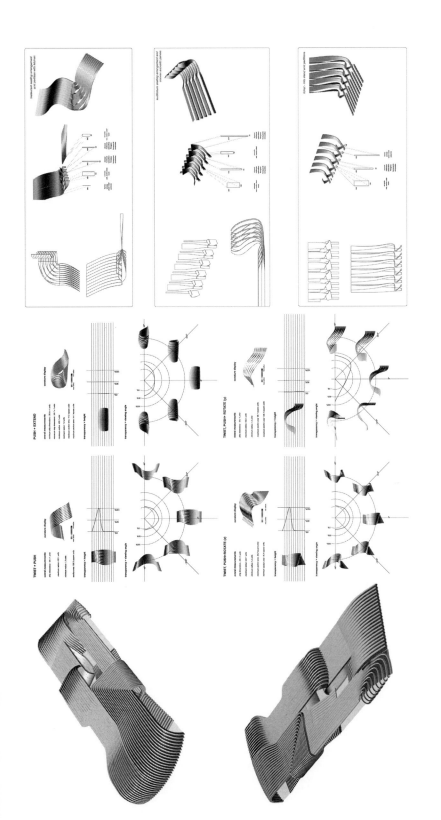

9.9
Copenhagen Playhouse Competition, Copenhagen, Denmark, 2001-02 by Nasrin Kalbasi and Dimitrios Tsigos under the supervision of Michael Hensel and Ludo Grooteman in the context of Diploma Unit 4 at the Architectural Association in London. Left: Two views of the digital model showing the transitions from closed surfaces to the striated organisation of the envelope and the semi-burrowed multiple ground configuration engendered by the project's continuous surface. Centre: Geometric study of striation density, orientation and curvature and the resultant viewpoint-dependent visual transparency of the envelope. Right: Study of gradual size-transitions of the striated envelope and its smooth transformation into a furniture and ergonomics-related scales. In this scheme the rotation of the elements along their longitudinal axis occurs in the areas of size transitions to accommodate the furnishing of space on a human scale.

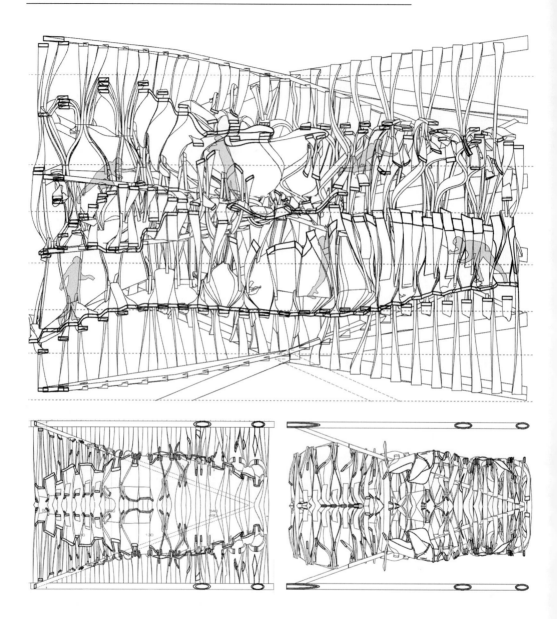

9.10a

Temporal Housing Study, The Netherlands, 2002-03 by Dimitrios Tsigos and Hani Fallaha under the supervision of Michael Hensel and Ludo Grooteman in the context of Diploma Unit 4 at the Architectural Association in London. Left: Longitudinal section and two plan sections displaying the striated tectonic scheme of the project. Due to the small scale of the housing unit the material strips that make up the surface relate to the scale of the human body. Right: Four samples of an extensive catalogue of geometric manipulations of the material strips and the resulting arrays, based on preceding material experiments.

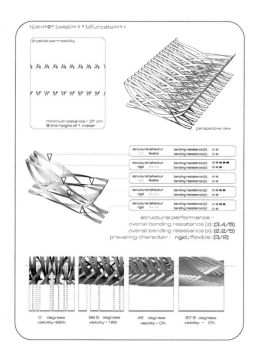

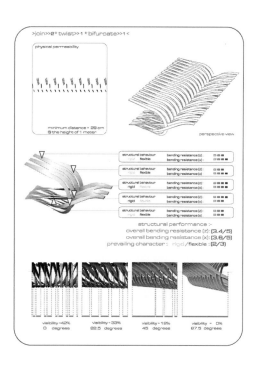

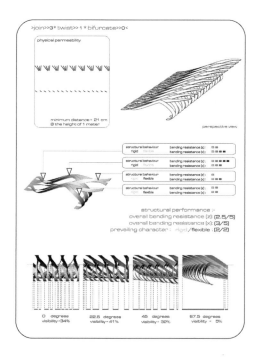

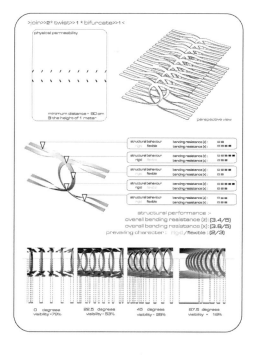

9.10b

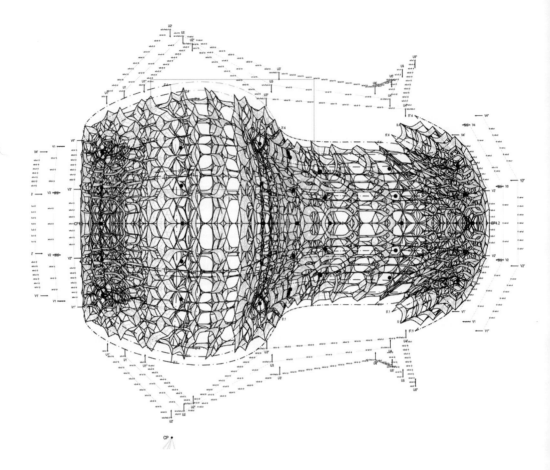

9.11a
Strip-Morphologies, 2004–05 by Daniel Coll i Capdevila under the supervision of Michael Hensel and Achim Menges in the context of Diploma Unit 4 at the Architectural Association in London. Left: This sample assembly with synclastic and anticlastic surface curvature shows a complex arrangement of bent and twisted metal strips. The permissible extent of curvature was established through extensive physical experiments. Right: The controlled deformation of strips made from different materials delivers the limits to the manipulation of an associative model. The top row shows a component made from three strips and their relation to an environmental input, i.e. light or sound. The middle row shows the same for a larger arrangement of strips. The bottom row shows the subdivision of the large arrangement into smaller areas that can each be articulated in a coherent and interrelated manner in response to a variety of environmental stimuli. In this way the material threshold can become extensive rather then remaining a hard division between an inside and an outside.

increasing baluster size, the cooling and humidification are increased. Furthermore, a larger baluster has not only more surface area to absorb water vapour and to serve as a surface for evaporation but also more volume, which means that it has more capacity and will therefore release the water for evaporation over a longer period of time.

(Fathy 1986: 48–49)

This becomes increasingly interesting when a more general design principle for larger building elements or entire building envelopes is derived from the insights

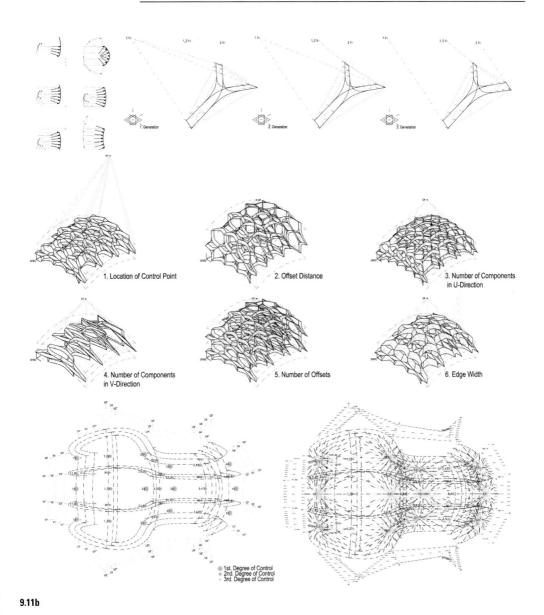

1. Location of Control Point
2. Offset Distance
3. Number of Components in U-Direction
4. Number of Components in V-Direction
5. Number of Offsets
6. Edge Width

1st. Degree of Control
2nd. Degree of Control
3rd. Degree of Control

9.11b

gained. David Leatherbarrow examined a particular type of louvered wall that he calls a 'breathing wall'. It is the interaction between this type of building element with the specific environment that it is set within that Leatherbarrow calls 'productive, because its settings supply what the given location is unable to supply on its own' (Leatherbarrow 2009: 33), and, moreover:

> Certainly the building's elements are passive – they do not move or change position – but they can also be seen to be active if their 'behaviour' is seen to result in the creation of qualities the world lacks. This is

to say, architectural elements are *passively active*. Seemingly at rest, they are secretly at work. The key is this: in their labour, architectural elements fuse themselves into the latencies of the ambient environment, adopting their capacity for change or movement.

(Leatherbarrow 2009: 37–38)

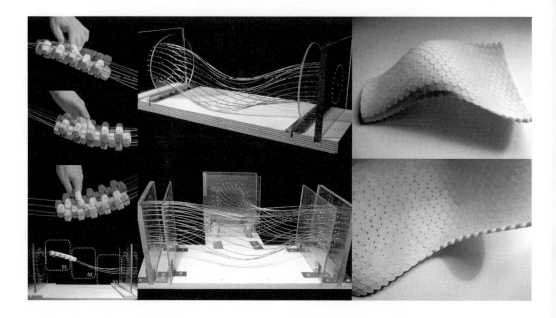

When the architectural boundary begins to acquire adequate space for inhabitation it furthers the performative capacities of architecture, as well as the possibility of entirely repositioning the relation between inside and outside. This is not a new thought. The history of architecture is rich with examples that are entirely worth re-examining from a performance perspective. The transitional zone between inside and outside introduced by such elements can serve sophisticated climatic modulation for the respective building and provide spaces for versatile use for the inhabitants.

Conclusion

Performance in architecture has once again become a vital discourse that can provide a relevant platform for developing an alternative approach to architectural design and sustainability. It does so from a systems-thinking perspective and by understanding the key domains of architectural designs as imbued with active agency: the human subject, the environment, and the spatial and material organisation complex. However, considering previous attempts it seems inadequate to pursue this endeavour from an exclusive hard systems and engineering perspective. Instead, an expanded scope of systems approaches needs to underlie performance-oriented architecture for it not to simply remain a post-design optimisation method geared only towards greater efficiency in functionality. Likewise it is necessary to develop a detailed theoretical and methodological framework based on key concepts

9.12
Complex Brick Assembly research by Defne Sunguroğlu Hensel.
Slender rods under torsional buckling serve as the means to induce pre-stressing into a complex double-curved brick assembly. Left: Experiments with slender rods and brick-like elements. Centre: Modelling set-up for inducing and measuring torsional buckling of slender rods. Right: Resulting structural double-curved brick surfaces.

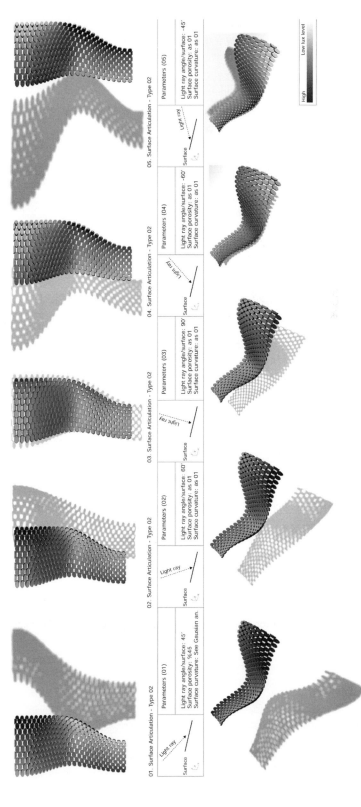

9.13
Complex Brick Assembly research by Defne Sunguroğlu Sunguroğlu Hensel.
Self-shading and shading pattern of a double-curved porous brick assembly at five different times of the day.

and concerns. This chapter introduced the notions of *auxiliarity*, desegregation of form and function, *extended thresholds* and nuanced microclimatic provisions. These constitute initial steps to the elaboration of a complex research programme that will rely on extensive research by design and collaboration with practice to gain broad relevance and to make a significant contribution to architecture and the built environment.

Bibliography

Ackoff, R. (1967) quoted in 'The Changing Aesthetic'. *Performance Design – Progressive Architecture*, August: 149–151.

Addington, M. and Schodek, D. (2005) *Smart Materials and Technologies for the Architecture and Design Professions*. Oxford: Architectural Press, Elsevier.

Austin, J. (1962) *How to Do Things with Words*. Oxford: Clarendon Press.

CIRET Le Centre International de Recherches et Etudes Transdisciplinaires (1994) *Charter of Transdisciplinarity*. Online: http://basarab.nicolescu.perso.sfr.fr/ciret/english/charten.htm (accessed 8 September 2011).

Fathy, H. (1986) *Natural Energy and Vernacular Architecture – principles and examples with reference to hot arid climates*. Chicago, IL: The University of Chicago Press.

Giampietro, M., Mayumi, K. and Munda, G. (2006) 'Integrated assessment and energy analysis: Quality assurance in multi-criteria analysis of sustainability'. *Energy,* 1 (31): 59–86.

Giampietro, M., Mayumi, K. and Ramos-Martin, J. (2008) *Multi-scale Integrated Analysis of Societal and Ecosystem Metabolism (MUSIASEM): An Outline of Rationale and Theory*. Working Papers, Department of Applied Economics at Universitat Autonoma of Barcelona. Online: http://www.ecap.uab.es/RePEc/doc/wpdea0801.pdf (accesssed 8 September 2011).

Hensel, M. (2010) 'Performance-oriented Architecture – Towards a Biological Paradigm for Architectural Design and the Built Environment', *FORMAkademisk* 3 (1): 36–56. Online: www.formakademisk.org/index.php/formakademisk/issue/view/6/showToc (accessed 8 September 2011).

Hensel, M. (2011) 'Performance-oriented Architecture and the Spatial and Material Organisation Complex – Rethinking the Definition, Role and Performative Capacity of the Spatial and Material Boundaries of the Built Environment', *FORMAkademisk* 4 (1): 3–23. Online: www.formakademisk.org/index.php/formakademisk/issue/view/8/showToc (accessed 8 September 2011).

Hensel, M. and Menges, A. (2008) *Form follows Performance – Arch* + 188, July.

Hensel, M. and Sunguroğlu Hensel, D. (2010) 'Extended Thresholds II: The Articulated Threshold', *Turkey: At the Threshold, AD Architectural Design* 80 (1): 20–25.

Kolarevic, B. and Malkawi, A. (2005) *Performative Architecture: Beyond Instrumentality*. New York: Spon.

Leatherbarrow, D. (2009) *Architecture Oriented Otherwise*. New York: Princeton Architectural Press.

Leatherbarrow, D. (2011) *Architecture Oriented Otherwise* – Lecture at the Oslo School of Architecture and Design, 28 April. The theme will also be further elaborated in David Leatherbarrow's forthcoming book *Building Time*.

Martens, P. (2006) 'Sustainability: Science or Fiction?', *Sustainability: Science, Practice & Policy* 1 (2): 36–41.

Marzluff, M., Shulenberger, E., Endlicher, W., Alberti, M., Bradley, G., Ryan, C., ZumBrunnen, C. and Simon, U. (eds) (2008) *Urban Ecology – An International Perspective on the Interaction between Humans and Nature*. New York: Springer.

Pickering, A. (1995) *The Mangle of Practice – Time, Agency and Science*. Chicago, IL: The University of Chicago Press.

Pitt, J. C. (2000) *Thinking about Technology – Foundations of the Philosophy of Technology*. New York, London: Seven Bridges Press.

Sevaldson, B. (2009) 'Why should we and how can we make the design process more complex? – A new look at the systems approach in design', *Shaping Futures – IDE 25 Year Book*. Oslo: Oslo School of Architecture and Design, pp. 274–281.

Sevaldson, B. (2010) 'Discussions and Movements in Design Research – A Systems Approach to Practice Research in Design'. *FORMAkademisk* 3 (1): 8–35. Online: http://www.formakademisk.org/index.php/formakademisk/issue/view/6/showToc (accessed 8 September 2011).

Songel, J. M. (2010) *A Conversation with Frei Otto*. New York: Princeton Architectural Press.

Chapter 10

The Research Centre for Architecture and Tectonics – implementing research towards performance-oriented architecture

Michael U. Hensel

The Research Centre for Architecture and Tectonics was inaugurated at the beginning of 2011 at the Oslo School of Architecture and Design in Norway. Some of its core activities had, however, begun several years earlier in the format of a series of research by design-oriented Master-level studios and seminar courses at the school, as well as a series of PhD stipends earmarked as 'research by design' in 2008.

The principal motivation in setting up a new research centre with focus on tectonics and performance-oriented design was driven by a number of key realisations:

1   Traditional Norwegian architecture displays a particular context-specific tectonic. Local differences in traditional Norwegian architectures had arisen over time from differences in local climate, materials, and skills.
2   While displaying a distinct tectonic contemporary Norwegian architecture and the underlying policies and regulations no longer react adequately to local differences, in spite of great differences in local climates across the country.
3   Norway stretches over a number of climate zones (in reference to the updated Köppen Geiger climate classification) and high local climate variation and can thus serve as a climate laboratory for research by design activities focusing on the relation between local climates and tectonics. Overall this can promote an alternative approach to questions of sustainability of the built environment that

extensively draws on the specificity of local conditions while at the same time employing non-standard design and fabrication to facilitate this endeavour.

4   Traditional local high-level craftsmanship is still present and can be brought into contact with the latest scientific knowledge about materials (in particular wood) and contemporary non-standard design and fabrication approaches to amount to a feasible and sustainable articulation of the built environment.

The goal of the new centre is therefore to pursue research projects based on the above relations. This is intended in a manner that will involve vertical and lateral research undertakings with the former being based in intense collaboration between Master-, PhD- and post-doc levels, and the latter taking advantage of the presence of four research centres at the Oslo School of Architecture and Design (AHO): the *Research Centre for Architecture and Tectonics* located at the Institute of Architecture, the *Centre for Urban Studies* located at the Institute of Urbanism and Landscape, *OCCAS – The Oslo Centre of Critical Architectural Studies* located at the Institute of Form, Theory and History, and the *Oslo Centre for Design Research* located at the Institute of Design.

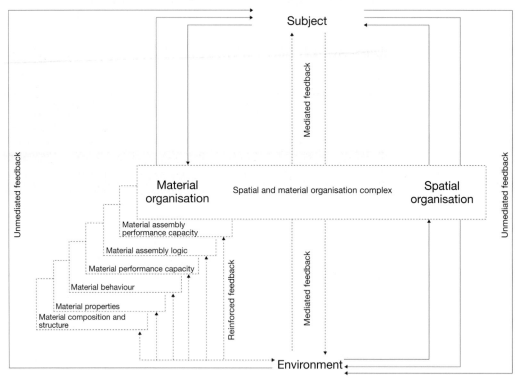

10.1
Performance-oriented architecture concerns the dynamic interrelation between four domains of 'active agency': the human subject, the environment and the spatial and material organisation complex. In order to derive an instrumental approach to the material constituent as 'active agent' material behaviour needs to be positively regarded and fully embedded in architectural design. When approaching this dynamic interrelation from a material perspective it is necessary to consider material properties and their potential range changes due to independent environmental variables in a different way and with main emphasis on deploying the resulting behaviour (i.e. dimensional variability). Material behaviour can in this way be instrumentalised as performative capacity. This entails reinforcing a nuanced feedback between material properties and independent variables and a fundamental repositioning towards the material constituents that make up the built environment. Illustration: Michael Hensel, 2010.

The Research Centre for Architecture and Tectonics focuses on research by design and in particular on full-scale construction and related analysis as a primary means of empirical knowledge production. This is done from a *performance-oriented architecture* perspective (Hensel 2011 and 2010). Physical experiments that examine material properties and resultant behaviour are frequently placed at the beginning of research by design efforts and focus on form-finding methods and self-shaping tendencies.

10.2
Restored hanging chain model of the Colònia Guell Church by Antoni Gaudí as displayed at the Sagrada Familia museum in Barcelona. For this project Gaudí invested years to develop a design method for form-finding that would have informed the design and structure of the building. The clear focus on an instrumental design method and modelling with regard to specific aspects of the building performance can be understood as a clear example of research by design. The free-hanging chains form under their self-weight optimum tension structures, so-called catenary curves that, when inverted result in freestanding optimum compression arches of constant thickness.

In this way the research by design efforts draw upon and advance methods developed by distinguished experts such as Antoni Gaudí, Frei Otto, Heinz Isler *et al*. This is done with the intention to introduce a material logic at the onset of the design process in order to ensure an integral logic of constructability, feasibility and sustainability. The findings of the material experiments are the basis for computational modelling and analysis, which serves to further elaborate the design as it gains in complexity. In most cases the design experiments culminate in full-scale constructions that can be further examined in order to empirically derive reliable data for the further development of the specific material system, working methods and approach to design.

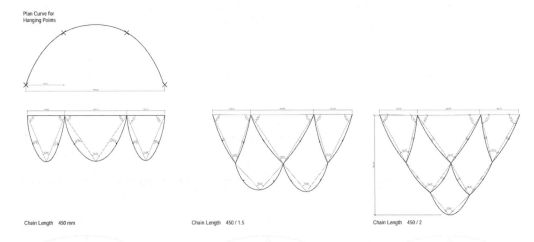

Plan Curve for
Hanging Points

Chain Length   450 mm   Chain Length   450 / 1.5   Chain Length   450 / 2

10.3

Nested Catenaries workshop directed by Defne Sunguroğlu Hensel in the context of the Auxiliary Architectures Studio 2010 at the Oslo School of Architecture and Design. This research focused on the structural use of brick and developing Gaudí's method further. The aim was to develop a system of interacting catenaries that are arrayed along a sinusoidal baseline, leading to a form-found inclined arrangement of catenary arches.

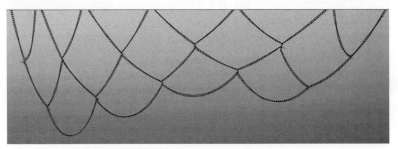

10.4 and 10.5

Nested Catenaries workshop directed by Defne Sunguroğlu Hensel in the context of the Auxiliary Architectures Studio 2010 at the Oslo School of Architecture and Design. Free-hanging chain model of the form-found final arrangement of interacting catenary arches to be constructed.

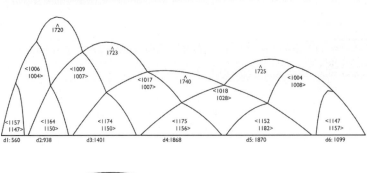

10.6
Nested Catenaries workshop directed by Defne Sunguroğlu Hensel in the context of the Auxiliary Architectures Studio 2010 at the Oslo School of Architecture and Design. Initial concurrent lines of inquiry: computational form-finding (top left), physical form-finding (top and bottom right), and test constructions (bottom left).

10.7
Nested Catenaries workshop directed by Defne Sunguroğlu Hensel in the context of the Auxiliary Architectures Studio 2010 at the Oslo School of Architecture and Design. Construction phase: test construction (top left), form-work preparation (bottom left), brick cutting (top right), and initial stages of final construction (bottom right).

Auxiliary architectures

We ought always to design with a number of nested, overlapped form-context boundaries in mind.

(Alexander 1964: 18)

Thus the object – be it a building, a compound site, or an entire urban matrix, insofar as such unities continue to exist at all as functional terms – would be defined now *not by how it appears, but rather by practices*: those it partakes of and those that take place within.

(Kwinter 2001: 14)

The *Auxiliary Architectures* studio course focuses on examining and developing the participation of architectures in many conditions and systems across spatial and time scales. It is principally a systems-oriented approach that aims for an alternative model of sustainability and distinguishes between:

1   First-degree *auxiliarity* which entails the overarching participation of entire archi-tectural schemes in various systems across scales (such as infrastructure, agriculture, etc.) and is of use for the design of new projects.
2   Second-degree *auxiliarity* which entails supplementary designs for entirely built-up contexts and is of particular interest for the intersection between architecture and industrial design.

10.8
Nested Catenaries workshop directed by Defne Sunguroğlu Hensel in the context of the Auxiliary Architectures Studio 2010 at the Oslo School of Architecture and Design. Final construction phase.

10.9 and 10.10
Nested Catenaries workshop directed by Defne Sunguroğlu Hensel in the context of the Auxiliary Architectures Studio 2010 at the Oslo School of Architecture and Design. Views of the completed construction.

Michael U. Hensel

In both cases the complex nature of the dynamic interactions that are central to the notion of interaction requires moreover a transdisciplinary approach and knowledge of first principles across a scope of disciplines to facilitate communication and collaboration between the members of a design team. This realisation is instructive with regard to the learning outcomes of a studio course that focuses on *auxiliarity* as a key concept in the context of performance-oriented architecture and design. In addition, the necessarily high level of context-specificity and interaction requires typically strong analytical skills, the ability to conduct focused research and to acquire and/or develop appropriate design methods. With regard to second-degree *auxiliarity* the ability to detect through suitable means relevant openings for intervention in a fully built-up context is of key importance. This involves more often than not the ability to proceed in a 'bottom-up' manner in a research by design process and typically challenges students to rethink inherited views and notions, as well as the problem-solving 'top-down' process that is typically taught.

Wood Studio

The *Wood Studio* shares principal concerns with *Auxiliary Architectures* studio, but focuses on material characteristics and behaviour as a starting point. Specific characteristics of wood that are commonly deemed negative are looked at from a fresh perspective that seeks new opportunities for innovation and design. These characteristics include: heterogeneous material make-up, cellular differentiation, anisotropy and hygroscopy. The culmination of such characteristics entails that wood displays variable behaviour and dimensional instability, two characteristics that lie at the core of the negative evaluation of timber as a material.

10.11
Shaping Wood industrial design diploma 2010 by Linn Tale Haugen at the Oslo School of Architecture and Design, supervised by Michael Hensel. Linn Tale Haugen researched the self-shaping capacity of laminated wood due to its hygroscopic behaviour and its utilisation of this form-finding method in design.
Left: Cover page of the dissertation based on research by design. Centre: The biological example of a seedpod of a Flamboyant tree that warps and twists due to moisture loss provided the initial idea for the research, as well as the realisation that wood laminates require an odd number of layers to be form-stabile. In turn wood laminates with an even number of layers can respond in a controlled self-shaping process for as long as reliable data on the behaviour can be extracted from experiments. Right: Experiments focusing on the controlled self-shaping of laminated beech veneer due to hygroscopic behaviour.

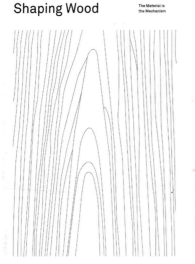

Shaping Wood

The Material is
the Mechanism

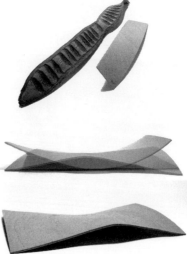

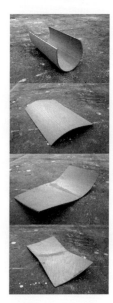

152

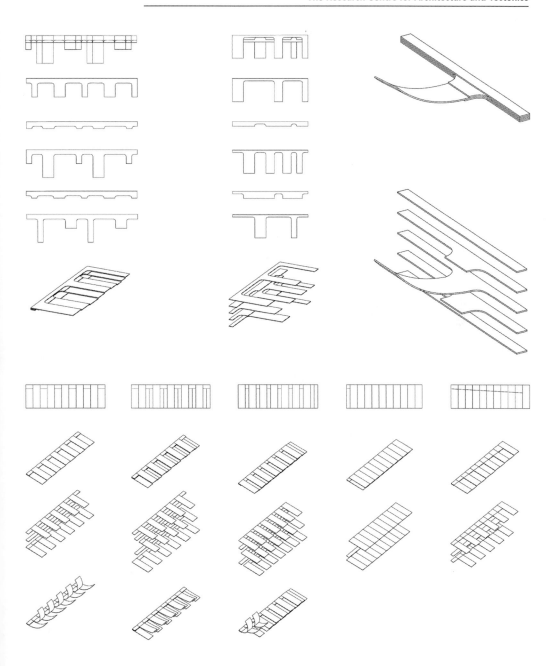

10.12
In the context of the *Auxiliary Architectures* studio 2010 Master students Daniela Puga and Eva Johansson developed Linn Tale Haugen's approach further. This involved the design of a design based on a building element of a laminate veneer strap with varying layers that permits dimensional variability due to hygroscopic behaviour wherever useful and prohibits it wherever structural capacity was of greater importance. This approach draws from the example of historical hay barns with timber shingles, where the warping of the shingle due to higher ambient humidity secured better ventilation of the interior of the barn.

The studio explores the utilisation of these characteristics in relation to specific environmental conditions that are extracted from a chosen context, and proceed 'bottom-up' with material experiments, leading towards material assemblies that instrumentalise variable behaviour and dimensional instability. The studio work is based on extensive material experiments and related computational modelling and analysis, material form-finding and modelling and the construction of full-scale prototypes.

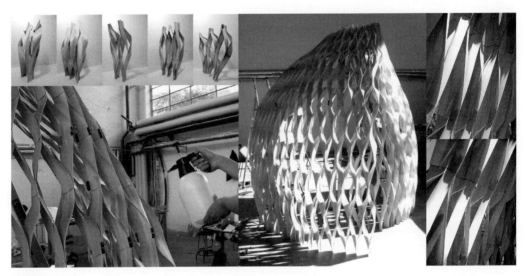

10.13
The *Wood Studio* 2010 focused on developing structures and spaces articulated by assemblies of thin wooden strips, a material element that is not usually associated with structural capacity. Self-shaping based on the hygroscopic behaviour of wood and traditional forming of wood were utilized for this purpose. Master students Wing Yi Hui and Lap Ming Wong constructed a small pavilion from 0.75mm thin pine veneer. The dome-shaped pavilion gains its structural capacity from both the global geometry of the assembly, as well as the multiple load-paths of the structural web.

In order to secure the necessary pre-conditions for a broad application of the positive approach to the internal differentiation of wood and its variable behaviour the work of the *Wood Studio* is set within a larger research effort by the Research Centre for Architecture and Tectonics that examines the entire supply chain of wood products for the built environment, including wood yards and, ultimately, the forestry industry. If a greater number of different kinds of wood are required this will need to first be grown. Given the time this takes it only makes sense to begin the necessary discussions and collaborations at an early stage. The Research Centre undertakes therefore to build up a wood expertise network involving numerous institutions in countries with similar climatic and environmental conditions as Norway. This is done in collaboration with the Norwegian Ministry of Agriculture (which includes forestry) and the information and communication company Trefokus, which covers the entire Norwegian forest-wood chain.

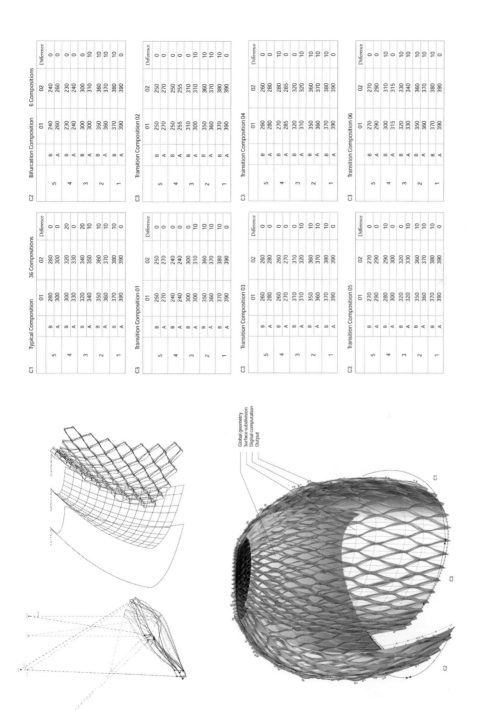

C1	Typical Composition		36 Compositions		
			01	02	Difference
5	B		280	280	0
	A		300	300	0
4	B		300	320	20
	A		330	330	0
3	B		320	340	20
	A		340	350	10
2	B		350	360	10
	A		360	370	10
1	B		370	380	10
	A		390	390	0

C2	Bifurcation Composition		6 Compositions		
			01	02	Difference
5	B		240	240	0
	A		260	260	0
4	B		230	230	0
	A		240	240	0
3	B		300	300	0
	A		300	310	10
2	B		350	360	10
	A		360	370	10
1	B		370	380	10
	A		390	390	0

C3	Transition Composition 01				
			01	02	Difference
5	B		250	250	0
	A		270	270	0
4	B		240	240	0
	A		240	240	0
3	B		300	300	0
	A		300	310	10
2	B		350	360	10
	A		360	370	10
1	B		370	380	10
	A		390	390	0

C3	Transition Composition 02				
			01	02	Difference
5	B		250	250	0
	A		270	270	0
4	B		250	250	0
	A		255	255	0
3	B		310	310	0
	A		300	310	10
2	B		350	360	10
	A		360	370	10
1	B		370	380	10
	A		390	390	0

C3	Transition Composition 03				
			01	02	Difference
5	B		260	260	0
	A		280	280	0
4	B		260	260	0
	A		270	270	0
3	B		310	310	0
	A		310	320	10
2	B		350	360	10
	A		360	370	10
1	B		370	380	10
	A		390	390	0

C3	Transition Composition 04				
			01	02	Difference
5	B		260	260	0
	A		280	280	0
4	B		270	280	10
	A		285	285	0
3	B		320	320	0
	A		310	320	10
2	B		350	360	10
	A		360	370	10
1	B		370	380	10
	A		390	390	0

C3	Transition Composition 05				
			01	02	Difference
5	B		270	270	0
	A		290	290	0
4	B		280	290	10
	A		300	300	0
3	B		320	320	0
	A		320	330	10
2	B		350	360	10
	A		360	370	10
1	B		370	380	10
	A		390	390	0

C3	Transition Composition 06				
			01	02	Difference
5	B		270	270	0
	A		290	290	0
4	B		300	310	10
	A		315	315	0
3	B		320	330	10
	A		330	340	10
2	B		350	360	10
	A		360	370	10
1	B		370	380	10
	A		390	390	0

10.14

Typically for the *Wood Studio*, Master students Wing Yi Hui and Lap Ming Wong progressed 'bottom-up' from physical experiments with single wood elements to increasingly complex assemblies. This informed an associative computational model that facilitated the design process, computational analysis and the production of the fabrication and construction instructions.

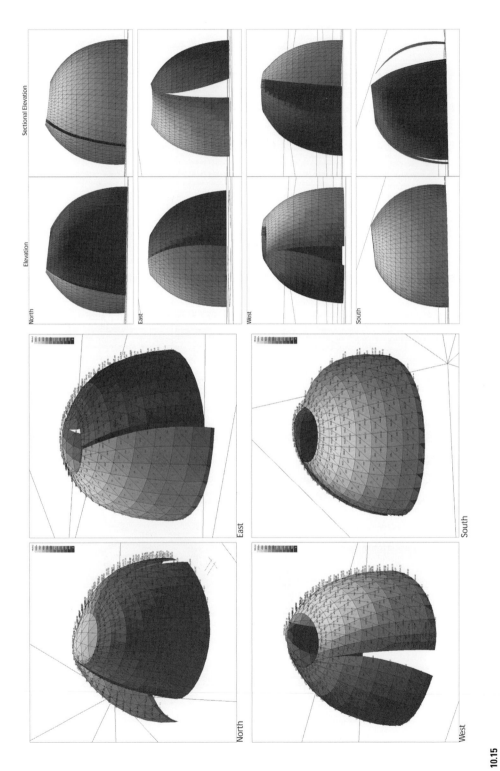

10.15
Environmental performance analysis informed the design experiments of Master students Wing Yi Hui and Lap Ming Wong as a key input for the articulation of the final design scheme.

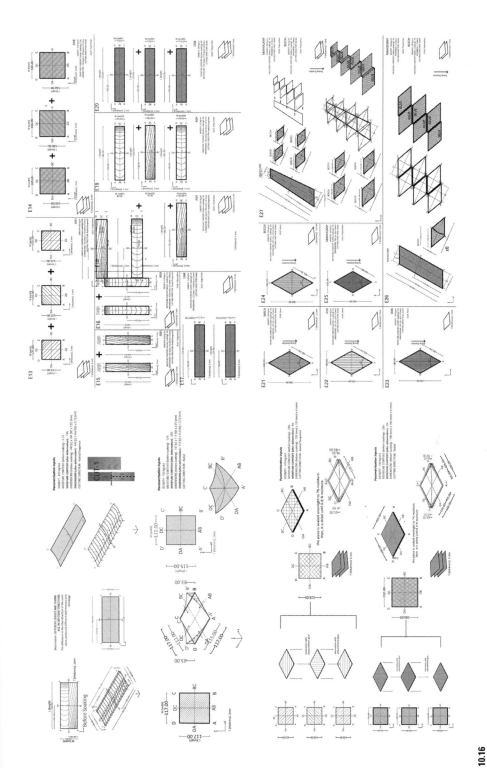

10.16

In the context of the *Wood Studio* 2011 Master students Rallou Tzormpatzaki and Juan Ignacio Hodali aimed to combine the approaches of responsive wood elements (Linn Tale Haugen, Daniela Puga, Eva Johansson) with the thin veneer structural web (Wing Yi Hui and Lap Ming Wong). In order to accomplish this within the given time a large number of experiments needed to be conducted and analysed in a systematic manner. This involved the careful registration of single experiments, as well as an overview over groups of experiments.

10.17
Partial full-scale prototype
made Master students Rallou
Tzormpatzaki and Juan Ignacio
Hodali in the context of the
Wood Studio 2011.

Biological systems analysis

> The relationship between biology and building is now in need of clarifi-
> cation due to real and practical exigencies. The problem of environment
> has never before been such a threat to existence. In effect, it is a bio-
> logical problem.
>
> (Otto 1971: 7)

> To call something a wing, a feather, a tissue, a cell, an organelle, a gene
> is to describe it, at least implicitly, in terms of its function, i.e. the
> purpose it serves in the behavioural economy of some larger system.
>
> (Brandon and Rosenberg 2000: 148–149)

The *Biological Systems Analysis* course focuses on examining the intricate relation between organisms and their specific environment and their related morphological expression and physiological processes. The aim is to introduce students to a far more complex set of interrelations than is typically done in the education of architects and designers. There are two key questions involved:

1   What can be learned from living systems? (This is a well-established field of inquiry associated with Bionics, Biomimetics and so-called bio-inspired design.)

2   What can be learned from Biology as a specific scientific discipline? (This is surprisingly not a very common question, in spite of the current interest in living systems.)

The long-term goal of the course is to inform and develop the concept of *auxiliarity* pursued in the *Auxiliary Architectures* studio towards a more inclusive and complex ecological model. This shows that the concurrent development of areas of inquiry can be pursued in such a manner as to enrich one another whenever relevant realisations and findings make it possible.

Outlook

The Research Centre for Architecture and Tectonic is just now in its initial phase and while several clearly defined research efforts begin to characterise the work a number of exciting other projects are on the drawing-board. These include, for instance, the *Small Building Project* initiated by Professor Marius Nygaard as a collaborative effort between numerous educational and research institutions and industrial partners. This effort takes advantage of a clause in the Norwegian building regulations, which allow the construction of buildings up to 15 square metres for non-permanent use without planning permission. The intention is to design and construct these small projects in different climate zones and local climates in order to study their environmental performance. Again a deep-systems approach underlies this effort, only this time it is focused on the necessary scope of education in such research efforts. In this case professional schools for craftsmanship are involved in the design and construction process so as to concurrently educate all those whose expertise needs to be coordinated in order to secure the possibility of turning the research findings into everyday architecture. This is done again by means of foregrounding full-scale construction as a primary means to gain reliable data on building performance, as well as the associated production of knowledge and skills. And this is after all a core intention of the Research Centre for Architecture and Tectonics.

Bibliography

Alexander, C. (1964) *Notes on the Synthesis of Form*. Cambridge, MA: Harvard University Press.

Brandon, R. and Rosenberg, A. (2000) *Philosophy of Biology. Philosophy of Science Today*. Oxford: Oxford University Press, 147–180.

Hensel, M. (2010) 'Performance-oriented Architecture – Towards a Biological Paradigm for Architectural Design and the Built Environment', *FORMAkademisk* 3 (1): 36–56. Online: www.formakademisk.org/index.php/formakademisk/issue/view/6/showToc (accessed 8 Sepember 2011).

Hensel, M. (2011) 'Performance-oriented Architecture and the Spatial and Material Organisation Complex – Rethinking the Definition, Role and Performative Capacity of the Spatial and Material Boundaries of the Built Environment', *FORMAkademisk* 4 (1): 3–23. Online: www.formakademisk.org/index.php/formakademisk/issue/view/8/showToc (accessed 8 September 2011).

Kwinter, S. (2001) *Architectures of Time*. Cambridge, MA: MIT Press.

Otto, F. (1971) *IL3 Biology and Building Part 1*. Stuttgart: University of Stuttgart.

Chapter 11

How can biology inform architects?

Julian Vincent

Biological extinction has been associated with events of geological magnitude. Events have been both exogenous (the meteor, for instance, which created the Chicxulub crater in Mexico, associated with the Cretaceous-Tertiary (K-T) discontinuity (Schulte *et al.* 2010) and the extinction of 95 per cent of all life on Earth including the dinosaurs) and endogenous (the eruption of the Deccan Trap, an outflowing of lava which probably exacerbated the K-T events)). In more recent times, variability of climate is associated with significant disruptions in European populations (Buentgen *et al.* 2011). Emerging successfully from these and other changes, biological life forms have shown great talent for survival. The nests and burrows which animals make provide shelter from changing external conditions (Hansell 2005). These structures are adaptive responses to local conditions and increase the survival of the organism. In some respects the same is true of the botanical survivors, in that although plants do not commonly build protective structures (except for their gametes) they can adapt their shape to local conditions and so are more durable (Mattheck 1998). One can therefore look at animal or plant structures with a trained eye and appreciate the problems of survival that have been overcome with the added realisation that in most cases the solution to those problems is integrated with the survival of the ecosystem rather than just the individual. But there is a difficulty: given a problem, it is not too difficult to arrive at a workable answer. However, given the answer (e.g. an organism) it is much more difficult to decide what the problem was! Biologists are used to this difficulty, but on the whole designers and engineers are not. Designers and engineers therefore need access to biological skills of translation.

Misapprehensions

The interplay between biology and design – especially architecture – has a long history. Most of the design has been decorative and has been called biomorphic or zoomorphic (Aldersey-Williams 2003). Such shapes can be immensely appealing but rarely give functional advantage. Biomorphism can also give rise to misleading stories. For instance, the story about the leaves of the lily *Victoria amazonica* inspiring Paxton in his design of the corrugated roof of the Crystal Palace is wrong. The roof was invented by horticultural journalist and revolutionary John Claudius Loudon sometime in the first decade of the nineteenth century (Colquhoun 2004). The 'ridge and furrow' glass construction maximised light and heat, particularly in the early morning and late evening, when the sun is low in the sky. It seems quite probable that Paxton used the leaf of *V. amazonica* (which he grew in his greenhouse in 1849) to suggest the design of the end walls of the great central arch on top of the building (Figure 11.1), but this is an architectural element and doesn't appear on Paxton's famous sketch of the original design made on a piece of blotting paper! Thus the Crystal Palace had biomorphic elements, but was certainly not biomimetic.

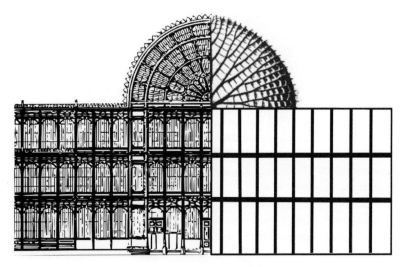

11.1
End view of Paxton's Crystal Palace (1851) showing the supposed origin of the semicircle motif based on the leaf of *Victoria amazonica* (shown on the right).

Similar stories have grown up about the Eiffel Tower. It owes nothing to biology. The original design came from Maurice Koechlin and Emile Nougire, two junior engineers who performed the preliminary calculations. The curvature of the uprights was calculated for least wind resistance (Anon 2010). Stories that the design had anything to do with the arrangement of the trabeculae (small bony supports) in the head of the human femur are laughable. Interestingly the Eiffel Tower is hierarchical (Lakes 1993), though the reason for adopting this form of design is obscure. But the parts for the tower were constructed in off-site workshops in lengths of 5m, which suggests problems transporting the components on site. Certainly hierarchical structures are expensive to make because of labour, but in coming days of reduced availability of material and increasing expense, they may become more common since they can be at least ten times more efficient in their use of materials (Lakes 1993).

Biological origins

This chapter concerns the implementation of functional design concepts derived from the study of biology. The desired outcome is living spaces that will be more 'sustainable', or will have the least net impact on the surroundings and allow us to continue living in a world which we now know is finite and which we can very easily destroy – at least in terms of our own survival.

Since biological phenomena occur as part of a system in a context, any biomimetic implementation must take account of the way in which it interacts with related factors in a system. In the biological paradigm, when a species of plant or animal is introduced into a new environment it both changes itself and changes its surroundings. This is studied in the ecology of invasive species, which often tend to be destructive since they have no natural enemies in their new habitat, and so can exploit resources unchallenged. Ideally, biological systems are in continual flux, keeping some sort of equilibrium with the environment. Nests are built up and torn down or abandoned, in response to local conditions. The ways in which that response might be mediated may be important. How does the organism come to the judgement that change is necessary? What is the behavioural trigger? Those studying animal behaviour have discovered some fairly simple rules by which animals respond to events and conditions around them, whose implementation leads to subtle and far-reaching conclusions.

1   Beavers flood areas of land and make their lodges in the centre of the lake. They are second only to humans in the impact they have on geomorphology (Butler 1995). The immediate effects for the beaver are protected living space and stimulated growth of young plants in the newly boggy areas. The environmental effects are deposition of sediment in the pond leading ultimately to the formation of rich meadowland, and the purification of water downstream as a result of the reduced sediment. Beavers are good. And their main behavioural cue is the sound of running water. Within limits, the louder it is the more they try to silence it by building or patching up their dam. They make the pond using the least and best directed effort.

2   Compass termites build a nest that presents a large profile to the rising and setting sun, but a narrow profile to the heat of the daytime sun. This shape and orientation can be obtained by the simple rule of placing material where the nest is warmest. Thus it grows fastest (and therefore thinnest) towards higher temperatures.

3   Pigeon nests from the area around Bath, UK, were tested individually in a wind tunnel, placing a thermometer and a heating element inside each and measuring the voltage required to keep the temperature in the nest at 40°C as the nest was rotated about its vertical axis. The least voltage, and therefore the most insulation, was registered when the wind in the tunnel was aimed at what had been the southwest quadrant of the nest (Figure 11.2). Since the prevailing wind around Bath is from the southwest it is clear that the nest was insulated maximally against this prevailing wind. One can imagine the bird sat on the nest feeling chilly down one side and repacking the nest material until it was comfortable again.

In all these three examples the structure is attuned to its environment as a direct result of simple behavioural feedback mechanisms.

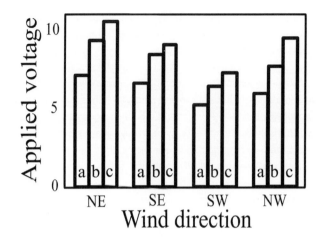

11.2
Heat loss from a pigeon's nest is the least from the SW direction. Tested wind speeds were (a) 3, (b) 5 and (c) 7 m/s. Applied voltage was used to keep internal temperature of the nest at 40°C.

In a somewhat different way of gauging the performance of a construction, a mole cricket makes a horn-like tunnel (Figure 11.3) in which it sits to sing its mating call (Bailey *et al.* 2001). The tunnel has to be tuned to the size of the cricket and the frequency of its sound. The cricket makes a rough tunnel, slightly too small, then sings within it repeatedly enlarging the tunnel until the impedance is correct. This is analogous to picking up the resonant frequency of a long stick that you hold in your hand and shake. The feedback mechanism is innate.

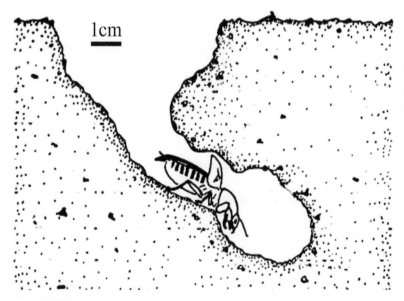

11.3
Section of a mole cricket's singing burrow. The cone-shaped opening sits like the horn on a loudspeaker, matching the impedance of the cricket's sound-producing organ to the outside air. After Bennett-Clark (1987).

These animal structures display other advantages: they tend to be made of locally sourced materials (the caddis larva is, and has, a case in point). Bodily secretions can be an important component. A continual cycle of re-formation tends to ensure best use of materials in dynamic and adaptive structures.

Plant structures cannot be modified so quickly or completely, although they have some interesting and relatively simple mechanisms. They are therefore better models for the relatively static structures, which architects design. Trees (and probably all plants) equalise stresses and avoid areas where fracture might occur (Mattheck 2004). If the plant detects localised high stresses, it tends to deposit more material in those places, thus reducing the stress. This is directly opposite to our designs where high stress can lead to accelerated rates of corrosion or erosion, giving a positive feedback that leads to disaster.

Analysis using TRIZ

In continuing efforts to introduce some rational analysis into biomimetics, rather than have it as an assemblage of case histories, I have been using the Russian system of solving problems inventively, known by its Russian acronym, TRIZ. This system was invented and developed by Genrich Altshuller, who based it largely on the Hegelian philosophy that Russians are taught at school. TRIZ is a collection of techniques that encourage objective and careful analysis of a problem, coding examples from the widest possible range of sources. It is ideally suited to problems that cannot easily be separated from their environment – systems problems – and so is peculiarly suited to biology and architecture. One of the techniques in TRIZ is an algorithm for selecting a transformative process that will solve the current problem. The list of transformations is supposedly exhaustive, derived from a very large number of the best patents, and grouped as the 40 Inventive Principles. This list is, therefore, also a compendium of best practice from within technology. Since it deals specifically with systems, TRIZ can subsume biology and thus can produce an abstraction of the mechanisms that drive life on this planet. These mechanisms are obviously sustainable within the constraints of planet Earth, so biomimetics in this form can provide a paradigm for the survival of a technical culture. Since natural selection has provided the quality control, this abstraction of biology is also a compendium of best practice. A comparison of biology and technology at this level should therefore provide formulations for truly sustainable technologies. Such a comparison should require a large amount of information, but a short cut is possible. The manipulations required to solve a problem can broadly be divided among six operational fields: substance, structure, energy, space, time, and information (Vincent et al. 2006). A sample of solutions to problems (about 2500 from biology, and 5000 from technology) along these lines, taken from sizes ranging from molecular through to a community of organisms (Figure 11.4), shows that, whereas technology solves 70 per cent of problems in the general area of materials processing (taken to be in the micrometre size range) using energy as a control parameter, in biology energy is the least significant control parameter over the entire size range.

Biology, meanwhile, uses information (derived at the molecular level from DNA) and structure as its main control. In the size range of buildings (roughly, 10 to 100m), technology is less dependent on energy to solve its problems, but certainly requires space. Biology by contrast needs even more information but more time and space to come to an agreeable solution. Although most engineers would

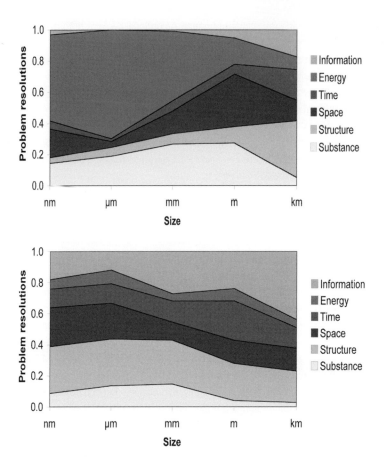

11.4
Diagrams showing the
proportion of problems solved
by using operational fields
listed, and how they vary with
the size of the object involved.
Problems in technology (top)
compared with biology
(bottom). From Vincent *et al.*
(2006).

not readily admit it, biomimetics presented in this fashion, far from being a miscellaneous collection of techniques and ideas for incorporation into the current engineering paradigm, is the first challenge to the way in which engineering is carried out. In many respects it finds engineering wanting, not least in its extreme reliance upon energy. This was already known in a vague sort of way, but the TRIZ-based analysis puts numbers to the differences.

Rules for biomimetic design

We can dissect biology's solutions to design in more detail. TRIZ classifies design problems into a matrix of about 1500 different examples and allocates up to four Inventive Principles to each design problem, yielding a large and complex database of solutions. The information was culled from a large number of good-quality patents. This is a process of description that can be applied to biological examples, so that life forms are treated as a sort of patent database. Recent research shows there are eight Inventive Principles used by biology to solve specific design problems, giving us design cues for a biomimetic technology. They are arranged here into the operational fields for convenience. Notice that these design suggestions say nothing about the means by which they can be delivered. That has to be the subject of another database and is related to the context of the final working design rather than its biological origins.

Structure

Fragmentation: Divide an object into independent parts, make it able to be dismantled or increase the degree of fragmentation or segmentation.

Local quality: Change an object's structure, environment, or external influence/impact from uniform to non-uniform; allow each part of an object function in conditions most suitable for its operation; allow each part of an object to fulfil a different and/or complementary useful function.

Mediator: Use an intermediary carrier article or intermediary process; merge objects temporarily.

Consolidation: Merge identical or similar objects or operations in space; make them contiguous or work in parallel.

Hierarchy: Place one or more object inside another; make a large object from smaller objects.

Information

Feedback: Introduce feedback to improve the process of action; change its magnitude, sign (+ or -) or influence in accordance with operating conditions.

Energy

Prior counteraction: When it is necessary to perform an action with both harmful and useful effects, this should be replaced with anti-actions to control harmful effects; pre-stress in opposition to known undesirable working stresses.

Space

Another dimension: Move into an additional dimension – from 1D to 2D, from 2D to 3D, etc.; increase the number of layers; incline an object, lay it on its side; use the other side of the object; use light falling onto the neighbouring square or onto the other side of the given square.

Asymmetry: Change the shape or properties of an object from symmetrical to asymmetrical, or to suit external asymmetries (e.g. ergonomic features), or increase degrees of asymmetry.

Implementation of biomimetic design

First, it is notable that biology and technology use pretty much the same design parameters based on time and substance. I have no explanation for this.

The rules above provide an objective set of guidelines that have been derived from biology. Will they work? In order to test such a system of guidelines we need to have a proper definition of success. This is probably easier than it appears, since the model, whose success is admitted, is biology. Therefore success can be defined as lack of environmental degradation, preferably improvement, although environmental diversification will always follow, which may not always be recognised as advantageous in the short term. The beaver is a case in point. The animal introduces controversial environmental change, but in the long term the outcome is positive – increased fertility (leading to increased diversity) and pure water.

Examining the use of these and the other 32 Inventive Principles of TRIZ in architecture, and deciding which architectural designs were biomimetically success-ful, would not be a trivial task but would yield an objective analysis. It would provide a sound basis for properly biomimetic/sustainable architecture. At the end of the exercise I would hope that the same eight Principles emerged as the most important!

Some successful structures use these principles, notably the Sagrada Familia, which exemplifies asymmetry of the columns in the nave, taking account of the local loading effects in the way they are designed around the fragmented projected lines of force from the roof. The Eiffel Tower is an example of hierarchy, being made of struts made of struts made of struts (Lakes 1993). Earthquake-proof buildings in Japan and China are fragmented and hierarchical, this time allowing the slight movements which can occur between so many layers to take up the major movement of the foundations. Feedback is another obvious factor in the stability and maintenance of a building (e.g. by moving large weights within the building, thus changing the loading lines), so is pre-stress which, combined, can provide another, more active, defence against earthquakes. Fragmentation is found in industrially designed buildings that can be provided as a kit of parts assembled on site. Some, such as Renzo Piano's IBM building, make use of this to be portable as well.

Salmaan Craig (Craig et al. 2008) is one of the few people to use our TRIZ system to suggest novel design. In this instance he used an earlier system which we called BioTRIZ (Vincent et al. 2006), a reduced version of Altshuller's Contradiction Matrix, populated with the normal 40 Inventive Principles but organised according to solutions derived from biology. The problem Craig addressed was that buildings in hot areas accumulate heat during the day. In order to reduce heat gain they are insulated, but this stops the building losing heat to the night sky, which is nominally at $-273°C$. The conventional answer would be to put in an air conditioner. But that is expensive and uses a lot of energy and requires maintenance. Biomimetic design argues against the manipulation of energy to solve a problem, suggesting information and structure as a route to solution. It turned out to be possible to make insulation that would keep heat out during the day, but provide a route for radiation during the night. This was achieved by structuring the insulation to provide an exit pathway for long-wave radia-tion from a concrete heat store (Figure 11.5).

This arrangement could reduce the temperature of a standard roof in Riyadh, Saudi Arabia, by as much as $13°C$ below ambient, averaging $4.5°C$ through-out the day. It is important to realise that this biomimetic solution has no natural prototype, so you would not be able to find it, or anything like it, in a catalogue of biological mechanisms and functions. This is a great strength of the TRIZ approach. It allows the use of biomimetic methods without being limited by the possibilities of biology. The basic reason that this is possible is that TRIZ isolates function from associated structures. Therefore the design concepts are considered in the absence of context, which makes them infinitely adaptable. This emphasis on pure function is a crucial strength.

If it is to be of any use, biomimetics must be able to aid in the design of a complete system – after all, that's the nature of biology. Other factors that have to

11.5
Roof section showing Craig's insulation (second generation). The concrete is a thermal store, radiating heat (LW radiation) through the parabolic holes, which have a larger entry hole than exit, so that the solar radiation is less likely to pass through.

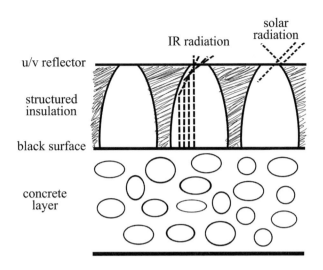

be taken into consideration are structural materials, energy, and water supply and waste control.

Biological materials are made from very few basic components yet can perform as well as man-made materials (Vincent 2008). The secret seems to be a combination of structure (at all size levels from millimetre up) and local quality. Material is placed only where it is needed and different materials (e.g. ceramics) are used sparingly as needed. Thus stress concentrations are avoided in relatively light-weight structures and costs of construction and maintenance are both reduced.

Energy is a difficult problem, if we confine ourselves to current tech-nologies. Biology stores energy inertly as starch or glycogen, polysaccharides which are essentially unreactive but chemically responsive. The major technical store of energy is electricity, which is basically ephemeral. Perhaps it would be better to store energy in a relatively inert object. Movement (air or water) is immediately obvi-ous, very traditional and capable of manipulation. A biological approach might be to encourage rainfall by planting trees at high points. This would also address problems of water supply.

Waste is a state of mind. Biology does not recognise the problem since it is based on a common chemistry that has relatively few basic reactions, which can all be performed at ambient temperatures. This makes recycling relatively easy through the medium of compost. Such an integrated system may be difficult to design, but there is nothing stopping us using natural systems, so long as we use them appropriately.

Much of the sustainability argument, as with climate change and other environmental problems, is not so much an exercise in technological progress – on the whole we have all the tricks we need – but in hearts and minds. It may be that anthropology and architecture will provide the best solutions.

Most architects want both to leave some heritage and to improve the lives of people around them in some way. With current climate problems the first problem to be attacked is 'How can architects be sure that there will be a heritage, and people around to enjoy and marvel at it?' If this is too apocalyptic, remember that 'hoping for the best' must always be married with 'preparing for the worst' and that progress is measured by performance, not hope. Taking these warnings and implied solution, if we wish to avoid extinction – from whatever cause – we should trust our nature and modify our technology.

Bibliography

Aldersey-Williams, H. (2003) *Zoomorphic: New Animal Architecture*, London: Lawrence King Publishing.

Anon (2010) *Origins and Construction of the Eiffel Tower*. Online http://www.tour-eiffel.com/everything-about-the-tower/themed-files/69 (accessed 8 September 2011).

Bailey, W. J., Bennet-Clark, H. C. and Fletcher, N. H. (2001) 'Acoustic of a small Australian Burrow Cricket: The Control of Low-frequency Pure-tone Songs', *Journal of Experimental Biology* 204: 2827–2841.

Bennet-Clark, H. C. (1987) 'The Tuned Singing Burrow of Mole Crickets', *Journal of Experimental Biology* 128: 383–409.

Buentgen, U., Tegel, W., Nicolussi, K., McCormick, M., Frank, D., Troet, V., Kaplan, J. O., Herzig, F., Heusser, K. U., Wanner, H., Luterbacher, J. and Esper, J. (2011) '2500 Years of European Climate Variablity and Human Susceptability', *Science* 331: 578–582.

Butler, D. R. (1995) *Zoogeomorphology: Animals as Geomorphic Agents*, Cambridge: Cambridge University Press.

Colquhoun, K. (2004) *A Thing in Disguise – The Visionary Life of Joseph Paxton*, London: Harper Perennial.

Craig, S., Harrison, D., Cripps, A. and Knott, D. (2008) 'BioTRIZ Suggests Radiative Cooling of Buildings can be done Passively by Changing the Structure of Roof Insulation to let Long-wave Infrared Pass', *Journal of Bionic Engineering* 5: 55–66.

Hansell, M. H. (2005) *Animal Architecture*, Oxford: Oxford University Press.

Lakes, R. S. (1993) 'Materials with Structural Hierarchy', *Nature* 361: 511–515.

Mattheck, C. (1998) *Design in Nature – Learning from Trees*, Heidelberg: Springer.

Mattheck, C. (2004) *The Face of Failure in Nature and Engineering*, Karlsruhe: ForschungsZentrum.

Schulte, P., Alegret, L. *et al.* (2010) 'The Chicxulub Asteroid Impact and Mass Extinction at the Cretaceous–Paleogene Boundary', *Science* 327: 1214–1218.

Vincent, J. F. V. (2008) 'Biomimetic Materials', *Journal of Materials Research* 23: 3140–3147.

Vincent, J. F. V., Bogatyreva, O. A., Bogatyreva, N. R., Bowyer, A. and Pahl, A.-K. (2006) 'Biomimetics – Its Practice and Theory', *Journal of the Royal Society Interface* 3: 471–482.

Chapter 12

Relational practice

Siv Stangeland and Reinhard Kropf

This chapter describes specific working methods for experimentation, which are tested, appropriated and adjusted, as illustrated in three projects: the Norway Pavilion at Shanghai Expo 2010, the Pulpit Rock Mountain Lodge and the Ratatosk Pavilion in London. These projects do not claim to represent a consistent theory of architectural form or processes, but share a common emphasis on the operation of making and fabricating by implementing theory into the materialization of complex tasks. The overall intention is to avoid a purely 'creationistic design' where a composition or form is imposed in one stroke over an inert matter and environment and the main agenda of the further design process is to defend and re-establish this form. A relational design practice, on the contrary, urges the creation of a mutual encounter with local conditions such as matter/energy properties, specific human resources and the environment. It constantly invents processes and experiments, which can help to trigger awareness of local, singular, specific, original space-generating possibilities. This does not mean that these projects merely emerge from bottom-up processes. Rather they gather different levels and constellations to achieve a more integrated relationship with their surroundings.

Levels of integration

At this point, it might be helpful to introduce the cybernetic model for natural systems by Francois Jacob (Jacob 1974). Consisting of 'integration levels', which are interlocked, the model describes how different elements joined together form one level on top of the next, from molecular activities, to the organization of cells, to tissues and organs, to breeds. Each integration level has its own characteristics and laws and therefore requires different means of observation and investigation. Communication systems must be explored, both between the different integration levels on the one hand and between the integration levels and their environment on the other. Connecting neighbouring integration levels to each other increases the system's complexity and thus its possible ways of interacting with its environment. In evolutionary theory this is seen as a success, because both perception and reaction skills improve.

This nested interactive model plays an important role in the design processes of the three projects described in this chapter. The common intention is to create the right conditions that promote possible interactions, between one another as well as with the environment, that might influence, advance or even constitute the design process. The design of the first integration level relates to contextual and pragmatic preconditions; it forms a spatial, structural and programmatic assemblage. It is designed on an intermediate scale, not as a large superordinate shape and not as an aggregate of small material units. This way, the structure is affected by top-down as well as bottom-up developments. It consists of several more or less similar parts, whose combination is relational and not figurative. Parts and internal relation are chosen in favour of process, to handle multiple changes and keep at the same time the overall robustness. In the described projects the 'trees' in the Norwegian Expo Pavilion, the ash trees in the V&A Pavilion and the timber ribs in the Pulpit Rock Mountain Lodge form the first integration level. The number, shape and internal relation of the trees, ashes and ribs were not fixed from the beginning and changed throughout the design process through top-down or bottom-up influences.

Then, further interlinked integration and design levels are developed, all of which together function as an elastic and geometric test field. Each individual level repeatedly gives feedback to the upper and lower design levels while at the same time extracting the information relevant to itself. The implicit material conditions such as development processes, internal cohesion, stress tests, etc. are different for each integration level. An important question is the degree to which the integration levels capture the entire project or whether there are additional elements. The 'trees' of the Expo were supposed to represent the entire Pavilion. However, it was not possible to integrate the business centre, a programmatic requirement, and the façade. As additional elements they became the weak point of the design. To compensate for this omission more top-down design and time-consuming compromises had to be implemented. In addition to the internal processes, each integration level stands in a different relation to its environment. The most important design tasks lie in formulating the right questions at each level and using empirical investigations to illuminate the space-generating potential of the environment. This structuring of specific relations for each level and the synergistic interacting of human behaviour, material and energetic capacities and environmental factors often resembles a long-winded odyssey. But it is precisely this repeated testing of the integration levels and the effort to tease out the multi-layered spatial possibilities of the environment, using digital and analogue models, that result in an intensity that can dramatically push the design forward.

Sequence of events

These experiments do not necessarily take place within a clearly demarcated temporality; they are rather multi-temporal and reveal a time, which is gathered together. In each project and on each level of integration, it is possible to rearrange or bypass the various developmental steps and invent new sequences of events. What is important here is to break away from a conventional design chronology such as sketch, preliminary draft, work planning and execution. This non-chronological temporal composition of developing processes can lead to new and unexpected spaces such as in the 'Ratatosk' Pavilion. Here the initial finding, scanning and digital modelling of the ashes led to information that is usually part of the detailed planning phase. As a result of this sequence of actions, we overthrew the design concepts of the sketch phase. Similarly, the after-use of the Expo Pavilion shaped the premise for the preliminary draft.

12.1
Ratatosk Pavilion: Sequence of material transformation.

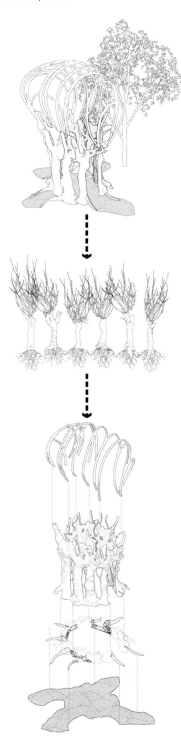

Synthesizing

Requirements and circumstances concerning the use, construction, building technology, material properties, etc. are identified and tested to show whether they can
be combined with each other and interlinked. This does not only imply multiple use
and function, and thereby reduced resources, it also allows a richer experience of
space. Spatial and programmatic hybrids are intense and evocative atmospheres
that appeal to all senses. In the Expo Pavilion, outer skin (membrane roof), construction, exhibition and infrastructure were combined into one 'tree' to create a simple
and at the same time complex multiple structure. This presupposes a synergistic
anticipation of different areas of knowledge that goes beyond mere interdisciplinary.
Rather, it requires the preparation of a fertile conceptual ground within the project
that allows for the active participation of different disciplines. The challenge here is
the 'translation effort', where the relevant information from the environment has to
be transferred step by step, to bring about specific changes to the space. When we
dealt with the trees in the *Ratatosk* Pavilion we roamed through Norse mythology,
dendrology, digital technology, behavioural research, etc., and we always tried to
connect the discoveries of our excursions with the trees.

Timber as a heterogeneous material

The choice of timber as the main structural material in nearly all of our projects is not
only based on its ecological advantages, but also on its specific qualities and
properties as an organic material. As Manuel De Landa states, timber as a heterogeneous material (unlike steel or concrete) has variable properties and
idiosyncrasies. The designer has to acknowledge and respect those pre-conditions
and make use of them as an integral part of his design process, which, it follows,
cannot be routinized (De Landa 2001). The design process of the following three
projects has been strongly influenced by the question of how to utilize the intrinsic
properties of the material timber within each specific case. In all projects the timber
elements maintain their anisotropic quality. The direction of the fibres within the
wood determined the processing and the assembly. In the *Ratatosk* Pavilion we
went even further: digital technology was applied to scan and analyse each tree's
characteristic anatomy and for the further form-finding process that led to complex,
heterogeneous shapes. Despite the use of high-tech tools, this is hardly a new
approach: the famous Wasa Museum in Stockholm exhibits an original drawing from
the sixteenth century that depicts how highly skilled boat builders used to look for
parts of trees that matched the shapes of elements they needed to construct boats.

The *Ratatosk* pavilion

We began our work on this project by recalling how we used to play in our favourite
trees in the forest. There was no differentiation between spaces created through
play and play in itself. This raised the question of how we can recapture this embedded interwoven reality of play, reflection and experimentation. In his book *The Five
Senses*, Michael Serres promotes a new topology of human perception, combined
with empiricism and scientific research. Instead of returning to an agricultural era he
claims that a new philosophy is needed, which includes bodily experience, art and
science. To achieve this, research and experimentation must be broadened. They

12.2
Ratatosk Pavilion: Sequence of
material transformation.

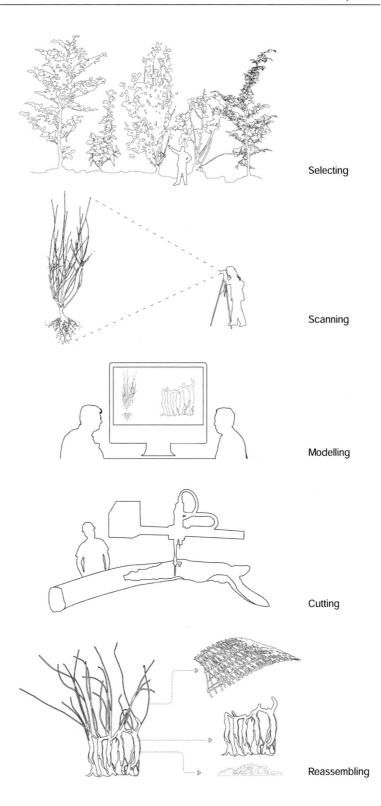

Selecting

Scanning

Modelling

Cutting

Reassembling

have to be applied in a synergetic, not reductionist and specialized way. This led us to the design of a heterogeneous sequence of empirical steps: searching and select- ing different living trees, digitally processing them (3D-scanning, 3D-modelling, CNC-cutting) and finally assembling and synthesizing them into a new whole.

The Norwegian Timber Research Institute helped us in our extensive research for a suitable tree species. In the end we chose pollarded/coppiced ash trees from our neighbouring municipality Strand. They have a preferred characteris- tic look, a short, thick trunk and numerous branches, that all protrude from one area on top of the trunk. The selected ash trees were growing on an old farm where the pollarding practice had been discontinued for several years, which resulted in thicker and thus stronger branches, ideal for climbing.

Finally, ten trees were chosen, and sawn in half, along the lengths of their trunks. The company responsible for the 3D-scan of the trees performed two jobs: the laser scanning of the original trees and the subsequent production of 3D models, also called re-engineering. In a first step, the scanner collected thousands of Cartesian Coordinates on the object's surface, forming a so-called point-cloud. Several point-clouds were combined to create a three-dimensional representation of the trees. We imported this data into our 3D programmes, FormZ and Rhino. Now that we had these real trees in a virtual format, we revisited our initial sketch models. Working with both the virtual model and a 3D print of all 10 half-trees, we experi- mented with the positioning of the 10 trees. We realized that, in order to create a stiff structure, one branch must always connect to another branch of an adjacent

12.3
Ratatosk Pavilion: Selected trees.

tree trunk. Similarly, the base of each tree should connect to its neighbour. We reassessed how we would achieve an intimate spatial quality but, at the same time, an airy and open assembly.

12.4
Ratatosk Pavilion: Digital model of the arranged halves of the ash tree trunks.

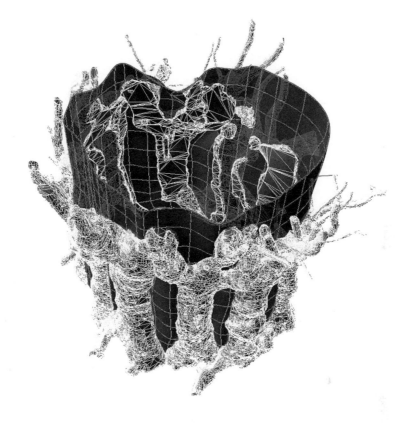

After positioning the trees, we designed the milling pattern of each tree in union with all 10 trees as a spatial topology spanning across several trunks. We placed very rough control lines relative to the branching, curvature and fibre pattern of the trees. The lines generated a three-dimensional NURBS (Non Uniform Rational B-Spline) surface that intersected with the model of each tree. By editing the control lines we adjusted the surface until we were content with the overall cut shape. Afterwards, heeding the inherent characteristics of the trees (such as knots, holes and fibres) we added details to the control lines to refine the surface in certain parts and to shape hand grips for climbing, signs to explore, seats to sit, etc. The resulting surface could never have been predicted in the sketch design phase and, once again, resulted in a feedback loop through the project's levels of integration. 'Roots', prosthetics connecting and stabilizing the trees at their bases, were modelled from existing branches, so as to interlock into milled joints in the trunks. Their forms were dictated largely by the shapes of discarded branches, and therefore could never have been predicted in a preliminary sketch. Once again, the design was adjusted through a bottom-up approach. The smooth, intricate NURBS surfaces of the trunks and roots were transmitted to the 3D mill workshop.

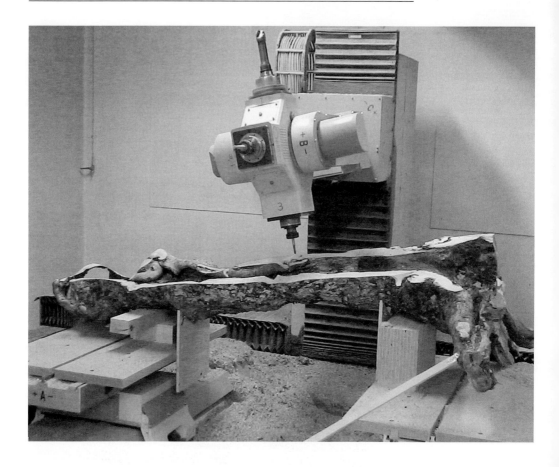

The milling process resulted in a continuous, furniture-finish interior plane, which included climbing grips, root connection surfaces and a continuous poem spanning all the trees. The pavilion was completed by a crown-like vaulted roof of sliced branches. The ultimate position of these elements was entirely dependent on the flexibility of each slice of timber, and therefore was in flux right until the element was fixed. While the roof was envisaged from the outset, the finished form could never have been predicted. A cushion of wood chips lined the base, providing a soft mat to protect playful children. The shape of the cushions was moulded to fit the interior space of the pavilion. All parts of the trees, that is, trunk, bark, wood chippings, roots and branches, have been refined and reassembled, according to their intrinsic qualities, into a new whole. We hoped to accentuate the contrast between the rough, untreated exterior and the refined interior and also between the heavy rhythm of the trunks and the delicate filigree of the woven roof. The result is a prefabricated kit, which was developed on a number of integration levels simultaneously, and challenged the traditional sequence of the design process.

12.5
Ratatosk Pavilion: Digital fabrication.

12.6
The *Ratatosk* Pavilion at the
Victoria and Albert Museum in
London.

12.7
The *Ratatosk* Pavilion at the
Victoria and Albert Museum in
London in its intended use as
a play-scape.

The Pulpit Rock Mountain Lodge

The Pulpit Rock Mountain Lodge, the winning design competition entry in 2004, accommodates 24 guest-rooms, a café, a restaurant and a conference room. The lodge is situated at the trailhead leading up to the Pulpit Rock, the sheer cliff overhanging Lyse Fjord, one of west Norway's best-known attractions.

12.8
The Pulpit Rock Mountain Lodge.

The initial scheme was based on the concurrent research of a large folded roof and a rib structure both in massive timber elements. These two levels of integration changed continuously and adapted directly to all inputs from the client and the consultant group. Our ambition was to solve all major requirements of the project with one move: double ribs and a roof of prefabricated massive timber elements, isolated and covered with a timber skin. The folded roof doubles as walls and protection for outdoor spaces around the building. Its profile and topological form relates carefully to the immediate environment with its undulating landscape and dramatic peaks. Internally, the double ribs separate adjacent guest-rooms and eliminate lateral sound transfer. As the main load-bearing construction of the project their spacing and form arose from static concerns, and also the spatial requirement of the guest-rooms. Hollowed out on the ground floor they create a generous public zone with intimate sitting areas in between the ribs along the façade. A 3D model was the common tool in the whole process and included, combined and constantly adapted to new circumstances and inputs.

The project's development accelerated and shifted through profound investigation within the two lower levels of integration: the massive timber elements and their constituent material Holz 100. Each element consists of several layers: one load-bearing vertical core, two diagonal stiffening layers and horizontal

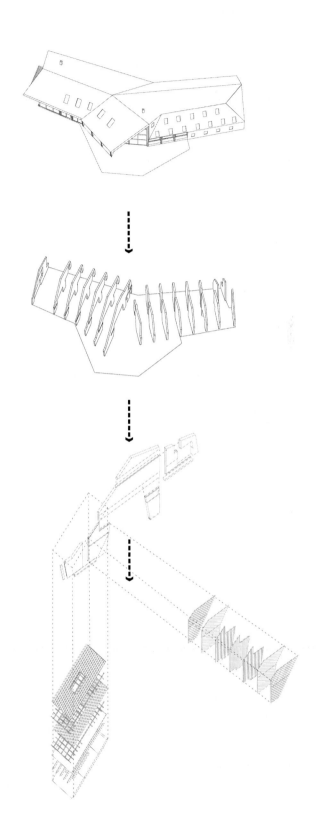

12.9
The Pulpit Rock Mountain
Lodge: Component logic of the
scheme.

exterior panels. These layers are dowelled together by peach taps, which swell after injection. The elements are produced without any glue or steel, and they are therefore not only more environmentally friendly but also keep the anisotropic qualities of the timber. The sizing of each element was calculated by the structural engineer and industrially mass-produced. Occasionally, adjustments were made in the factory, according to their specific performance. These discoveries had a major impact on the design of the two higher levels of integration, that is, the total 15 ribs and the overall shape of the building.

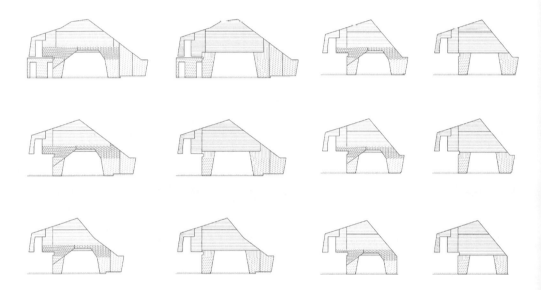

The structural challenge in the use of the Holz 100 elements was the large span over the public spaces; the café and restaurant area which measures 6 metres at its widest. This was too lengthy a span for the load of the second floor that the ribs had to support. We wanted to avoid an additional reinforcement of the Holz 100 system with, for example, a laminated beam and therefore investigated possibilities to increase its load capacity. We solved this in collaboration with the engineer Wörle Sparowitz by turning the build up of the elements inside out, exposing the diagonal layers which then could extend into the room at a higher level and thereby increase the static quality and stiffness of the rib. At the same time, the shift of the timber elements' layers changed the entire form and, subsequently, the geometry of the public rooms while exposing the unique construction principle and the intrinsic qualities of the timber assemblage.

12.10
The Pulpit Rock Mountain Lodge: Differentiated massive wood sheer-walls.

The Norwegian Pavilion for the Expo 2010 in Shanghai

The theme of the Expo 2010 Shanghai dealt with the future possibilities of sustainable urban development. With this ambition in mind the extended use of resources to erect a 1900m² exhibition pavilion to last only 140 days would be difficult, if not impossible to legitimize.

12.11
The Pulpit Rock Mountain Lodge: Interior view of the restaurant.

Subsequently, our competition project emphasized awareness on extending the life span of the pavilion through the proposal of an after-use as described in the introduction. We investigated less the formal or figurative design of a pavilion than a loose constellation of self-sustained components, which can be easily erected, dismantled and transformed. At the same time they had to reach aesthetic and narrative qualities to qualify for representing Norway in the Expo. This led us to introduce a field of 'trees' which would fulfil most requirements of the programme and could adapt to the huge number of external inputs in a relatively short design process. During the Expo period, the proposal assembled the trees in a sensory and multifunctional 'forest'. After Expo each individual tree would be reused as a multifunctional installation, for example, as social meeting place, playground, climbing tree or recreation and relaxation tree. Each tree consists of a laminated timber construction, with four CNC cut and milled branches, one trunk and four roots, which serve as foundations. The load-bearing construction was produced in Norway, the rest of the pavilion in China. The four branches uphold a pretensioned four-point sail; a membrane roof in Teflon calculated by the engineers Julian Lienhard und Jan Knippers. The trees and the membrane roof were designed and dimensioned in such a way that each of them could stand free after the Expo. A main intention in the project was to avoid the split between the interior and the exterior of the pavilion, so often designed as a black box with a fancy façade, with

the exhibition designed separately and put in afterwards. Instead we intended to weave together skin (membrane roof) infrastructure (air-conditioning, water and energy supply, lighting, etc.), furniture, exhibition and information display into every single tree. To achieve this, we designed a layer extending the main construction; CNC-cut plywood plates in bamboo, so-called 'add-ons' along the branches, trunk and roots. Between these add-ons lay the rain-water pipes, sprinkler pipes and electrical ducts. In the roots, monitors and screens were integrated in another form of specially designed add-ons, which together create the entire exhibition of the pavilion. In addition they contain the technical infrastructure and air chambers for the supply of air, which enters the pavilion through a perforated add-on. The division of the pavilion into 15 trees on one hand and the merging of all the main functions of the pavilion in each single tree on the other hand means that each single tree was influenced both from the top down and from the bottom up. The internal exchange of information and interdependency in between the different levels of integration was highly complex and constantly changing until the very end of the construction phase. Directions given on a higher integration level, like the constraints of the site, the layout of the overall outer form and floor plan and the design of the exhibition were rudimentary and less important than the material constraints and static limitation of the free-standing tree, the connection in between the trees and local information on lower levels of integration.

For example, the Teflon membrane on the first level of integration required a pretension so that the difference between the two high points and the two low points at the ends of each branch of a tree (level of integration 2) should not drop below a minimum value. This dependency affected the whole roof and established parameters for the overall size of the fourth level of integration. Changing one point changed the whole roof. The form-finding included static considerations, the room height of the different zones, and the perception of the pavilion from different angles from the outside and the drainage of rain-water.

To grasp the functional demand of the after-use we initially planned to not only start with the design of the after-use but also combine that process with the design of the exhibition in the pavilion. The idea was to develop the trees and the

12.13
The Norwegian Pavilion for the
2010 Expo in Shanghai:
Component logic of the
scheme.

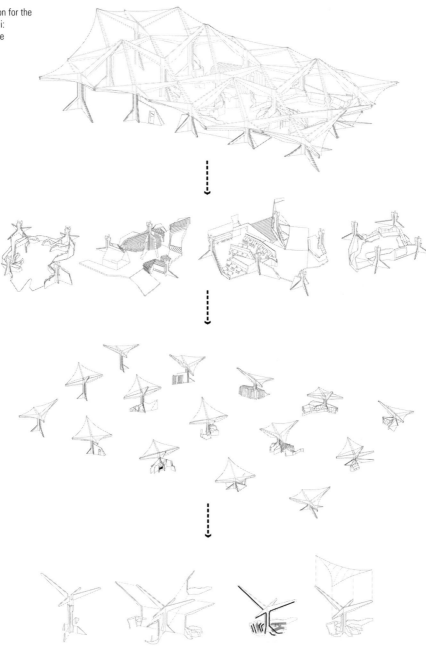

exhibition in neighbourhoods and include inhabitants that were relocated from the Expo site by the Chinese authorities together with different professional Norwegian milieux. To merge the different design processes, which are normally temporally and geographically separated, was not accepted by our Norwegian client. This reaction points out a general problem: an initial design would benefit from confrontation with

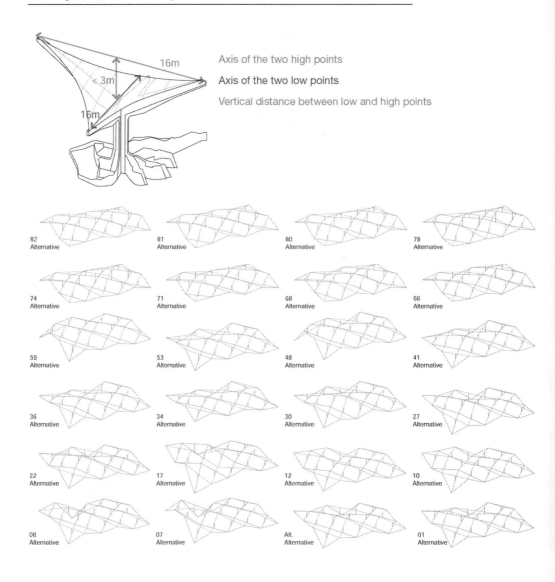

Axis of the two high points

Axis of the two low points

Vertical distance between low and high points

information which emerges normally later in the process, like the construction phase, the future use or transformation. But this would imply legal, organizational or economical complications; the client does not want to commit him/herself too early and take the risk of making a wrong decision. If economic, legal and organization models had been seriously considered from the beginning our chances to follow our initial ideas would have been better. Nevertheless, we had several workshops with students from the Huazhong University of Science and Technology in Wuhan, GAFA in Guangzhou and Tongji in Shanghai about the programmatic, figurative and financial possibilities of the reuse, as an alternative to the original concept for the exhibition.

12.14
The Norwegian Pavilion for the 2010 Expo in Shanghai: Differentiated tree columns and the varying undulation of the membrane roof.

12.15
The Norwegian Pavilion for the 2010 Expo in Shanghai: Workshops with students from the Huazhong University of Science and Technology in Wuhan, GAFA in Guangzhou and Tongji in Shanghai.

12.16
The Norwegian Pavilion for the 2010 Expo in Shanghai.

Conclusion

There are two compelling and substantial questions to be answered within each project: Which are the design methods that guide you through a process allowing feedback loops to occur and influence while still keeping the idea? What are the all-encompassing concepts and premises that are relevant in most parts of the project? The difficulty in answering those questions lies, among others, in the interdisciplinary and compound nature of our profession. Concepts are often either too limited to be expressed in every part of the architectural scheme, or they are too rigid to be adapted to different situations. The method applied in the three projects could be described as a 'toolkit' that helped us to grasp and traverse different disciplines, cultures and agendas. Interweaving different spatial concepts with design and production processes can ultimately lead to multi-functionality as well as to richer experiences and unexpected spatial inventions. This can include the redesign of usual relations between building components and its functions and uses. This process of synthesizing requires a timely reconfiguration of the usual working and feedback procedures. Extensive iterations of design and modelling steps are required, while expert knowledge and detailed planning have to be integrated from the beginning. As a result, a project can be defined on different levels of integration. Each of those levels has its own implicit possibilities and internal communications. This is by no means intended to create a formal hierarchy within the project. Rather, the different conceptual layers increase the project's adaptability towards its environment and users, as well as to material properties and assemblies.

Bibliography

De Landa, M. (2011) 'The Case of Modeling Software'. *Verb Processing*, 132–136.
Jacob, F. (1974) *The Logic of Life – A History of Heredity*. New York: Pantheon.

Chapter 13

Studio Integrate – interview with a young practice focusing on research by design

Michael U. Hensel in conversation with Mehran Gharleghi and Amin Sadeghy

MH: *Starting up a new practice is always a considerable challenge, yet certainly more so when the aim is to pursue research by design in every project, given the related resourcing implications. Studio Integrate has this aim. Please describe your practice and mode of operation. What distinguishes you from standard practice?*
MG & AS: Studio Integrate is a small practice that recruits on a project basis and according to need. We have been careful to select a focused path through architectural education and working in practice so as to facilitate our specific research interests in architectural design by both boarding and deepening these interests. Likewise we built up a network of experts we can call upon. Design and research by design is in our case always related to projects or teaching engagements leading to physical construction. Our studio is equipped with specific fabrication technologies so that projects or parts of projects can be made to inform the design development.

We place great emphasis on synthesizing spatial quality, material performance and the building's interaction with its context and environment, even if other criteria, such as economic considerations, seem to preclude such an effort.

In the *Saba Naft* commercial office complex project, for instance (a collaboration of Studio Integrate and Nasrine Faghih – Local Architects: Archen co.), we developed a multi-criteria approach that responded to the strategic location of the site in a cutural urban development with unique views, climatic characteristics, material performance and the physical programme. The site is located in a future cultural and commercial development area. The project will potentially be an important urban node by way of creating a public platform overlooking the east and south scenic views.

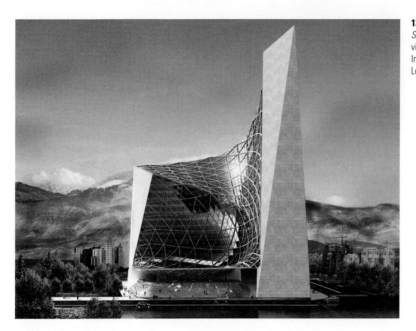

The public platform provides the entrance to the hypermarket, as well as several other entrances on different sides of the building, making it highly accessible along all the edges. Spectacular north, south and east views suggested an L-shaped building volume. In order to maximize the amount of daylight within the office building the depth of the building was differentiated. Office buildings with dual north/south views were the result of the narrow building depth.

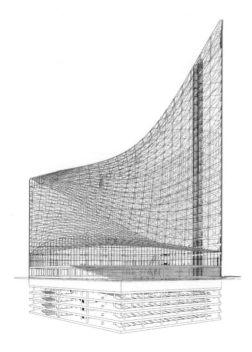

13.2
Saba Naft Complex: Schematic axonometric, collaboration of Studio Integrate and Nasrine Faghih- Local Architects: Archen co.

The location of the building called for maximum visibility, which is in contradiction with the climatic characteristic of the region. To tackle the issue, a second pneumatic skin was introduced reducing south and east sunlight, while maintaning a high level of transparency of the envelope. The climatic skin then turns over the public platform improving spatial quality and environmental conditions. The lightweight ETFE cushions along with high level of differentiation capacity make the complex geometrical arrangement possible that is required to negotiate the numerous criteria that govern the design of the layered envelope.

13.3
Saba Naft Complex. Rapid-prototype model, collaboration of Studio Integrate and Nasrine Faghih- Local Architects: Archen co.

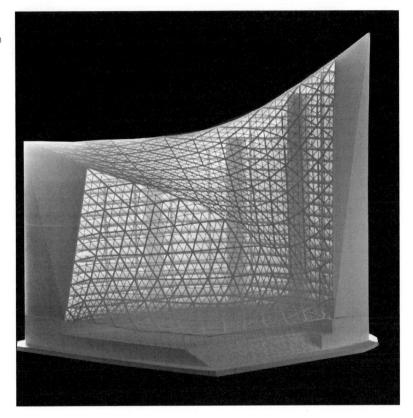

MH: *Please describe the mix of expertise that characterizes Studio Integrate.*

MG & AS: Our brand of research by design necessitates knowledge in a range of fields. This is necessary in order to establish the links between and to integrate the different research interests and experiments. We establish these links from the very early stages of the design process and acquire skills and expertise accordingly. This includes expertise in material, computation, mathematics, environment and also Building Information Management (BIM) software.

In the *Adaptive Pneus* project, for instance, we required a range of skills and tools in different stages of the project to tackle different issues and questions. The project started by extensive material research to understand inherent structural

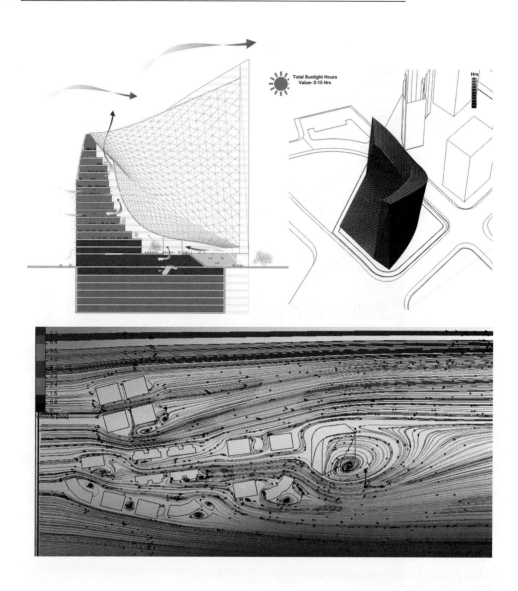

and adaptive characteristics of the pneumatic material system. The purpose of the research was to achieve a lightweight self-supporting system that is inherently capable of reacting to the external environmental stimuli without resorting to electrical-mechanical actuators. In this instance the environmental stimuli was direct sunlight causing different pressure in the air-filled cushions throughout the day. Once material knowledge was established and reliable empirical data concerning the behaviour of the pneumatic material system were established, the computational design and environmental simulation process commenced, testing and developing the system's performance in micro-, meso- and macro-scale in different environmental set-ups and geometrical arrangements. This process required extensive knowledge in computation and environmental analyses.

13.4
Saba Naft Complex.
Environmental analysis,
collaboration of Studio
Integrate and Nasrine Faghih-
Local Architects: Archen co.

Another example for our approach is the *Benetton HQ* project, which was a redevelopment of a central courtyard typology suitable for the project's specific climate. The central courtyard was designed through a three-dimentional rotation of a U-shape around the vertical axis, leaving one edge of the building open at the entrance and public level, while creating an almost enclosed central courtyard for climatic purposes.

13.5
Benetton HQ – Competition
entry 2009: Rendered view.

13.6
Benetton HQ – Competition
entry 2009: Rendered view.

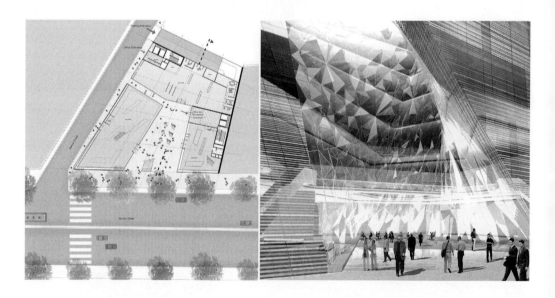

The complex overall geometry of the building volume was further articulated through Penrose patterns that cover the doubly curved interior façade with only three different elements. In so doing, environmental knowledge, digital simulation and mathematical expertise made it possible to arrive at an exciting and feasible answer to a complex design problem.

13.7
Benetton HQ – Competition
entry 2009: Left: Ground plan,
Right: Rendered view of the
central courtyard.

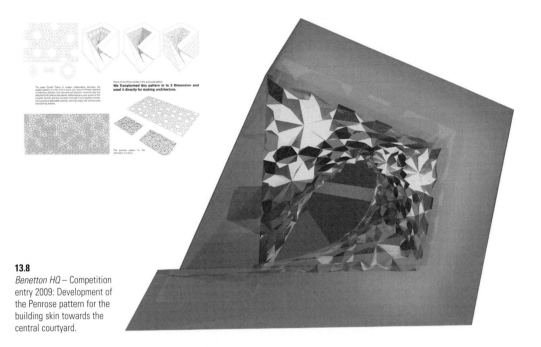

13.8
Benetton HQ – Competition entry 2009: Development of the Penrose pattern for the building skin towards the central courtyard.

Total Sunlight Hours
Average Daily Value
:Value 0 - 10 Hrs

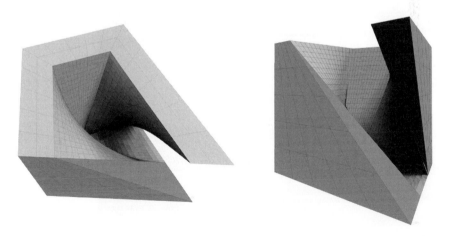

13.9
Benetton HQ – Competition entry 2009: Environmental analysis.

MH: *Please describe the specific research interests that underlie Studio Integrate's work.*

MG & AS: Questions regarding spatial quality and the inhabitant's comfort level interest us the most. Materials, geometry and environmental studies that are in the service of these interests comprise the most important areas in our research. The ways in which material organizations under different conditions can significantly affect the geometry and performance of buildings or building parts fascinate us. One major area of study are vernacular buildings. Vernacular buildings demonstrate a fundamental integration of material, structural and environmental performance, which results in rich spaces that make provisions towards the inhabitant's lifestyle. In some cases through the evolution of civilizations and having the opportunity to reconstruct those buildings for several hundreds of years they have provided stunning spaces as well as perfect responses to climatic needs. Through careful studies and analyses we try to understand the principles of operation under certain climatic conditions and material choices to be able to apply and develop them whenever suitably in our projects.

Our material and geometry research usually starts via rigorous physical and digital small-scale experiments. As soon as we understand the behaviour of material in small scales, experiments proliferate upwards in scale towards construction-scale installations. This is done in order to test structural and environmental performance, as well as spatial articulation. When suitable projects come up we try to apply our findings to full-scale buildings. This indicates that we pursue two lines of research, one that is directly geared towards tackling a building design and another that results in realizations and empirical knowledge to be utilized when suitable opportunities present themselves. The latter is an investment into the creative and knowledge capital of the practice.

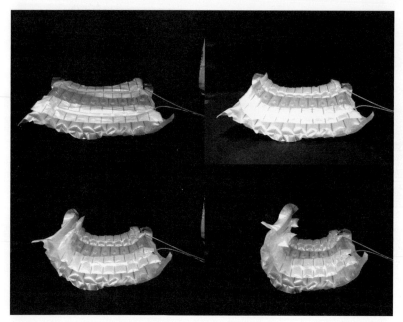

13.10
Adaptive Pneus: Full-scale prototype at different stages of response.

Our pneumatic studies started with extensive physical experiments that led us to a reliable understanding of the circumstances under which the material works as a self-supporting structure or an adaptive cell. Through specific material arrangements we achieved a self-supporting system that is simultaneously capable of reacting to environmental stimuli without a need for electrical-mechanical devices.

13.11
Adaptive Pneus: Digital model of a double-curved arrangement of the pneumatic elements.

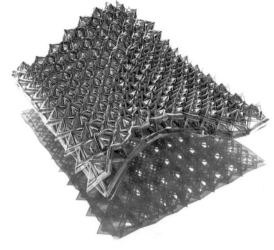

13.12
Adaptive Pneus: Environmental analysis of a double-curved arrangement of the pneumatic elements.

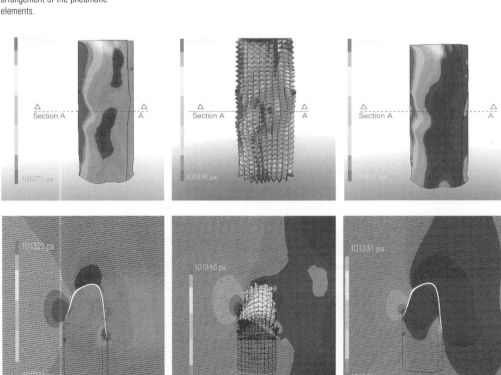

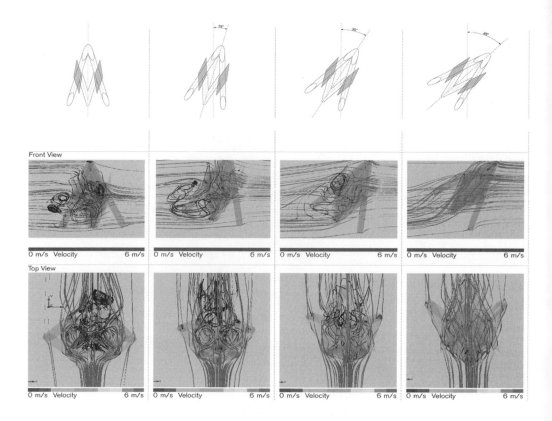

The adaptive capacity of pneumatics was derived from the inherent characteristics of the material system that is width reduction after being inflated. In the closed state the component comprises two layers of pneus. The bottom layer is inflated while the top layer is deflated. As the direct sunlight hits the component the turgur pressure within the cell increases. Higher air pressure allows the air to travel through a pressure valve to the top layer and inflate the top layer. As a result of this process the component opens and allows airflow through the envelope and thus delivers natural ventilation. As the orientation and angle of the sun changes throughout the day, cells that are under the direct sunlight vary. In order to create cross-ventilation, the geometry needs to be doubly curved creating different patches of openings in the right spots at different times.

In so doing, the complex geometrical arrangement is directly informed from the material performance and the immediate surrounding environment that affects the lighting conditions around the building. In fact, this results in a different environmental set-up for each building; therefore, different morphology.

Material limitations and boundaries also open various research opportunities in different areas for us. In this example, one of the limits of the material systems was their ability to open only if the component is flat. In order to obtain doubly curved surfaces, essential to the performance of the building, we had to use quadrilateral geometries, a mathematical solution, which allowed us to achieve

13.13
Adaptive Pneus: Environmental analysis of a single pneumatic element at different stages of response.

13.14
Adaptive Pneus: Full-scale prototype made for the London Design Festival 2010.

doubly curved surfaces via simple flat elements. A full-scale prototype was made for the London Design Festival 2010, to test the self-supporting capacity and its performance. This project later won honourable mention for the international sustainable award.

We are continuing our explorations into pneumatic systems. In a recent workshop done with students in the Technical University of Graz, we designed and built an installation entitled *Airbone*. We aimed to explore more complex geometrical arrengements and smoother joints to achive better structural performance, while obtaining more complex spaces. The design process included advanced computational form-finding, material logics, and fabrication. One of the challenges involved was to prepare flat cutting patterns out of double-curved surfaces. This is still ongoing research and there are a few issues that have to be resolved until the system is fully operational.

13.15
Airbone Installation: Developed in a workshop at the Technical University of Graz, view of the gallery workspace.

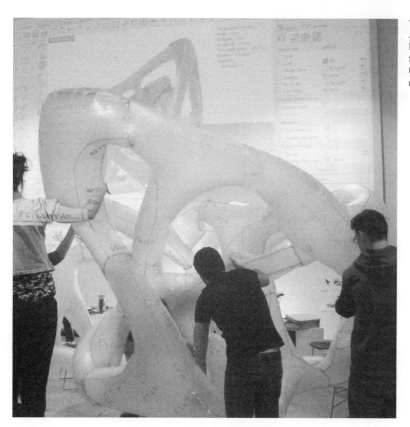

13.16
Airbone Installation:
Developed in a workshop at
the Technical University of
Graz, view of the prototype in
construction.

This research into pneumatic systems enabled the use of pneumatics in the above-described *Saba Naft* project. The advantage of pneumatics became immediately clear once the criteria for the design of the envelope of the building were defined: lightweight construction in a seismically active area and advanced climatic performance in a harsh climate with great temperature differentials.

MH: *How do you identify research potentials in projects with a given brief?*
MG & AS: We find it quite exciting to adapt researched subject matter into certain boundary and spatial conditions introduced by a given programme. In so doing, research goes beyond generic solutions and may result in a unique project. In addition, every project introduces certain unanticipated difficulties that normally help the research go further by reacting to a specific problem. *Saba Naft* and the *Benetton HQ* projects are useful examples of that.

Our research into the reutilization of Islamic geometric patterns, for instance, commenced five years ago and culminated recently into a specific design solution for the *Benetton HQ* project. This line of research started with our diploma project and continued in a book entitled *Conversation with a Young Architect* authored by Nasrine Faghih, which received the best Iranian architectural book of the year award. The research started by realizing the potentials that the mathematics behind Islamic geometries present. Peter J. Lu, a PhD reseacher from Harvard, found that by 1200 CE a conceptual breakthrough occurred in which so-called *girih* patterns were reconceived as tessellations of a special set of equilateral polygons (*girih* tiles) decorated with lines. These tiles enabled the creation of increasingly complex periodic *girih* patterns, and by the fifteenth century, the tessellation approach was combined with self-similar transformations to construct nearly perfect quasi-crystalline Penrose patterns, five centuries before their discovery in the West. This was a starting point for studying the underlying rules of Islamic geometries and readapting them to doubly curved surfaces and complex volumes, seeking novel integrated spatial, structural and environmental opportunities. We developed this research in two architectural projects: the *World Carpet Trade Centre* (2007, third prize in the related design competition) and later in 2009 in the *Benetton HQ* competition, both as joint collaborations between Studio Integrate and Nasrine Faghih. In the design for the *Carpet Trade Centre* we were studying and experimenting with transitions of patterns into different forms of geometry to modulate spatial and lighting conditions. The project presented a great opportunity to put the findings into practice. The envelope was informed by the redevelopment of a motif in Persian carpets into different densities to modulate views, lighting conditions, and interior quality.

13.17
World Carpet Trade Centre – Competition entry 2007: Third prize, joint collaboration between Studio Integrate and Nasrine Faghih, Night view of the building with emphasis on the envelope as a redevelopment of a motif in Persian carpets into different densities to modulate views, lighting conditions, and interior spatial conditions.

The programme of the project was split into two main sections, generating a public ramp-platform leading to the exhibition halls, which are located at the top volume. Spectators were given the opportunity to see the volume from various angles in order to experience different spatial conditions while walking through or under different densities and porosities of the developed geometry.

When the *Benetton HQ* competition was done, we had already reached the stage in the research where we could apply quasi-Crystalline Penrose geometry on complex doubly curved surfaces using only a few base modules. This served to ensure the feasibility of fabrication of the complex envelope facing the central courtyard. Here again, we synthesized environmental studies with mathematical knowledge to respond to a given brief in a dense urban environment.

MH: *What kind of external expertise do you value and bring into your projects?*

MG & AS: We try to collaborate with various groups of experts at various stages in the projects to be able to reflect their feedback into the design process. Valued areas of expertise include:

1   Culture, heritage and architectural history of the region in which we are designing a project: We have always benefited from collaboration with senior designers such as Dr Nasrine Fagih who has a thorough knowledge in vernacular and historical architecture of Iran, as well as worldwide history and theory of architecture.

2   Fabricators: We tend to seek advice from specialized fabricators from a very early stage in design. Sometimes this communication takes place before the projects as part of our research and at other times we find experts relative to the specific question of the project. Benefiting from constructors and fabricators included in the design team expands the dynamic design process from the first few months of the project into almost the entire length of design to fabrication and construction.

3   Material researchers: As mentioned, material research is one of the core areas of our research and plays a significant role in our design process. So far we have been undertaking studies in pneumatics; fibre-reinforced concrete, with Professor Shin Enshigra and Rubez Azavedo; and also fabrics. Our future material studies will include fibre-reinforced inflatables, wood and new high-performance materials.

4   Mathematicians: We use mathematics to find elegant and simple solutions to complex questions. Currently we are studying more mathematical solutions for panelizing *Saba Naft's* climatic skin, to find a more meaningful, structural and economic solution, in which we are collaborating with some external mathematicians and computational experts.

5   Environmental specialists: We collaborate with environmental experts on our research on vernacular buildings and design projects. We consider local climate a crucial part of our design process and it is not a post-design optimization approach that we follow. Instead, environmental input informs the geometry of our projects from the onset.

6   Structural engineers: Creative structural advice in the early design stages is the area where we need external expertise the most. To obtain innovative structural solutions, we try to work with creative engineers who help us with the behaviour analysis of material systems.

Chapter 14

Multiplying the ground

Eva Castro and Alfredo Ramirez

Introduction

This chapter introduces the work which the practice GroundLab has been developing in the last three years, and which stems from the academic research undertaken in the Landscape Urbanism Master programme at the Architectural Association and the applied strategies worked out from the branches of specific professional projects.

The aim is to examine general questions about the methodology, operability and relevance of a practice that is mainly addressing contemporary urban conditions, including highly urbanised contexts, places susceptible to high migration rates and huge developmental pressure; therefore, demanding immediate responses to urban sprawl, rapid urbanisation, post-industrialisation, and natural disasters.

Where traditional urban planners around the world still propose masterplans akin to twentieth-century compositions and sensibilities, GroundLab works actively to propose alternative models of urbanisation, rethinking organisational structures, diagramming new urban networks, indexing sensitive readings of territories and exploring the generative potential of material and drawing techniques. The capacity of these strategies to articulate new structures, logics and territories is tested and confronted within frameworks with specific briefs, critically addressing its viability and pertinence within the contemporary urban panorama.

On landscape urbanism

GroundLab work is rooted in the relatively new discipline called *Landscape Urbanism*, and more specifically the methodology developed in the Landscape Urbanism Master programme at the Architectural Association in London, which unlike its North-American counterpart focuses on the 'Urbanism' aspect, deploying architecture as the driving model for spatial articulation, conceived as an urban, cultural, political and social device from its inception and focusing on the built environment. At the same time, it incorporates models, methods and techniques from landscape practices, hence the ability to engage at different scales, required in large-scale projects. Landscape allows the use and manipulation of the ground, as the raw material to work with, taking advantage of its time-based qualities in the staging of various sequences and phases. GroundLab aims at the entwining of architecture as spatial structure with landscape and ecological processes through ground manipulation, in its widest sense:

> Landscape as a model of connective, scalar and temporal operations through which the urban is conceived and engaged with: the urban is diagrammed as a landscape; a complex and processual ecology. With this model the urban can be connected to local, regional and global scales and understood in terms of its future orientation and performative potential.
>
> (Castro *et al*. 2011: 6)

And

> Although the urban might be 'diagrammed' as a landscape, in terms of scale, connectivity, process, etc., we don't think of the urban as itself a landscape, i.e. as some pastoral space for middle-class people to go for a pleasant walk in, or something that looks pleasingly 'green' and 'environmentally sustainable'. We recognise the urban as a social, political, and economic intensity fraught with all sort of tensions, conflicts and competing agenda.
>
> (Spencer 2010)

This implies considering the city as part of a wider metabolic ensemble, where the metabolic and time-based processes of landscape and 'nature' become devices for human interaction and relationships. Thus the critical engagement with the environmental conditions becomes the crucial driver of a design process that is grounded on the experimentation of form as an operational/political device.

Processual design: from abstract thought to concrete production

GroundLab operates based on the understanding that regardless of the size of a territory, it is paramount to engage all scales contained in it to achieve a substantial spatial resolution. The definition of the scale(s) to engage with is revealed through the same process by which the dynamic systems are unfolded and assimilated, allowing us to identify hierarchies and crucial agents embedded. Thus the chosen scales to operate with are symptomatic of specific issues pertinent to the site conditions, denoting key areas that are intrinsic to the whole and that can have a transformative effect on it. In this manner the work develops through a dialogue among different scales.

From macro ...

We work with an inclusive design process, which acknowledges in full contemporary conditions, whether physical, social, economic or environmental, and through the use of a wide range of techniques, mainly material and representational. These techniques perform as tools to decode, synthesise and process the various conditions, shifting from exclusively explorative into propositional devices, hence, directly informing the designs.

to micro ...

We employ the notion of the prototype as a mediator that can operate locally at a more tactical level, both as a mode to manipulate the territory – understood as a dynamic system, and to create a finer grain of resolution. This is done to address the articulation of the proposed changes, affecting the overall system and recording its responses.

The prototype arises after existing typologies, addressing, for example, infrastructural issues, but it moves away from the remedial take of a purely efficiency-driven element to include other roles and ultimately a new purpose. Thus, its scale, form and general attributes are not predetermined and variable by definition; its robustness develops as 'more than one' start to operate in combination with each other.

and back ...

The prototype, as a mediator, has the double 'task' of affecting the overall, whilst also tracing the effects generated through measuring its own performance. Thus we use it operatively as a tool to carry out the design and as a recorder of the changes in the whole, to further adjust the proposed strategies.

Techniques

GroundLab strongly engages with design techniques, as these constitute the way to bridge from abstract thoughts and design intentions, into concrete production and proposals. Design techniques are a tool to tackle the problems of homogenisation in urban fabrics and the lack of responsiveness within contemporary accelerated urbanism. At the same time, they test and confront strategies developed in academia against real projects and client requirements.

Representational techniques, developed within academia, find their application in actual projects and competitions. Large-scale projects offer the perfect test-bed for these tools, which have traditionally been used solely to understand and clarify different aspects of the territory.

We enhance the use of design techniques beyond the solely analytical or explanatory tools of the site. We boost these territorial readings to translate environmental, topographical and geographical parameters into more propositional and explorative mechanisms. Indexes are thus understood as a construct/an alchemy/an amalgam among the territory's existent parts, that rather than prioritising one over the other, facilitates the interaction – and further manipulation of the system by which they are held together and ultimately operate as a whole. This facilitates the generation of strategies that take at their core the affection of relationships instead of the remedial approach to the discrete parts.

The transit between the index towards the hyper-index is maintained as a continuum or zone of action that allows us both to (infra)structure the ground as a mean for spatial organisation and to return for feedbacks and readjustments. Hence, natural systems (rivers, green corridors, water channel systems), urban flows (pedestrians, vehicular), exchange of goods and products, networks of local interactions, existing urban patterns, are used to establish new frameworks from where nodes, axes, routes or paths are accentuated, enhanced or weakened; while others become spines to connect, separate or differentiate from existing and new developments. This methodology does not lead us towards a blank canvas completely free for experimentation, but to one that is full of information with which to work, negotiate and experiment. The purpose is to acknowledge the presence of *an existent* materiality within the territory and to propose modes of relating to it.

Augmented infrastructures

The role of infrastructure in cities is crucial in order to organise and manage complex systems of flow, movement and exchange. Commonly, though, they have remained static underground structures covered and hidden below a number of layers to avoid contact with them. Recently, the often-cited design shift in architecture from 'what it means' to 'what it can do' becomes relevant in urban projects, especially in infrastructures, given its performative nature within the cities.

GroundLab seeks to explore infrastructures through the research of landscape and engineering techniques, with the objective of integrating them within the urban design process. Beyond the problem-solving and remedial capabilities, landscape and engineering techniques, such as soil remediation, water-cleansing strategies, traffic control, earthworks, to name a few, become the medium through which diagrams and indexes find the material constraints to emerge as highly designed spatial structures. Infrastructures thus constitute the raw materials that by definition respond to performance and efficiency. They articulate the networks for movement, communication and exchange. The intertwining of both techniques and infrastructure results in a material model of organisation, which from its inception understands how the site works or might work. Thus, it allows the integration of infrastructures with other programmes and activities that can share similar spatial requirements and components to perform.

As we consider cities as dynamic systems in constant change and evolution, the understanding of their performance becomes essential for the viability of the proposed urban environments. The utilisation of these engineering techniques, to structure the city, presents numerous opportunities to reshape the public realm. The insertion of green space, for instance, with simultaneous leisure and productive capabilities, or the design of waterscapes, both providing water-cleansing devices and visual attraction, offers a multi-functional and adaptable framework for rapid urban environments, through the acknowledgement of the performance qualities of infrastructures.

Critical forms

The design industry is very permeable to external influences and it is probably neo-liberalism that has 'recently' had a strong effect particularly on urbanism. Possibly as an outcome of the exhaustion of public funds, the government's incapacity to diligently respond to the growing cities and an ever-increasing urban population, the identity of the city has gradually been subjected to the interests of the private developers' pockets. We believe that it is under this constellation that a 'new' urban discourse was born, which advocates an extreme connectivity, flexibility and adaptability and that is capable of catering for indeterminacy of programmes. In other words, this is a discourse that happily complies with the overall uncertainties of the free market. And whilst we acknowledge the necessity of adaptable and flexible strategies to respond to unknown futures, we don't renounce form as a means to design our environment. Form becomes the vehicle through which we challenge and face the different possible urban scenarios.

The objective is on the one hand to avoid the pitfalls of traditional master-planning as deterministic, controlled and inflexible and on the other the looseness of an open framework catering to an infinite number of scenarios, able to host any brief or given future. Thus the interest in form as both the medium that embodies and facilitates performance and the means to privilege spatial specificity is intrinsically related to our material experimentation. In short, GroundLab advocates highly articulated environments that commit themselves to specific scenarios, briefs and contextual needs, building up a sense of identity that rather than being imposed, arises from a dialogue between the territory's requirements (infrastructure) and our capacity to respond to current trends not purely as service providers, but as cultural producers.

Ground as a design paradigm

As the name GroundLab and several projects such as *'deep ground', 'ground_n', 'ground ecologies'* suggest, we are concerned with the ground as one of the main substances from where to explore the material potentials of urbanism. Central to this interest is the belief that the ground is the last bastion of public space: the territory within the city that needs most urgently to be addressed as it has the political capacity to deeply affect its surroundings.

Thus our work seeks to redefine the geologically self-contained solidity often associated with the ground, shifting from notions of monolithic finitude towards multiplicity. We propose a morphological engagement with the ground and in doing so we recognise the importance of positioning ourselves as designers in relation to the city and generate responses to the existing fabric, interacting with it instead of dissociating from it, establishing strategic links, and forming new affiliations.

We understand the ground as an artificial construct that although generated by simple operations derived primarily from pragmatic approaches to address technical demands it soon expands from the purely utilitarian state to acquire further spatial specificity. The objective is to create diversity, identity, place: a fertile environment capable of fostering a more complex set of interactions among environmental, cultural and social conditions, thus triggering alternative models of urbanisation that privilege the public realm over the private one, democratise mobility and accessibility in the city. Operations such as thickening, lifting, bifurcating, duplicating and stacking of the ground may foster a synthesis between landscape and architecture: semi-public podiums, infrastructural green spaces, urban patios, land bridges, pedestrian networks, urban terraces and so on, promoting new spatial arrangements and adjacencies.

By intensifying social interactions, they create new realignments of programmes and functions; in short, they provide a fertile ground to rethink new urban configurations, challenging existing notions and current trends of public, private and semi-private space in the city.

We believe it is important to articulate a finer spatial resolution as a means to enrich the ground beyond its performance and basic necessities into the formation of an extended public realm. We endeavour to de-commodify it in order to free it from pre-assigned definitions and prescriptive activities. We believe that to reconnect the user with his environment and foster an active engagement with it, it is vital to think about 'time for leisure' and concurrently, *to develop* spatial arrangements that can cater for it; environments with abstract qualities that cannot be codified or functionally predetermined, 'awkward' conditions that relate more to the ludic, the intuitive and the haptic than merely the rational.

Transdisciplinarity

At the core of GroundLab's organisation lies the idea of transdisciplinarity, a concept that defines Landscape Urbanism as a new discipline. In order to address the dynamics of contemporary urbanism, different expertise and backgrounds are combined to complement each other and borrow knowledge and techniques, to foster a more comprehensive urbanism. In this way transdisciplinarity informs the development of projects so that they become the medium to propose alternative urban scenarios whilst building up new and correspondent relations between the different parties normally involved in large-scale projects as well as in between the acting disciplines.

GroundLab members' expertise ranges from architecture, urban design, landscape architecture and civil engineering, which form the basis for any given project. Through these means GroundLab projects new material interventions that operate within an urbanism conceived as social, material, ecological and continually modulated by the spatial and temporal forces in which it is networked.

Ultimately this highlights a research process that focuses on discovering a modus operandi inbuilt in the Landscape Urbanism agenda that could serve as a catalyst for contemporary modes of practice. A process to describe new ways in which all professions dealing with the city may be reconfigured and adjusted to meet the contemporary social and environmental conditions that pose the most significant challenges to normative design practices.

Deep Ground

Deep Ground is GroundLab's winning entry for the international design competition of Longgang City Centre and Longcheng Square. The project deals with the regeneration of 11.8km² of the urban fabric in the centre of Longgang, northeast of Shenzhen in the Pearl River Delta, China, with an estimated population of 350,000 and 9,000,000m² of new development.

The project radically expands the scope of urbanism in order to deal with the contemporary challenges of modern China – rapid urbanisation, huge developmental pressure, highly polluted landscapes, and their local implication in the province of Shenzhen, China. Through this project and the workshops that took place with the local authorities and the various other bodies in Shenzhen, we gained a significant understanding of both the local and global conditions in China, allowing us to develop a series of concepts that condensed the different issues and agents involved into a set of operative design tools that shaped three main strategies.

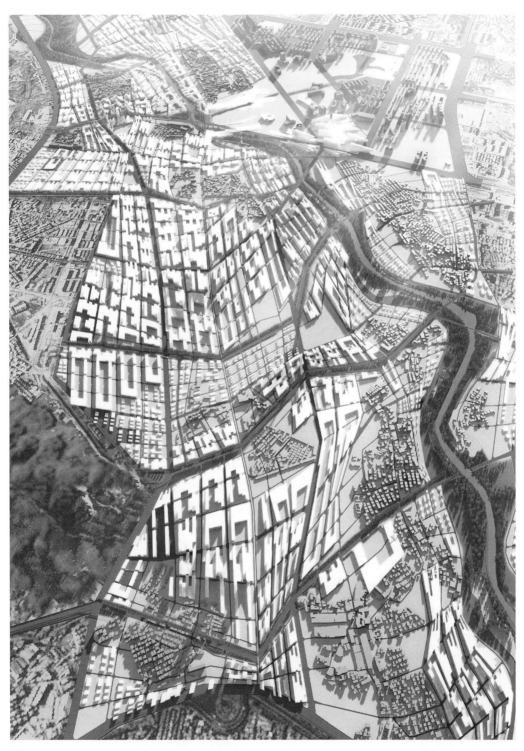

14.1
Deep Ground-Longgang master-plan, bird view. © 2008 GroundLab Ltd.

These design strategies are specific to the local requirements in Shenzhen and can be understood also as responses with a certain degree of typicality, addressing conditions that are symptomatic of the top-down, centrally controlled urbanisation process found today throughout China. In this way the strategies acquire a relevance that expands from the specific to the general and from the singularity of one situation to the plurality of a series of instances, thus allowing us to re-tailor them through successive iterations.

14.2
Deep Ground-Longgang
master-plan, bird view.
© 2008 GroundLab Ltd.

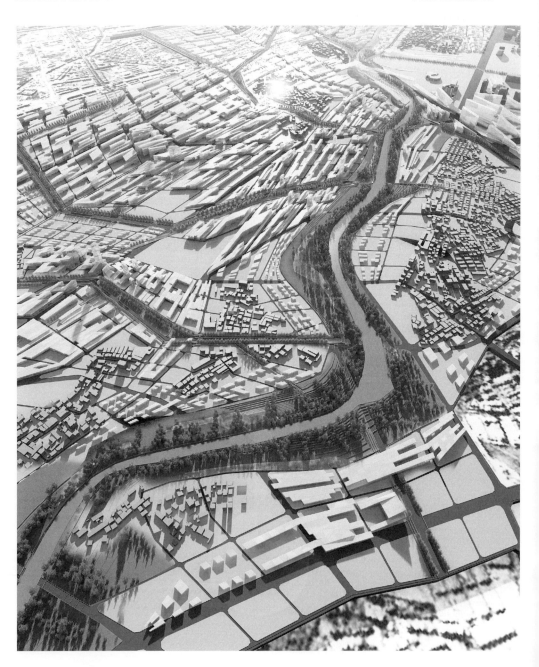

Within Longgang's scenario, three strategies took shape:

1   The '*thickened ground*', where multiple ground datums are fused to foster intuitive orientation and connectivity in the city, whilst generating more commercial
area and a higher revenue for the developer, thus enabling a financial mechanism for both its implementation and subsequent maintenance.

14.3
Thickened ground
development, top view.
© 2008 GroundLab Ltd.

2   The '*Infrastructural Landscape*' regenerates a polluted river and reinstates it
into daily life, transforming it into an ecological corridor that hosts a series of
public spaces, both along its main axis and across, splitting secondary lines that
permeate the urban fabric.
3   The existing '*Urban Villages*', which were going to be demolished, were
retained to form nuclei to lend identity, vitality and human scale to the new
development.

Thickened ground

Part of the competition brief was the redevelopment of the main square and the
introduction of a series of public programmes (book store, parking, etc.) to be placed
underground below the square, and the integration of the river crossing. The strategy of the thickened ground describes the spatial scheme of a morphology that
attempts to understand this space as a surface, acquiring depth and spatial complexity as the different functions and land uses start to combine. In this way, the strategy

seeks to produce a mixture of programmes rather than the compartmentalisation of functions, working towards an open-ended spatial result that combines good-quality open space with otherwise isolated infrastructural elements.

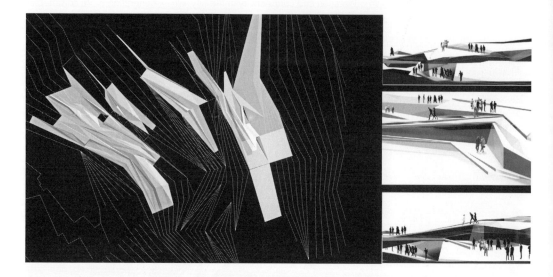

For the case of this project, the thickened ground emerges out of the bridge over the Longgang River and highway, crossing north to LongCheng Square to then become a folded surface containing both public programmes, underground access and parking for the CBD. The thickened ground becomes a prototypical strategy that challenges the traditional building/landscape opposition, managing to introduce surprisingly high density and programmatic diversity into areas that are currently underused, increasing the overall value, open space usage and intensity of life at street level.

14.4
Thickened ground schematic views. © 2008 GroundLab Ltd.

14.5
Thickened ground, bird view. © 2008 GroundLab Ltd.

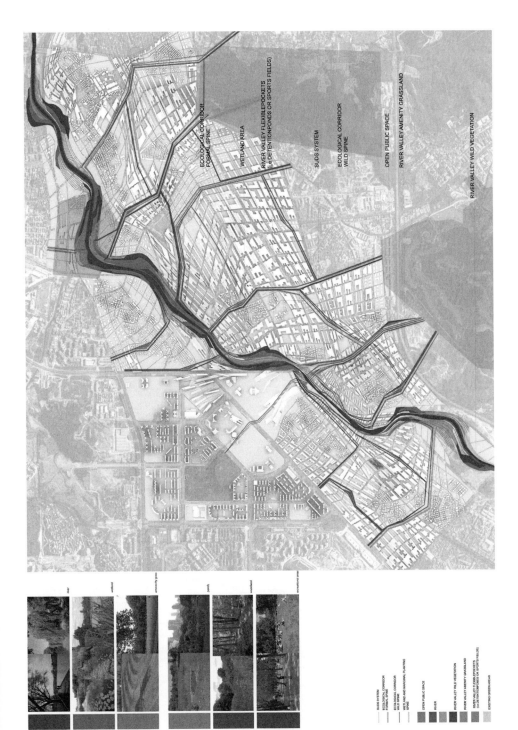

ECOLOGICAL CORRIDOR
FORMAL SPINE

WETLAND AREA

RIVER VALLEY FLEXIBLEPOCKETS
(i.e. DETENTIONPONDS OR SPORTS FIELDS)

SUDS SYSTEM

ECOLOGICAL CORRIDOR
WILD SPINE

OPEN PUBLIC SPACE

RIVER VALLEY AMENITY GRASSLAND

RIVER VALLEY WILD VEGETATION

river

wetland

amenity grass

fields

woodland

recreational areas

SUDS SYSTEM

ECOLOGICAL CORRIDOR
FORMAL SPINE

ECOLOGICAL CORRIDOR
WILD SPINE

WETLAND AND MARGINAL PLANTING
SPINE

OPEN PUBLIC SPACE

RIVER

RIVER VALLEY WILD VEGETATION

RIVER VALLEY AMENITY GRASSLAND

RIVER VALLEY FLEXIBLEPOCKETS
(i.e. DETENTIONPONDS OR SPORTS FIELDS)

EXISTING GREEN AREAS

14.6
Infrastructural landscape, master-plan. © 2008 GroundLab Ltd.

Infrastructural landscape

The Longgang River is located in the core of the city, while being strongly separated from it, with no interaction other than its use as an open air wastewater sewer for the city. The landscape strategy used this contradictory condition to propose the recovery of the river, triggering not just the revitalisation of its banks and surrounding areas, but also its integration into the urban environment, driving the landscape strategy, green space and river as one interactive and interconnected system.

The infrastructure designed along the river will serve as an anchor point to deploy cleansing strategies, rain-water collection and flooding defence while creating green areas, ecological corridors, public open spaces, sports fields and leisure areas. This is paralleled by the integration of a network of a sustainable drainage system that stems from the river towards the urban fabric. The system collects and distributes storm water to different areas for a variety of uses in the city. This network extends the benefits of the river regeneration towards other parts of the fabric at different scales, by becoming river tributaries that adjust to the different conditions and necessities it encounters.

14.7
Infrastructural landscape, exploded axo. © 2008 GroundLab Ltd.

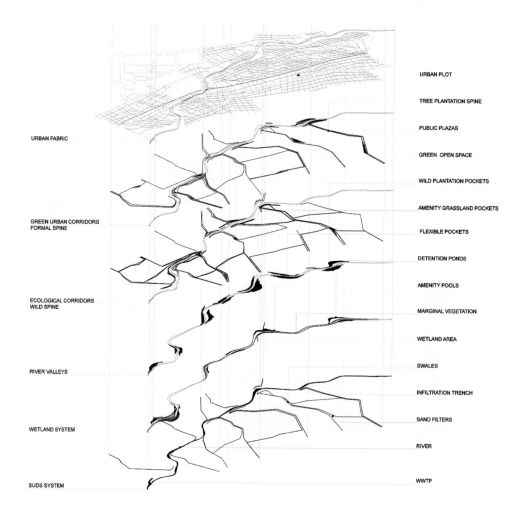

URBAN FABRIC

GREEN URBAN CORRIDORS
FORMAL SPINE

ECOLOGICAL CORRIDORS
WILD SPINE

RIVER VALLEYS

WETLAND SYSTEM

SUDS SYSTEM

URBAN PLOT

TREE PLANTATION SPINE

PUBLIC PLAZAS

GREEN OPEN SPACE

WILD PLANTATION POCKETS

AMENITY GRASSLAND POCKETS

FLEXIBLE POCKETS

DETENTION PONDS

AMENITY POOLS

MARGINAL VEGETATION

WETLAND AREA

SWALES

INFILTRATION TRENCH

SAND FILTERS

RIVER

WWTP

The complete landscape network creates a major framework that weaves the urban fabric with open space and infrastructure, and connects the river with additional programmes, producing a coherent system. The strategy generates ecology within the city and highlights the existence of the river not just as an aesthetic element, but also as a strategic, active and vital contribution for the present and future viability of the city.

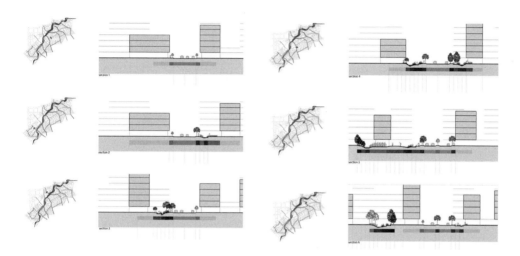

14.8
Infrastructural landscape,
SUDS's schematic sections.
© 2008 GroundLab Ltd.

Urban villages

Urban villages were key in the inception and development of the Deep Ground project. They are an urban typology that defines the character and recent history of many cities in China in general, and in Longgang in particular. And whilst, at a governmental level, there is an ongoing discussion on their relevance and its permanency inside China's urban environments, in this specific case, the local authorities' overall land use map proposed the erasure of the urban villages contained in the area. However, from our perspective these 'traditional' enclaves presented certain qualities that defy top-down conventionalisms. They foster pedestrian-oriented urbanism, having a strong character based on the very local activities that exist, always within walking distance and generating a sort of inner ecology that establishes links among their inhabitants and creates a sense of identity among the community. We therefore carried out a survey of the existing villages to assess their current condition both in terms of their material and social construct and identified some that should be retained, treating them as an anchor point for the overall proposal.

All pedestrian networks, public and private spatial configuration, radii of influence, frequency of access nodes, etc., were seen as parts of a wider assemblage that works at a macro scale, networking existing urban villages, whilst consolidating and enhancing their urban qualities at a micro scale.

MAIN ACCESS POINTS AND PUBLIC SPACES

Type C

Type B

Type A

Type D

Type C

Key Area

Type A

Type B

Urban-Villages. Phenomeno-logical study.
Evaluation of main access points and internal circulation patterns, as well as open spaces within the urban villages.

● Main access from vehicular and pedestrian streets

● Access points from lots

● Public space within the urban village

MAIN VEHICULAR AND PEDESTRIAN GRID

Type D.

Type C

Type B

Type A

Key Area

Type D.

Type C

Type A

―――― Vehicular Paths

―――― Pedestrian Paths

EXISTING CONDITIONS

INTERVENTION STRATEGIES

Porosity and connectivity between CBD area and main rail way, the creation of commercial corridors within the urban village

Intensifying and nesting the urban spaces within the village, site boundary condition

Expanding the village_connections with MRT and the Longgang river

Public space enhancement
Site boundary villages

Bridging condition, 1. connections with MRT and the Longgang river 2. connections between village -railway-village

river connections

Type A

Vehicular paths
Pedestrian paths
Public space UV ● 24%
Access from streets ● 38%
Access from lots ● 38%

Type B

Vehicular paths
Pedestrian paths
Public space UV ● 45%
Access from streets ● 17%
Access from lots ● 38%

Type C

Vehicular paths
Pedestrian paths
Public space UV ● 40%
Access from streets ● 26%
Access from lots ● 34%

Type D

Vehicular paths
Pedestrian paths
Public space UV ● 37%
Access from streets ● 10%
Access from lots ● 53%

URBAN VILLAGES BRANDING STRATEGIES

14.9
Urban villages, diagrammatic studies. © 2008 GroundLab Ltd.

Parametric model

Parallel to these strategies we developed a parametric model, on the one hand to control built mass quantities tested against a 3D model of the built fabric and on the other to promote an inclusive decision-making process in terms of design, by facilitating the communication between all the parties involved; clients, stakeholders, developers, architects, etc.

Through the parametric model we acknowledge the necessity of building tools that within a specific framework-territory's requirements and strategies are able to cope with and adjust the enormous amount of data that keep fluctuating during the design process. These data being GFA, density, projected population, to name a few, inform the overall massing which in turn is used to produce and evaluate a range of urban patterns while studying their effects in terms of spatial arrangement.

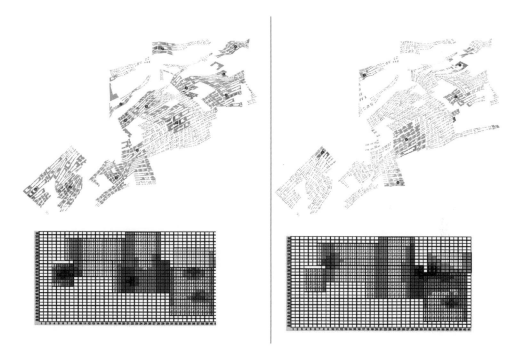

14.10
Parametric model, massing iteration studies. © 2008 GroundLab Ltd.

At the same time it allows an inclusive decision-making process, whereby programme adjustments and its intrinsic impact into the overall scheme can be integrated as part of an iterative process that derive into different scenarios. In this way client requests and/or planning requirements, which cause changes such as new allocation of centres of intensity or overall quantities for buildings, can be modified in order to get a different, yet related, urban configuration, so that further discussion on the urban fabric and architectural qualities can be put forward at any given moment within the design process.

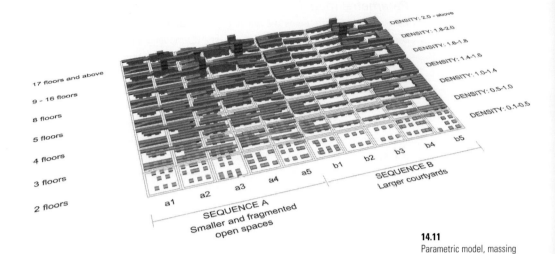

14.11
Parametric model, massing
parameters. © 2008
GroundLab Ltd.

Bibliography

Castro, E., Ramirez, A. and Spencer, D. (eds) (2011) *Critical Territories: From Academia to Praxis*,
    Barcelona: Actar: 6.
Spencer, D. (2010) *Opening Remarks* for AALU Open Day at the Architectural Association,
    London, 3 November.

Chapter 15

Building communication by design: mobile fiction and the city

Andrew Morrison and Henry Mainsah

Setting
Introduction

Digital media have expanded rapidly from desktops and the distributed networked communication of the Web to mobile, wireless technologies and popular cultural practices and professional uses. Consumers and users are increasingly involved in producing and participating in what are now broadly labelled social media. These media have already seen widespread use. These are media that connect with social interaction, shifting from a broadcast mode of mediation to a polyvocal and conversational framing of dynamic and emergent communication (Jenkins 2006). Developments in mobile technologies, such as Global Positioning Services (GPS), Bluetooth protocols and radio frequency identification (RFID), now make it possible to include geo-locational features in social media. This has major implications for the uses of mobile technologies and collaborative expression, including narrative, place and space in the built environment (Morrison *et al.* in press).

In urban settings, digital cameras and smartphones are in widespread use. This is apparent in all seasons as visitors to the Oslo opera, designed by the architects Snøhetta, stroll and run up its ramps, clamber over its marble surfaces and sit on its edges (Figure 15.1). There they pose and pause for photos, videos, calls and messages. Mobile communication is a highly visible part of people's dialogues and perambulations on this open-to-the-air public opera building.

A number of related implications arise in considering social media and the city (e.g. Galloway 2004). These need to be understood in relation to both communication and lived experience in urban settings (Léfèbvre 1991/1974). First, social media are becoming increasingly place-based or locative. Second, in 'locative media' we experience a mix of space and place. Third, this hybrid is realised via social uses of locative social media tools as we toggle between physical and digital environments. Fourth, for most of us, our uses and practices of situated and distributive tools are connected to the types of locative services and applications, or apps,

15.1
Glass and marble meet in the Oslo opera and provide a public space for activity and reflection. Photo: Jens-Christian Strandos.

that are provided. In short these are often already designed 'tools'. Fifth, commercial services (often firmly functional) and urban gaming applications (typically instrumental and tending towards the competitive) also influence our uptake and practices of locative media in urban everyday life. Sixth, in contrast to games, there are beginning to appear more culturally situated, 'playable stories' (Ryan 2009) that resituate earlier notions and conceptualisations of imagined cities (e.g. Blum 2003) into co-designed, creative and often collaborative narrative experiences.

The communication design of social media tools and applications or 'apps' (e.g. Apple App store) needs attention in relation to locative media and the built environment. In short, apps are constructed tools that allow for composed mediations of aspects of our lives in cities (Mitchell 2005; Shane and McGrath 2005). Little attention has been given to them at the level of design research and analysis. Such apps may also be developed to help us shape and articulate narrative accounts of the city. In this chapter, we take this up concerning the design of the design of affordances for the making of a mobile fictional narrative. We focus on fictional narrative in locative media and the city as one way of moving beyond locational information and services functions that often predominate. Drawing on work on imagining cities and imagined cityscapes, we extend the reach of locative technologies to communication design of mobile fiction.

Below we look into the development of one locative fictional narrative app co-designed for cultural expression by adult African immigrants to Oslo. Our designing and researching has drawn on the growing body of work into research by design (e.g. Morrison and Sevaldson 2010). In a research by design approach one switches between known and emerging practice and given research and emerging analytical reflection. Overall, we argue that approaches to research by design now established in various areas of design research may be extended to research by *communication* design. Communication design needs to be understood as reaching beyond earlier framings of it as graphic and visual design largely related to design practice (e.g. Frascara 2004). Research frameworks are being developed in communication design that link technologies, multimodal mediations across and between media types and cultural contexts of use. This perspective places weight on the design of means to cultural and mediated articulation in which the main motivation is to enable communicative articulation (see e.g. Morrison *et al.* 2010a; Morrison 2010).

Key concerns

Given these 'settings', in the following sections we address a number of linked key questions on research by communication design, locative media and narrative and the built environment: What might comprise and inform a research by *communication* design view on locative media and the city? In what ways may the development of an imaginative and fictional perspective on urban spaces, identity and character offer? How might a developmental narrative-oriented communication design process and completed product help us understand the role and importance of both genre and 'platform' concerning locative media in the built environment?

We take up these questions by reflecting on an experimental production-based and analytically framed case study into research by communication design of one playable story 'app' called *NarraHand*. This app sits in the sub-domain of expressive mobile narrative (Rushton 2010). It was designed for GPS-enabled smartphones. The app was developed through a collaborative, developmental communication design process by a team of programmers, media, narrative, cultural and computing specialists. This team worked in tandem with a small group of experimental authors made up of students, city workers and researchers. Through iterative design, the app was developed first as a prototype for the then leading GPS-enabled Nokia N95 handset and, more recently, as a fully functioning app for the iPhone.

Motivations

Communicatively, the design of *NarraHand* focuses on providing means for cultural expression by African immigrants in Oslo via mobiles. African adults were part of this design process at various levels; the two authors have been involved in design, trialling, authoring and research. Although African immigrants to Oslo come from different parts of the African continent, what they all have in common are experiences of displacement, resettlement, nostalgia and loss. Described varyingly as either 'black', 'African', 'immigrant' or 'outsider', they are often subjected to an increasingly dominant public discourse that is negative, stereotypical and exclusionary. Alternative spaces for self-expression become crucial. It is in this light that our project focuses on designing tools for Africans in Oslo to engage in identity expression through expressive mobile narrative by participating in and in part appropriating an established cultural public arena.

We have discussed this as part of a wider understanding of locative media and post-coloniality (Mainsah and Morrison in press). We examined issues of identity, voice and character in designing towards the articulation of expressive narrative in *NarraHand*. We have centred on the early co-designing of communicative affordances for locative narrative on the handset without 'touch' technology (Morrison *et al.* in press). Here, we extend these to situating locative narrative relation to urban studies and locative media, with focus on designed communicative affordances in *NarraHand* and their potential as a wider scaffolding for communication by design and its related research. In the next section we look into the wider contexts of locative media and the city, designing for performative use and a number of related tools and inspirational projects.

Scene
After the mediated city

New cultural communication complexities are emerging in and through the flow of data and their symbolic mediations in city spaces (Abrams and Hall 2006). New technologies contribute to a remediation both of urban social practices and relations, and of existing urban infrastructures. These tools and mediations are located in our cultural and social practices as citizens but also our activities as consumers (Lash and Lury 2007). They are formed through a mix of the 'real ' and the 'virtual' and in our embodied interaction that connects our sensing and critical selves to actual practices of mediated and situated use.

Shane (2005) conceives of the city as a layered, spatial matrix. He argues for a heterotopic system of urban elements whose transformative and recombinant elements are activated by urban actors. This too is to move beyond framings of the pervasive reach of media into urban spaces as the 'media city' (McQuire 2008) that refers to media architecture and urban space in and as media, to seeing cities in terms of mediation. This takes place in a 'network city, a wired and mediated environment' (Shane 2005: 11). This is not a techno 'cybercity' notion, but one where we engage with the 'senseable', moving and mobile in urban settings (Zardini 2005). We concur with Mitchell who (2005: 9) writes: 'the introduction of technologies for inscribing physical objects with text, and the associated practices of writing, distribution, and reading, created a new sort of urban information overlay.' Socio-spatial practices need to be seen in this co-mingling of electronic and physical space, while meeting the material potentials and constraints of the physical world and the demands of presence and flow.

Culture and communication design

Overall, in studies of space, place and culture, locative media need to be understood not only as relating to technology or to information (Lemos 2010) but also to modes, means and messages, in short, as mediations. However, these mediations are also linked to embodied interactions that take place in the world of the built environment that in sum add up to communicative enactments and exchanges. It is important to acknowledge that locative media are in fact designed tools; to a considerable degree, their designs influence the ways we apply them communicatively in contexts of urban use. However, these designs may also be examined and critiqued and knowledge about them may be gleaned from practice-based inquiry in which ecological and participative design activities may be included in their development.

Designing tools, platforms and affordances for cultural identity expression does not feature greatly in current research publications on social media and mobile communication, or in that on electronic literature. Similarly, few studies exist into the design of these means to mediated expression and exchange in communication and interaction design that vigorously connect to research in 'new' media and electronic arts more generally. Writings on electronic narrative extend to the construction of affordances for computer-generated discourse and processural texts; a research literature is also emerging on the design of mobile gaming (e.g. Mäyra and Lankoski 2009).

Humanist views, championed earlier by scholars such as Murray (1997), Ryan (2004) and Hayles (2008), do prevail in these studies, but often missing are robust frameworks for connecting the interdisciplinary technical and cultural foundations and intersections at the level of design for communicative use. Rarer still is mention of the substantial literature of mediated identity that centres on perspectives of mobile media and migration that begin with design and work towards expression that includes immigrants in design processes of their mediated relocated lives.

Designing for locative social media use

The rapid expansion of mobile media also presents designers with challenges: how are we to design spaces, tools, and 'communicative affordances' (Knutsen and Morrison 2010) for mobile, wireless and distributed use that also pertain to identity formation and expression? 'Apps' developed for smartphones cover many needs and domains, from functional and informational ones, such as weather feeds and news, to social networking tools such as Facebook Mobile, and a host of location-based games. Little research exists into the communicative and cultural design of mobile media applications and services; a large body of publications can be found on the uses of mobile media in museums or in daily life such as studies on SMS. Mitchell (2005: 11) reminds us that 'Acts of use and inhabitation and acts of textual production and consumption cannot be separated neatly into functionally distinct categories, but should be understood as parts of the same system of meaning.'

Research into locative media has tended to focus on services and functions and on art and on games. As a result, the affordances, limitations and constraints of both given hardware and software development are often bypassed. However, research is beginning to appear on design-oriented issues. This covers locative games (e.g. Nova and Girardin 2009), communication design matters in designing for performative use in social media services, such as the Oslo-based calendar and networking social software service *Underskog* (Undergrowth) (Morrison *et al.* 2010b), and on the uses of communication design in shaping tools for identity expression in locative mobile narrative (Morrison *et al.* in press).

Selected works and projects

We now present a variety of locative media projects, not all fiction based, that informed and inspired *NarraHand* and notions and practices of the design and appropriation of digital public space. In the category of geo-mapping, in the MILK project (www.milkproject.net) artists developed a multilevel representational web of personal and industrial perspectives built on the use of GPS devices by dairy trade workers and sellers between Latvia and the Netherlands. Such a mapping of self and space was also carried out in the Biomapping project in which Nold designed the co-patterning of body data with geo-location. Concerning the category of locative, annotation and measurement, a leading app is Layar (www.layar.com) that enables location-based tagging in smart screen overlays on the physical world. In locative gaming, the work of Blast Theory (www.blasttheory.co.uk) has been influential (e.g. *Uncle Roy All Around You*). More recently, social locative networking has blossomed, such as Foursquare (http://foursquare.com).

Taken together these developments may be seen in relation to ones that are specifically narrative in character. *[murmur]* by Micallef and collegaues (http://murmur.info) uses audio to build a documentary voiced by local residents that is accessed by ringing a mobile phone number displayed at a location. *34 North 118 West* (http://34n118w.net) uses GPS to explore and document the early industrial history of a part of Los Angeles and mixes fiction and fact. *Textopia* (http://textopia.org) has place-based audio narrative in Oslo as its theme and uses a wiki to allow participants to both browse literary texts that are deictically connected and add their own comments, notes and contributions.

Earlier work by Morrison on a stand-alone polyvocal hyperfiction *Just Eating The Progressing* was developed in an African capital city and trialled with higher education humanities students as part of enabling multiple reader pathways and routes to locational engagement in movement between the city and rural areas (Morrison 2003). One inspiration for *NarraHand* was the co-authored situationist inflected novel *Implementation* (http://nickm.com/implementation) by Montfort and Rettberg that was transferred into stickers that participants then placed in a variety of international urban settings and photographed along with the wider contexts of location. *NarraHand* takes such a view over the design of affordances for narrative articulation via mobile, locative technologies. This is the focus in the next section.

Scripting
A developmental process
The development of much locative media draws on notions of the ludic city (Stevens 2007). In contrast to more instrumental and directed approaches to urban planning and policy making, this is an approach that views play as an important emergent feature of people's engagement with public space in cities. In following a mode of play in creative construction with locative technologies, *NarraHand* placed the co-design of culturally oriented expression at the centre of the design of affordances for mediated communication. Authoring was devised to allow for text and still image entries and narrative connection to the 'material' of locative technologies as we present below. The *NarraHand* tool and the experimental articulation of a mobile collaborative fiction it enables may be seen as a form of 'cloud computing' related to the built urban environment. This is the name given to the abstract relations between points of annotation on remote devices and their connections to Web and server infrastructures and services that allow access to archived and current content.

NarraHand was developed through an iterative process involving researchers and developers from media studies, computer science, electronic narrative and communication design. The project spans co-design, multimodal story making and transdisciplinary research. This article is one of several that take up communication design aspects in Phase 1 of the project. The second phase of the project, now underway, looks more closely at the actual narrative work and its social and cultural contexts of composition, participation and use.

Interface and affordances

We draw together these developments in the confluence of the computational, place, space and mediation, but with a focus on 'playable story'. In shaping locative media technologies to enable playable story making we designed a two-level system. *NarraHand* has a splash screen with two main options: Context and Story. Context leads to a wiki that provides background to the project, links to related sites and projects, and a set of experimental short research papers. It also provides space for comments. Story leads to the actual space for authoring and reading. In Phase 1 of the project we concentrated on the co-design of a map-based interface for the generation of a collaborative voiced and distributed narrative. The log-in is for characters or authors. A character makes a locative entry either on site with GPS or from their location using their emap interface to locate the entry with the result that the entry is marked at a point of choice. The entry is then retrievable by GPS. Using the convention of the map pin or demonstration of a Point of Interest (POI) used widely in locative services such as Google Maps, the entry automatically shows a character icon logged to a specific location on the map of the selected core central city zone around the Oslo opera, central station and waterfront development area.

In developing the system we were also motivated to use the potential of locative media to design a number of meta-discursive narrative affordances. These are embodied in a main menu. They cover Identity, Location, Recency, Relation, Proximity, Theme and Comment. Identity provides a pointer to the named entrant, location allows the author and reader to see where an entry is situated, and recency points to the last made entry. Relation offers a link to a related entry by the same character. Proximity points to the nearest entry, regardless of character. Theme allows a character to tag an entry with a fresh lexical item or to select from the list that emerges in collaborative composition. Comment offers the author and the reader a space to leave a written comment. As a whole, these metanarrative affordances make it possible for authors of characters to situate their entries on the physical site, and to refer to the most recent narrative contribution prior to making a new one. Links between related entries and themes are realised through the selection and generation of labels.

Identifiers, map modes and mobile tools

The presentation parameters of the map served by the partner developer company, Faster Imaging, were developed specifically for *NarraHand*, enhancing the visibility of the character Points of Interest (POIs) and emphasising their importance in the application. POIs are widely used in locative technologies to provide orientation to specified services, landmarks and activities. In contrast to their more functional qualities and their being provided by service providers and companies, focus may be placed on who and what is being appointed by what we have called Markers of Identity or MOIs (Mainsah and Morrison in press). This helps orient our understanding and use of mappings that are culturally voiced and oriented.

In the map interface underlying the *NarraHand* system, the mode 'Normal' refers a schematic map with street names and main roads highlighted. This may be seen either as a flat representation or a '2D' view, one that that in addition shows the main built structures that are rendered in a titled view offering some idea of major physical volumes together with key transport spots.

'Tools' has two options. The application has a built-in update feature, the changes that were made since previous version(s) may be seen by invoking the 'Changelog' option. 'Send map' allows authors to send the current image on their device screen to members of their contact list as an MMS. 'Settings' offers options for titled display of buildings, GPS as active, if GPS is in follow mode, and what functions are assigned to keys. 'Help' provides fundamentals of using the application and navigating the map.

These developments that began on the Nokia N95 phone with in-built GPS did not include collaboration with that company. From the start we were bent on developing an independent 'application'. This was well ahead of the arrival of the commercial app stores of Apple or Nokia. We decided to shift the app to the iPhone due to its improved communicative potential. In doing this we have been able to effect further iterations of earlier prototyping and take them over into a fully framed app. This has meant considerable redesign of the interface to account for improved size, resolution, inbuilt interface conventions and given affordances. However, our initial motivation and design intentions have prevailed.

Siting
Reimaging the city

In 'African clouds over the Oslo opera' we have discussed the co-design of *NarraHand* as centred on shaping affordances for the expression-mediated identity via locative media narrative (Mainsah and Morrison 2011 in press; Figures 15.2 and 15.3). In contrast to a focus on maps and the delivery of locative services out of the ether, we used this metaphor to orient the means of cloud computing and GPS to a view on the articulation of a co-composed locative media tool. The clouds we have generated are both spaces and places connected to the application of the tool in collaborative narrative authoring by African immigrants at and above a leading cultural landmark in Scandinavia:

> Today there are new clouds over the Oslo opera. Against the scale of weather in Norway, these clouds are wisps and pinpricks of hidden, cultural condensation. They float experimentally above this startling building. These clouds are African in origin. As compositions, they are designed, digital formations. Metaphorical more than meteorological, these are techno-cultural formations, ones that are less climatically predicted than culturally seeded.
>
> (Mainsah and Morrison, in press)

15.2
Map interface in *NarraHand*.
Map mode 3D view.

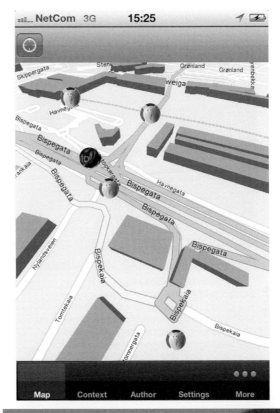

15.3
Henry Mainsah making an
entry in his character role in
an onsite workshop session.
Photo: Andrew Morrison.

From authoring to reading

It's stinking hot. Glare dances off the building. I feel the sweat of the day behind my knees. I try not to fan my ears too visibly, giant spans of African elephant skin. Joe said he'd meet me here at 3. And I'm still waiting. My tongue's hanging out for an iced latte. Joe. Joe. Joe-no-show!

Edit | Narrative no-show | Delete

15.4
Experimental entry by character called Ella, a small white elephant, waiting to meet another character in *NarraHand*.

Phase 2 of *NarraHand* moves more explicitly into the co-construction of a collaborative, locative fictional narrative level using GPS. The communicative affordances we have designed and trialled will now be explored further compositionally. They are still being shaped through narrative expression (e.g. Figure 15.4). Fictional narrative composition takes place on smartphones, out in the city, and in relation to proximity, relational tags and spatial story threads (Figure 15.5). Readers will have the opportunity to process the story and comments about it on the physical site of the opera building. They will have the narrative in their hands as they physically clamber over and relax on the built structure. At the points at which they access the work in the world, space and place will be co-axially intertwined, yet the characters they meet will be from other climes, now present, now 'remote'.

Staging
Platforms for communication

The built urban environment has rapidly become an arena for experimentation with digital technologies and their eventual use in many day-to-day operations. As mentioned earlier, many of the products and services on offer are firmly functional; at the same time, aspects of play and participation have emerged and are growing in use and popularity. Greenfield (2009) observes that:

15.5
NarraHand – two trial authors,
Lawrence Ssekitoleko and
Henry Mainsah, in an
experimental workshop
session, Oslo opera, summer.
Photo: Andrew Morrison.

15.5
NarraHand – two trial authors,
Lawrence Ssekitoleko and
Henry Mainsah, in an
experimental workshop
session, Oslo opera, summer.
Photo: Andrew Morrison.

If we're reaching the point where it makes sense to consider the city as a fabric of addressable, queryable, even scriptable objects and surfaces – to reimagine its pavements, building façades and parking meters as network resources – this raises an order of questions never before confronted, ethical as much as practical: who has the right of access to these resources, or the ability to set their permissions?

In *NarraHand*, we took up such challenges through a collaborative investigation in research by communication design that involved not only mediation in the form of electronic billboards or giant projections in open squares that often predominate in discussions of media technology in public spaces. We selected the new landmark of the opera as a site for symbolic and cultural appropriation and expression with locative media. We were motivated to also investigate through processes of research by communication designing how the transformation of the mediational potential, or mediatisation (e.g. Couldry 2008) of locative media might be enabled via the co-construction of locative tools.

Researching by way of communication design has highlighted the need to constantly re-emphasise the need for attention to what can be articulated. This too is a matter of access, as Greenfield notes. Importantly this is not simply a matter of access to communicative resources but to their shaping, by design, through collaboration and iterative experimentation in contexts of actual use in research by communication design. In this we have needed to work closely with programmers and systems designers. This has helped us look up, as it were, beyond our single project, despite its collaborative qualities, to consideration of matters of networked and distributed design. As a result, given the use of GPS in the project, we have explored the character and qualities of cloud computing. It offers interaction and communication designers new means to shaping mediated communication. Issues to do with 'building platforms' for communication may literally arise!

Where the *NarraHand* was part of an original project into genre and mobility, we have been able to focus on new features in expressive mobile narrative. Here we have coined the term 'reflexive expressive narrative' to account for the moves between space and place in locative story making, including more factual narrative (Mainsah and Morrison in press). While we have arrived at such a specific locative narrative category, the research by communication design experience and outcomes in *NarraHand* have led us to also look at it as a heuristic for understanding and building genre in locative media.

15.6
Window cleaning and inspection apparatus, Oslo opera. Photo: Jens-Christian Strandos.

Scaffolding potential articulations

The notion of genre as social action (Miller 1984; e.g. Yates *et al.* 1999) has been critical in relating experimentation in research by communication design to a wider understanding of locative. This is to see one project as providing a form of scaffolding for reflecting on the communication by design of locative media in the city (Figure 15.6). We have taken this up by reorienting the 'app' developed in *NarraHand* and supported by a related project into social media, performativity and the city, called YOUrban. Similar thinking lies behind the *Datascape* project (http://datascape.info; Kabisch 2010) that provides means of layered looking at and annotation of urban settings.

Applying such scaffolding helps lift the communication design of one application and project to wider, generic matters of designing and 'staging' with locative media in – and as part of – the changing built environment. This is to work with not just the built but processes of building through communication by design. Yaneva (2005) claims the building is a 'multiverse'; so too may we see experimental projects into creative and imaginary uses of locative media as part of building diverse cultural articulations and multimodal compositions into research by communication design in urban settings.

Acknowledgements

Our thanks to participants in the *NarraHand* project, Jonny Aspen and the two reviewers for comments. *NarraHand* is part of the Inventio project funded by the VERDIKT programme, Research Council of Norway; this chapter was supported by the YOUrban project into social media and performativity in urban environments (both projects funded by the Research Council of Norway, VERDIKT programme).

Bibliography

Abrams, J. and Hall, P. (eds) (2006) *Else/Where: Mapping New Cartographies of Networks and Territories*. Minneapolis: University of Minnesota Design Institute.

Blum, A. (2003) *The Imaginative Structure of the City*. Montreal: McGill-Queen's University Press.

Couldry, N. (2008) 'Mediatization or mediation? Alternative understandings of the emergent space of digital storytelling'. *New Media & Society*, 10(3): 373–391.

Frascara, J. (2004) *Communication Design*. New York: Allworth Press.

Galloway, A. (2004) 'Intimations of everyday life: ubiquitous computing and the city'. *Cultural Studies*, 18(2–3): 384–408.

Greenfield, A. (2009) 'Digital cities: words on the street'. *WIRED* magazine, Vol. 11. Available: http://www.wired.co.uk/magazine/archive/2009/11/features/digital-cities-words-on-the-street (accessed 11 September 2011).

Hayles, C. (2008) *Electronic Literature: New Horizons for the Literary*. Notre Dame: University of Notre Dame Press.

Jenkins, H. (2006) *Convergence Culture: Where Old and New Media Collide*, New York: NYU Press.

Kabisch, E. (2010) 'Mobile after-media: trajectories and points of departure'. *Digital Creativity*, 21(1): 51–59.

Knutsen, J. and Morrison, A. (2010) 'Have you heard this? Designing mobile social software'. *FORMakademisk*, 3(1): 57–79. Available: http://www.formakademisk.org/index.php/formakademisk/article/view/66 (accessed 11 September 2011).

Lash, S. and Lury, C. (2007) *Global Culture Industry. The Mediation of Things*. Cambridge: Polity Press.

Léfèbvre, H. (1991/1974) *The Production of Space*. Trans. D. Nicholson-Smith Malden, MA: Blackwell.

Lemos, A. (2010) 'Post-mass media functions, locative media, and informational territories: new ways of thinking about territory, place, and mobility in contemporary society'. *Space and Culture*, 13(4): 403–442.

Mainsah, H. and Morrison, A. (in press) 'African clouds over the Oslo opera'. Special issue in interaction and communication design: *Computers and Composition*.

Mäyrä, F. and Lankoski, P. (2009) 'Play in hybrid reality: alternative approaches to game design'. In de Souza e Solva, A. and Sutko, D. (eds) *Digital Cityscapes: Merging Digital and Urban Playspaces*. New York: Peter Lang, pp. 129–147.

McQuire, S. (2008) *The Media City: Media Architecture and Urban Space*. London: Sage.

Miller, C. (1984) 'Genre as social action'. *Quarterly Journal of Speech*, 70(2): 151–167.

Mitchell, W. J. (2005) *Placing Words: Symbols, Space, and the City*. Cambridge, MA: The MIT Press.

Morrison, A. (2003) 'From oracy to electracies: hypernarrative, place and multimodal discourses in learning'. In Liestol, G., Morrison, A. and Rasmussen, T. (eds) *Digital Media Revisited*. Cambridge, MA: The MIT Press, pp. 115–154.

Morrison, A. (ed.) (2010) *Inside Multimodal Composition*. Cresskill: Hampton Press.

Morrison, A., Mainsah, H., Sem, I. and Havnør, M. (in press) 'Designing location-based mobile fiction: the case of NarraHand'. In Jones, R. (ed.) *Discourse and Creativity*. New York: Longman.

Morrison, A. and Sevaldson, B. (2010) 'Getting going' – Research by Design. *FORM Akademisk*, 3(1). Available: http://www.formakademisk.org/index.php/formakademisk/issue/view/6/showToc (accessed 11 September 2011).

Morrison, A., Stuedahl, D., Mörtberg, C., Wagner, I., Liestøl, G. and Bratteteig, T. (2010a) 'Analytical perspectives'. In Wagner, I., Stuedahl, D. and Bratteteig, T. (eds) *Exploring Digital Design*. Vienna: Springer, pp. 55–104.

Morrison, A., Westvang, E. and Skøgsrud, S. (2010b) 'Whisperings in the undergrowth: performativity, collaborative design and online social networking'. In Wagner, I., Stuedahl, D. and Bratteteig, T. (eds) *Exploring Digital Design*. Vienna: Springer, pp. 221–260.

Murray, J. (1997) *Hamlet on the Holodeck*. Cambridge, MA: The MIT Press.

Nova, N. and Girardin, F. (2009) 'Framing the issues for the design of location-based games'. In de Souza e Solva, A. and Sutko, D. (eds) *Digital Cityscapes: Merging Digital and Urban Playspaces*, New York: Peter Lang, pp.168–186.

Ruston, S. (2010) 'Storyworlds on the move: mobile media and their implication for narrative'. *Storyworlds*, 2: 101–120.

Ryan, M. (ed.) (2004) *Narrative Across Media: The Languages of Storytelling*. Lincoln: University of Nebraska Press.

Ryan, M. (2009) 'From narrative games to playable stories. Toward a poetics of interactive narrative'. *Storyworlds*, 1(1): 43–59.

Shane, D. (2005) *Recombinant Urbanism*. Chichester: Wiley-Academy.

Shane, D. and McGrath, B. (2005) *Sensing the 21st-century City*. London: John Wiley & Sons.

Yaneva, A. (2005) 'A building is a "multiverse"'. In Latour, B. and Weibel, P. (eds) *Making Things Public*. Karlsrhue: ZKM/ Cambridge: The MIT Press, pp. 530–535.

Yates, J., Orlikowski, W. and Okamura, K. (1999) 'Explicit and implicit structuring of genres in electronic communication: reinforcement and change of social interaction'. *Organization Science*, 10(1): 83–103.

Zardini, M. (ed.) (2005) *Sense of the City*. Baden/CCA; Montréal: Lars Müller.

Chapter 16

Making material of the networked city

Einar Sneve Martinussen

16.1
A Wi-Fi network on a street in Oslo.

Figure 16.1 shows the strength and reach of a common Wi-Fi network on a street in Oslo. To create photographs like this we have developed a technique using long exposure photography and a specially designed measuring rod that visualises Wi-Fi signal strength as a bar of glowing lights. The height of the bar corresponds to the strength of a network in a specific location, and, when moved through space, the measuring rod displays the changes in the Wi-Fi signal. This is captured using long exposure photography and the narrow bar of light is stretched into a cross-section of the network that shows how it changes through the physical environment.

This chapter investigates and discusses phenomena of interacting with wireless networks in the city through practice-based design research. Using tools and methods from interaction and communication design, a small team of design researchers have developed instruments and techniques that can reveal qualities of wireless networks that we cannot normally see. This allows us to get closer to some of the spatial, contextual and material aspects of everyday networked technologies, and how these may be used to unpack, communicate and discuss our interactions with devices and networks in the city.

Wireless networks in cities

Wireless networks and increasingly sophisticated mobile phones are becoming an interwoven part of daily life in many cities. Our interactions with personal technology are moving into urban contexts and starting to influence how we understand and experience our environments. These developments are taken up in a broad range of research fields and studied and discussed within and across multiple disciplines, including urban studies (e.g. Graham and Marvin 2001), architecture (e.g. Mitchell 2004; McCullough 2004), anthropology (e.g. Galloway 2009) and computer science (e.g. Paulos *et al.* 2004; Foth 2009). In this chapter I approach wireless technologies and network material in cities through practice-based design research. I focus on discussing and contextualising some of the phenomena that surround our interactions with network technologies, and explore their material qualities through visualisation.

Many of our activities based around network technologies are already becoming mundane, like using our mobile phones to take our online lives with us into the streets, cafés and buses, and finding our way around the city guided by online maps, GPS and real-time public transport updates. An increasing number of new services and applications are being designed and marketed around everyday urban activities such as shopping, commuting and socialising. Behind these novel products and activities are complex technologies and infrastructures that are only vaguely understood by common consumers and designers alike.

The design research presented in this chapter investigates and unpacks spatial, contextual and material qualities of one of the basic background phenomena of the networked city: the Wi-Fi network. Wi-Fi, or IEEE 802.11, is a standard form of wireless network that is typically used to distribute internet connection to laptops and mobile phones within a limited area (Wi-Fi Alliance 2011). Wi-Fi communication uses high-frequency radio waves to send and receive data between a base station and a mobile device. The base station shares an internet connection with mobile devices through setting up a radio field. This field is often called a wireless zone or hotspot, and is the space where a mobile device can detect the radio waves coming from the base station and create a two-way data connection. The size of a Wi-Fi zone depends on the strength of the base station and the antennas in the mobile devices; it can vary between 30 metres and 100 metres or more. The reach and shape of the wireless network also depends on how the physical environment absorbs and reflects the radio waves. This can have unforeseen effects and make Wi-Fi networks seem spatially unpredictable.

Wi-Fi networks have qualities that make them an interesting topic for this study. In several respects, Wi-Fi is a part of popular culture that stretches far beyond the technical basis of wireless communication standards. Wi-Fi base stations are inexpensive consumer products that allow people to create their own networks. This has made them almost ubiquitous (Mackenzie 2010). Wi-Fi networks are popular in homes, offices, businesses and in institutions. They are especially numerous in urban contexts. The radio waves from all these networks reach out into the environment, which makes it possible to detect and identify any number of domestic and institutional networks in most urban settings. If you can find a network without password protection, or if you know the password, you can therefore connect to the network while sitting outside in a park, in a café or in your own apartment. This density of overlapping networks is occasionally experienced by most Wi-Fi users as a list of network names in the network settings of the phone or computer. Access to Wi-Fi networks has itself become a resource in the city, and this is especially true when it comes to cafés and coffee bars. For many the wireless internet is already a taken-for-granted aspect of cafés and the quality of the Wi-Fi influences where you choose to drink your coffee. Wi-Fi networks play an important role in contemporary urban life. Even if better technologies or new pricing models may make it obsolete in a few years, this technology is an interesting one of the first ways in which the Web is brought into the city.

Wi-Fi networks are just one example of how digital phenomena are becoming a part of the urban landscape. Our interactions with mobile devices, applications and services generate, and are surrounded by, invisible technical phenomena like data from embedded sensors, bluetooth connections, signals from GPS satellites, and numerous forms of wireless networks. The inner workings of these technologies are often opaque and black-boxed, but we use them and experience them in our daily life in ways that are already becoming mundane. Importantly for design research, we also design with and around these phenomena. We therefore find it especially interesting to develop techniques for bringing the invisible digital structures and the physical environment together in order to spatialise and contextualise some of the material aspects of the networked city.

Investigating wireless networks

Figure 16.2 shows how the Wi-Fi network of the Oslo School of Architecture and Design reaches through a neighbouring park making it possible for the students to bring their laptops outside when the weather allows. What we see here is a 100-metre-long cross-section from the corner of the campus (on the right), where the signal is relatively strong, diagonally across the park to where the signal disappears behind a small mound. The reason for the meandering curves of the cross-section is that the Wi-Fi measuring rod used to create the visualisation is 4 metres tall, and therefore has to avoid the low branches of the trees.

The measuring rod is reminiscent of the poles used by traditional land surveyors to map and describe the topography of physical landscapes. Similarly, our equipment and technique allows us to survey and visualise the immaterial landscapes that surround our interactions with mobile devices. Mitchell describes this landscape of digital networks as an 'electromagnetic terrain' that is both intricate and invisible, and only hinted at by the presence of antennas (Mitchell 2004: 55). Visualising and representing invisible technological phenomena have previously been explored at the intersections between design, art and studies of technology. Our design research is inspired and informed by work such as that of Dunne and Raby's 'Tuneable cities' (1994-97) and their discussions of 'hertzian space' (Dunne,

16.2
A university Wi-Fi network stretching across a park.

2005; Dunne and Raby, 2001), Jarman and Gerhardt's 'Magnetic Movie' (2007) and Chalmers and Galani's discussions of the physicality of wireless networks and their concept of 'seamful design' (2004). The investigations presented in this chapter are also grounded in our own research into visualising the material qualities of RFID – another ubiquitous and immaterial technology (Arnall and Martinussen 2010).

Our photographs of networks in urban contexts are the result of the interplay between the lights on the Wi-Fi measuring rod and the optics and exposure times of the camera (Figure 16.3). The rod has been specifically designed for creating the Wi-Fi visualisations through an iterative process of developing electronics and code, and taking photographs. For common Wi-Fi users the strength of a network is displayed on the screen of their device as a fan of 4 bars that indicate reception. Our rod measures the strength of a network in a similar way to a smartphone, but displays it with much more detail. The rod has 80 bright white LEDs that

16.3
Detecting a Wi-Fi signal indoors.

are connected in 40 pairs along a 4-metre-long wooden beam. This means that we can display the signal strength with a resolution of 40 levels, which allows us to make detailed graphs of the network reception in the environment on a scale of 0 to 4 metres. The reason for drawing out the graphs at this large scale is to show the architectural scale at which Wi-Fi operates.

The Wi-Fi measuring rod is a stand-alone, battery-powered instrument that consists of three connected parts: a Wi-Fi module, a microcontroller and a row of LED lights. The Wi-Fi module is relatively small and similar to those found in smartphones. The microcontroller is called Arduino and made for prototyping and development, and allows us to write our own code in a lightweight programming language. The microcontroller is programmed to use the Wi-Fi module to scan the environment for a specific network identity and measure the signal strength of this network. The signal strength is then translated into how many of the 40 LED pairs to turn on (Figure 16.3).

Scanning for Wi-Fi networks does not give instant feedback, but depends on factors such as the number of available networks and the speed of the Wi-Fi module. We have programmed the measuring rod to scan for signal strength every three seconds and draw straight lines between each new scan-point (Figure 16.4). This means that if the rod is moved at a speed of 1 metre per three seconds over a chosen area, the Wi-Fi mapping gets a resolution of one reading per metre. The LEDs also flash on and off every 100 metres to create dashed lines rather than solid ones. This effect creates a texture that makes the cross-section semi-transparent. Consequently, it is possible to see through the graph and allows the visualisation to appear within the physical environment without covering the background scene (Figure 16.4).

When photographing the moving measuring rod we use a photographic technique called light painting. Light painting involves long exposure photographs of a dark environment and painting or drawing by moving a light source. Light painting

16.4
The texture of the cross-section is made of dashed lines and linear transitions.

has a background from photography and art, which includes early examples by Man Ray, and Mili and Picasso (Baldassari 1997). Light paintings were also used early as a technique for analysing movement, for example, the Gilbreths' studies of work processes (Marien 2006). Light-painting photography has several characteristics that make it an interesting technique for visualising invisible phenomena like Wi-Fi. First, it lets us photograph both the physical environment and the light-painted representation of the network in one picture. This means that the detailed qualities of the phenomenon of the network are captured in the physical space where it occurs. The photographic visualisations spatialise the phenomenon and through contextualising it in the situation gives the phenomenon a material quality. Second, the process of creating the light paintings requires us to both develop instruments for revealing invisible networks, and find and photograph these networks in the city. This process of investigation also acts as a way of contextualising the phenomenon of Wi-Fi through finding and revealing it in the spaces and environments where it exists. This practice-based design research involves the interplay of interaction design and the development of electronics instruments, urban and architectural photography, and explorative fieldwork.

In the field

Figure 16.5 shows the measuring rod being moved across the foreground of the Oslo School of Architecture and Design (AHO). Here we see some variation in the signal strength of the Wi-Fi coming out of the building, but we also see the blurred image of the rod operator. This gives an impression of the scale of the visualisations as well as the size of the equipment. To create a successful visualisation we needed to be three people: a photographer, an operator carrying the rod and one person to keep it balanced and pointed towards the camera. As well as working technically and photographically, the measuring rod also has to work practically while outdoors. The rod has handles and a shoulder-rest for keeping it upright, waterproof housing for the

16.5
Walking with the Wi-Fi measuring rod.

electronics and a hinge in the middle to make it easier to transport. The LEDs and electronic components are kept in place with solderless miniature screw connectors to make it possible to quickly maintain and fix the rod while in the field. The rod is designed and built specifically for fieldwork, and discussing this fieldwork can be a good starting point for exploring the material level of the phenomenon of Wi-Fi in a city. Our explorations have taken place in and around Grüerløkka in central Oslo, which consists of residential areas, educational institutions, cafés and shops.

As we are taking our equipment with us through the streets, we continuously scan for networks with a smartphone, looking for places with interesting network qualities. The lists the smartphone gives us reveals that the density of networks is high and that we are rarely completely without some form of Wi-Fi contact. When we start to photograph these networks we typically get pictures like the one shown in Figure 16.6. In Figure 16.6 we see a network that comes out of someone's apartment. The signal we get from this network is not very strong, but it reaches across the street and into a hedge. When we photograph the same network from a different angle, and move the rod along the facade, we can see how the network spills out onto small sections of the pavement (Figure 16.7). Larger institutional networks give us very different visualisations than the domestic networks extruding from apartment buildings.

16.6
A domestic network reaching out into the street.

Figure 16.8 shows cross-sections of the Wi-Fi network of AHO reaching from the library on the left, to the Akerselva river on the right. This image gives an impression of the extent of the digital footprint of the building and how the open park allows the Wi-Fi radio waves to be cast far out of the large windows.

Wi-Fi networks at Grünerøkka in Oslo are ubiquitous, but highly local and qualitatively different. The strength, consistency and reach of the networks tell us something about their host, but also something about the built environment where

16.7
A domestic network spreading
out along the pavement.

16.8
A large institutional network
stretching across the park and
into the river.

the network is set up. The open park around AHO is one example of this (Figure 16.8); another can be seen in Figure 16.9 where a high and street-long brick wall creates a shadow in the network.

Here the network comes from the Oslo National Academy of the Arts (KHiO), which lies behind the wall to the left. The brick wall absorbs the radio waves coming from the KHiO base station and creates a small shadow. The urban land-scape, typology of buildings and building materials shape the way networks spread into the environment. This shows how these technological phenomena are highly contextual and behave differently when localised in different urban settings.

A related aspect is where and to whom the network is spread. In the case of the AHO network reaching through the neighbouring park, this makes it

16.9
Brick wall creating a shadow
in the network.

possible for AHO students to use the park as a networked area when the seasons
allow it. For anyone else, this network is both technically invisible and practically
unavailable (as it is also password protected).

Figure 16.10 shows the same far-reaching AHO network covering a
nearby street and a busy bus stop. Here we have the overlapping of one invisible
digital structure, the network, with the highly visible infrastructure of public transport. This unplanned overlap allows students and employees of AHO to use this bus
stop as a space for accessing the Web while waiting. Here the wireless network
connects the semi-private indoor work spaces with the public outdoor commuting
environment. This illustrates how wireless networks, both practically and metaphor-
ically, can connect different environments and settings.

16.10
Bus stop and Wi-Fi.

The phenomena that are generated by and surround our interactions with networked devices are complex and often black-boxed. Latour describes black-boxing as when 'technical work is made invisible by its own success' (1999: 304). When technologies work efficiently we only focus on their inputs and outputs, and their internal complexities become opaque and obscured (ibid.). Interestingly, Wi-Fi networks are both physically invisible and technically obscure, which makes them black-boxed on multiple levels. The detailed technical level of the infrastructures, data traffic and electromagnetic fields that our mobile devices are built upon are obviously complex and difficult to understand. However, there are also interactional and material aspects to how we experience these technologies that are similarly opaque and vaguely understood. This material level is especially important for design research as it is not only related to the technical and infrastructural properties of the technologies, but also to how they are experienced as spatial, material and interactive phenomena in the city. Through photographs and the process of creating them we have unpacked some of the qualities of Wi-Fi networks and make them understandable as spatial and contextual phenomena. This process of making the phenomena material through visualisation shows how digital structures and physical environments are interwoven elements of the urban landscape. It also illustrates how our interactions with devices and networks are a part of the fabric of everyday urban life.

In the discourse

Our investigations and visualisations of wireless networks work towards unpacking and discussing the immaterial landscape of interacting with devices in urban environments on multiple levels. First, they explore the material level, and as described above show how the phenomena can be visualised and contextualised, how Wi-Fi networks are a part of the urban landscape, and how the networks are both shaped by the environment, and shapes how the urban spaces can be used. Second, the visualisations and the process of creating them can also be used as illustrations on a conceptual or metaphorical level, connecting the interactive and technological phenomena of urban life to the macro-discourses around urban technologies and networked cities.

The contextualising of digital technologies in urban life is an emerging field of research that spans multiple disciplines and takes up a broad range of topics, including the development of new devices, services and infrastructures, and studies of how technologies affect city life. The design research presented in this chapter can be situated within these discourses, and it relates specifically to critical perspectives on research and development of new and emerging technologies.

Our visualisations show how Wi-Fi networks are highly local, informal and fragmented, but it also illustrates how these networks make up a highly evolved urban infrastructure that is largely created by its users. This connects with research and discussions from Bell and Dourish on how computing, digital networks and urban environments can be understood as interwoven layers of the city experience:

> The spaces into which new technologies are deployed are not stable, not uniform, and not given. Technology can destabilise and transform

these interactions, but will only ever be one part of the mix. Digital technology is only another layer in the already dense and complex context of the city.

(Bell and Dourish 2004: 2)

Bell and Dourish argue for designing not just for urban settings, but for the behaviours and practices of the city and how these evolve (ibid.). These writers represent critical perspectives from within computer studies and human–computer interaction (HCI), and have used studies of daily uses of devices and networks to argue for new approaches to technology development that focus more on 'the messiness of everyday life' of the present than the envisioning of seamless infrastructures of the future (2007: 131).

Similar perspectives are also addressed in urban studies and cultural geography that work with urban life and technologies. Crang et al. (2007) discuss how people are reshaping daily life through the possibilities and limits of digital networks and communication technologies, and how the information landscape and daily life co-evolve. In their research detailed ethnographic studies are used to demonstrate how technology-based urban change 'involves a layering, tangling, and imbrication of new practices and new possibilities alongside old ways and enduring demands' (ibid.: 2407). Crang et al. discuss how interacting with new technologies is happening in between, alongside and within existing practices. The network photographs we show here can be seen as a way of spatialising this discussion through visualising how the technological phenomenon is situated within existing spaces and across urban environments, or as Bell and Dourish (2007) put it, as yet another part of the messiness of everyday life.

Architect Malcolm McCullough argues along similar lines for media urbanism to move from studying macro-infrastructures to focusing on the micro-scale of personal, situated bottom-up embedded computing. He claims that 'there is urbanism in how people obtain, layer, and manage their connections. Like attention itself, any belonging to community or place is made continuous, partial, and multiple by this mediation' (2006: 29).

These perspectives come from different backgrounds and have different research agendas, but have a number of central issues in common. They come out of a critique of technology-driven arguments that have dominated the discourses around digital technologies in the city, and move to demonstrate how interacting with digital technologies is interwoven with daily city life in many different ways. Significantly, they bring forward an understanding of technologies in urban contexts that take daily practices and everyday environments as a starting point.

In the design and research presented in this chapter we have taken up this thread and investigated phenomena of networked city life in the everyday environments where these occur. Through visualising, situating and spatialising the phenomena of wireless networks we contextualise and materialise otherwise invisible technological materials that make up the urban landscape. In doing so we suggest ways of unpacking and discussing networked technologies as a highly physical and interwoven part of daily life in cities, and grounding the discourses of technologies in urban life within the environments where this takes place. Seeing our built environment populated with networks and data is one way of understanding the networked city. This could point towards new means for design research to discuss relationships between our interactions with devices and our interactions with our cities.

Acknowledgements

The work presented in this chapter has been developed together with Jørn Knutsen and Timo Arnall at the Oslo School of Architecture and Design. The work has been supported by Andrew Morrison and the research project YOUrban, funded by the VERDIKT programme, Research Council of Norway. More detail on this work and extended bibliographies can be found at the project's website: yourban.no.

Bibliography

Arnall, T. and Martinussen, E. S. (2010). Depth of field – discursive design research through film. *FORMAkademisk*, 3(1): 100–122.

Baldassari, A. (1997). *Picasso and Photography: The Dark Mirror*. Paris: Flammarion.

Bell, G. and Dourish, P. (2004). Getting Out of the City: Meaning and Structure in Everyday Encounters with Space. Workshop on Ubiquitous Computing on the Urban Frontier (Ubicomp 2004, Nottingham, UK),

Bell, G. and Dourish, P. (2007). Yesterday's tomorrows: notes on ubiquitous computing's dominant vision. *Personal Ubiquitous Computing*, 11(2): 133–143.

Chalmers, M. and Galani, A. (2004). Seamful interweaving. In *Proceedings of the 2004 Conference on Designing Interactive Systems Processes, Practices, Methods, and Techniques – DIS '04*. Cambridge, MA, 243.

Crang, M., Crosbie, T. and Graham, S. (2007). Technology, Time – Space, and the Remediation of Neighbourhood Life. *Environment and Planning A*, 39(10): 2405–2422.

Dunne, A. (2005). *Hertzian Tales: Electronic Products, Aesthetic Experience, and Critical Design*. Cambridge, MA: MIT Press.

Dunne, A. and Raby, F. (1994–97). *Tuneable cities*. Available: http://www.dunneandraby.co.uk/content/projects/67/0 [accessed 13 January 2011].

Dunne, A. and Raby, F. (2001). *Design Noir: The Secret Life of Electronic Objects*. Basel: Birkhäuser.

Foth, M. (ed.) (2009). *Handbook of Research on Urban Informatics*. Hershey, PA: Information Science Reference, IGI Globale.

Galloway, A. (2008). *A Brief History of the Future of Urban Computing and Locative Media*. PhD. Carleton University Ottawa, Ontario.

Graham, S. and Marvin, S. (2001). *Splintering Urbanism: Networked Infrastructures, Technological Mobilities and the Urban Condition*. London: Routledge.

Jarman, R. and Gerhardt, J. (2007). *Magnetic Movie*. [Film] Available: http://www.animateprojects.org/films/by_date/2007/mag_mov [accessed 13 January 2011].

Latour, B. (1999). *Pandora's Hope: An Essay on the Reality of Science Studies*. Harvard, MA: Harvard University Press.

Mackenzie, A. (2010). *Wirelessness*. Cambridge, MA: MIT Press.

Marien, M. W. (2006). *Photography: A Cultural History*, 2nd edn. London: Laurence King Publishing.

McCullough, M. (2004). *Digital Ground: Architecture, Pervasive Computing, and Environmental Knowing*. Cambridge, MA: MIT Press.

McCullough, M. (2006). On the urbanism of locative media [Media and the City]. *Places*, 18(2): 26–29.

Mitchell, W. J. (2004). *Me++: The Cyborg Self and the Networked City*. Cambridge, MA: MIT Press.

Paulos, E., Anderson, K. and Townsend, A. (2004). UbiComp in the urban frontier. *Human–Computer Interaction Institute*. Available: http://repository.cmu.edu/hcii/213 [accessed 25 May 2010].

Wi-Fi Alliance. (2011). *Five Steps to Creating a Wireless Network*. Available: http://www.wi-fi.org/knowledge_center/kc-fivestepsforcreatingwirelessnetwork [accessed 13 January 2011].

Index